AMERICAN INDIAN CEREMONIES

Medicine Hawk
Grey Cat

Inner Light Publications

ACKNOWLEDGEMENTS

The authors wish to particularly recognize the assistance of the following individuals many of whom put themselves to considerable trouble to help us write this book. Carmin Waller, who posed for many pictures; Pat Santhuff, who loaned many books and magazines; Laira Ragan, who helped sort sevens; Harragano, who taught us about wigwags; Amber K. who shared her guidelines for teacher selection; Grey Wolf, Gilden, and Beket Asir Edithsdatter, who helped with proofreading and corrections; Mouse, who managed to see the pictures in our minds; and Wil, Tommy, Wren, Circe, Gillan and Pat who somehow kept us going. And most of all, we thank Grandfather Wallace Black Elk who shared his visions.

Cover: "Our Prophets Vision" by Barthell Little Chief, c/o Little Chief Art, Rt. 3, Box 109A, Anadarko, OKlahoma 73005.

Editorial Direction: Timothy Green Beckley

Typography: Jeffrey Goodman

Published by:
INNER LIGHT PUBLICATIONS
BOX 753
NEW BRUNSWICK, NJ 08903

ISBN:
0-938294-72-5

ABOUT THE AUTHORS

MEDICINE HAWK is Dr. Douglas Wilburn, born in Olive Hill, Kentucky. He has been published in over fifty metaphysical periodicals, including WILDFIRE, and CIRCLE NETWORK NEWS. In 1987 he received the Silver Salamander Award for Excellence in Journalism. Hawk is the author of twenty five cassette tapes and three books: TOTEM, THUNDERHEAD, and NATIVE AMERICAN ANIMAL SPIRITS. He graduated from Mercer University, Georgia State University with BS, MED and PhD degrees. Medicine Hawk is Council Chief of the Shadowlight Medicine Clan, International, and professor of education and psychology at three California universities. He lives in Riverside, California with his wife, Ramona, and two step children.

GREY CAT is founder of NorthWind, a tradition of American Wicca. She has published widely in New Age and occult periodicals including CIRCLE NETWORK NEWS, HARVEST, and COG NEWS. She is a two time winner of the Silver Salamander Award for Excellence in Journalism. She is Members' Advocate of Arn Draiocht Fein, an association of neo-Druids; and the editor of THE CRONE PAPERS, a periodical exploring the wisdom and mysteries of the Elders. She is the author of a correspondence course, HERBS FOR MAGICK AND MEDICINE. She has led workshops and rituals at a number of gatherings. An enthusiastic convert to computers, she has compiled a data base on magickal and medical uses of herbs. Grey Cat resides in the hills of Tennessee near the place where she grew up.

AMERICAN INDIAN CEREMONIES

A PRACTICAL WORKBOOK AND STUDY GUIDE TO THE MEDICINE PATH

In a medicine wheel there are two roads: east and west runs the black road, the road of hard lessons and the struggle for understanding. North and south runs the good red road, the road where each of us may find our happiness.

CONTENTS

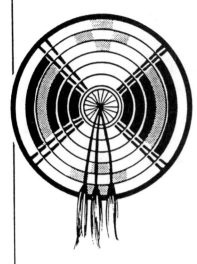

Myth: Smudging comes to the Cherokee. Explanation of smudging and description of equipment used. Methods of smudging. Construction and use of the personal spirit bag.

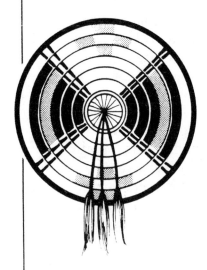

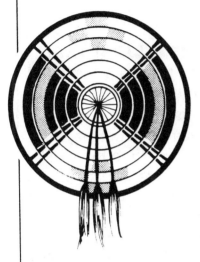

Why the mineral kingdom is considered "alive". Contacting the spirits of the rocks. A mineral kingdom meditation. The magick of ordinary rocks. List of some totem minerals: technical name, descrpition, mythology, powers, associated concepts.

17. CONCRETE CANYONS WITH MANY COLORED LEAVES

Urban medicine

Practicing medicine path within a modern, city-based life style. A "new" concept of just what environment really is. Totems of the urban environment. The invisible medicine wheel. Urban pipe ceremony. The underground railroad of the spirit: freeing the spirits of Turtle Island.

18. CHRONICLES OF SAND, ROCK AND SKIN

Magick in letters and symbols

Drawn and painted symbols of Indian spiritual observance. Pictographs, runes, sand painting, the Cherokee alphabet, non-verbal communication. Wigwags, color associations.

19. THE SEARCH FOR THE LODGE OF YOUR GRANDSIRES

Continuing along the path

Book list: a number of books which the authors have personally found useful in Indian studies. Methods of finding a teacher. List of mail-order sources of American Indian lore and objects.

A GREEN AND BLOOMING COTTONWOOD

What is medicine path?

"Walking a medicine path means being truly at one with your environment. This is what your personal medicine is. If your environment is the city there is no reason why you cannot walk a good, solid medicine path right where you are. You may take the concept of the sacred pipe, the medicine wheel, right into your business life with you — into your everyday life in the city. That is where you are to express and manifest your medicine. That's what walking the medicine path is.

"We are all put here on the earth to help heal and free things. That's why we are here. We aren't meant just to be born here in this lifetime and sit watching TV. We are here to do work. We are here to heal and free the things of the earth.

"We are supreme beings; we create, we heal, and we free with our voice, with our being, with our thoughts. A thought goes out from us, out of our spirits. If it's strong enough, that thought goes out and touches. That's how we create things, how we make these things happen. We say, "Let there be light, and light, and light." Our thought goes out, touches these things, and frees them.

"We are all instruments of freedom. We are the breakers of chains. We are put upon this earth to free and heal and create. This power is not confined to any one thing: it must reach the cities, the animals, the plants, the mountains, the people." [Medicine Hawk, Full Thawing Moon, 1988]

WHAT, AFTER ALL, IS MEDICINE PATH?

Medicine path is a term for a number of systems developed by followers of the pre-invasion spiritual beliefs of Native Americans. There is some disagreement about the use of the word "medicine" applied to these religions and/or their recognized leaders (medicine men or women). Perhaps the original use of the term, as it was translated into English, was due to a deliberate misunderstanding of the role and functions of these leaders. Perhaps the original Indian words would support such a translation. It doesn't really matter a whole lot. As long as we understand what WE mean by the term and that understanding is not inharmonious with the meaning of the original term in the Indian languages, mistakes in translation and application may be left to bury themselves.

Medicine path as taught by Medicine Hawk and the Shadowlight Clan is a method of seeking spiritual growth and enlightenment in a manner totally harmonious with the environment in which we each live. It is based upon the living traditions of the original inhabitants of this particular geographic area (Turtle Island).

In addition to being a method of seeking the spiritual realization of individuals, medicine path is also a way to the increased harmony of all with, and on, the earth. All followers of this path are not just expected, they are required, to fully realize the commitment - in fact, the intrinsic relationship - they have with all which constitutes their environment. This specifically includes such living things as other humans and the animals, minerals, and plants with whom we share it.

THE COSMIC UNDERSTANDING OF THE AMERICAN INDIAN

The spirituality of the American Indian is completely identified with all facets of the individual's surroundings. The Lakota (Sioux) greets the sunrise: "Here am I, behold me, I am the sun, behold me."

Each individual is literally a cousin, a brother, a sister of EVERYTHING! And not just Sister Hawk, Brother Eagle, Sister Bear; but Brother Mountain, Sister Cloud, Brother Sun, Sister Cottonwood. In everything is some of the "spirit stuff" which is the true existence of the cosmos: the same spirit stuff is within each individual human.

Wakan Tanka, Great Spirit, Manatu, Galunlati: these concepts have at times been said to indicate that the Indian believed in a single, monotheistic, all-powerful God such as Jehovah or Allah. While in one sense this could be said to have validity, it isn't really what the Indians meant. Other translations of these terms such as "Great Spiritual", "Great Mystery", and "Great Mysterious" have been offered. These translations give us a slightly better understanding of what was originally meant.

While the Great Spirit lives in everything, animate and inanimate, it also exists as itself. It is neither totally within us nor something totally outside us. It is above us and at the same time Is us. It is not a "God" in the European sense of God. Neither are the totems "Godlings", separate, pantheistic Gods. However, there may in some ways be a comparison to the concept of the guardian angel. To the Indians there is no separation of religion from life. All acts are religious acts.

Indians understand time in different terms. Industrial culture perceives time as linear: past — present — future. We, ourselves, are seen as disconnected dots on this line. The American Indian sensed time as cyclical, a circle or spiral. He saw himself as the axis of this cycle. He had an enduring place in it; he was not an unconnected, ever-moving dot.

WHAT DOES SHADOWLIGHT TEACH?

Shadowlight does not attempt to "recreate" the primal, pre-invasion religious beliefs, customs, or life of the American Indians. The teachers of this tradition live in modern houses, do their writing on computers, and wear clothes manufactured by semi-automatic machinery. They drive iron ponies and hunt most of their meat at Kroger's.

These teachings are offered as a path to enable each of us to live in harmony with life as IT IS, not as it should be. They offer us methods of remedying those things which violate the fabric of life on earth. Medicine path is a "militant" philosophy in that all followers must fight for the good of all their brothers and sisters. Medicine path is a contemplative philosophy in that its followers discover that they have a true place in the cosmos and a purpose in their lives and deaths.

The Shadowlight teachings are eclectic. They do not reflect either the ancient practices of just one particular tribe or group of Native Americans, nor one of the careful (or not so careful) modern re-creations of such practices. Our teachings emphasize Cherokee traditions somewhat but are by no means limited to them.

Medicine path is foremost and most importantly an intensely personal endeavor. The prime ethic of the Indians has always been that "the dogma of tribal rituals is always secondary to the guidance one received from personal visions." [Indian Medicine Power, Brad Steiger]

No individual or tribe attempted to force another to follow any particular practice. "...there is no evidence in North or South America that any Native peoples, even those who were otherwise militaristic and expansionist (the Aztecs, for one), ever tried to impose their particular religious philosophy on anyone else, friend or foe." [North American Indian Art, Jill and Peter Furst]

The ceremonial practices of the American Indians have always been mutable, changing to fit changing lives and circumstances, changing to meet the new needs of the tribe and of individuals. Black Elk, who has told us much of the ceremonies of the Lakota (Sioux), was present at the "invention" of rituals of major importance to that people.

Shadowlight teaches no cut and dried rituals which must be followed word for word. Reasonably detailed guidelines are given. Instructions are given such as a child might have learned through living in the culture in which these ceremonies were a part of everyday life. Shadowlight does not have nor teach the One True Right and Only Path [Real Magic, P.E.I. Bonewits] to salvation, true Indianness, and a better life.

WHY DO WE WALK THE MEDICINE PATH?

The medicine path does not cry to everyone. For some it may be a long and difficult journey, for others the short way home. There is much to learn and much to be done. It will take time from your usual amusements and it WILL change your life if you choose to follow it. The Ancestors have given us medicine path and we are provided with rough guidelines on how to follow that path. Exact instructions cannot be passed on to you from another human because each one of us walks his or her own path.

Medicine path has currently taken the interest of many people as the latest fad in alternative spirituality. This isn't necessarily a bad thing; however, the path is much, much more than that. If you are reading these pages in order to have a general understanding of Native American spirituality, this is welcome. The study of the medicine path, even if only out of curiosity, will help bring to you a greater understanding of the ancient spiritual presences here in Turtle Island.

For you who have heard or felt the call to the medicine path as the direction for your life, we can only help set your feet upon that path. The true medicine path is yours alone: it is within you. The knowledge of it is preserved for you by your own totem spirits. You, alone, must learn who they are and what they have to teach you.

The Great Spirit, Galunlati, has set his hand upon this land. His spirit keepers live within its trees and rocks, its streams, lakes and mountains. Whatever path to spirituality you are called to follow, it should move upon the land in harmony with these ancient ancestors.

SYMBOLS OF THE MEDICINE PATH

Most spiritual systems depend greatly upon symbolism. Some symbols are as simple and universal as a light in the window to welcome a loved one home. Most symbols, however, are complex and their explanations may run many pages.

In medicine path there is very little symbolism. The medicine wheel is not a symbol of the Gods, the Universe, the elements, and the moons. It is only itself and, in itself, it IS the Great Spirit, the universe, the spirit keepers and the year.

The sacred pipe particularly is not a "symbolic" instrument. The pipe IS the earth and sky. It IS the heart and spirit of its People, their blood and their bone. The cleansing of the smudge or the sweat lodge is not "symbolic" cleansing such as dipping a finger tip in water. They do in reality cleanse the body, the mind, and the spirit. The animal which may appear to you when you cry for a vision does not symbolize the direction of your life. The animal who appears to you is itself and because it is itself, it has real meanings which then become a part of your life and your path.

When you spread the seed and blessings of Turtle Island, giving them back to the Island or finding new homes in far lands, the Hokshichankiya is a reality. These seeds, blessed and filled with a special life and purpose, will grow to bring a special newness to the land.

I empty my spirit bag here before me. The objects which fall from it are not symbols of my life or my spirit: they are actually participating in the building of my life. The silver dime which has somehow grown to two dimes, the broken crystal which was given to the fire on the longest night - they are the embodiment of the changing in me. A wildcat claw, independent, the hunter of hidden things, surrounded by its own invulnerability. A clear crystal point—a spiritual goal. A bead, a penny are traditional for luck and prosperity. These are all symbolic objects and yet they are real; I can touch them. They exist. My spirit does not live in this bag, but the bag does indeed live in my spirit.

SPIRIT BAG
Following the medicine path is not a simple

matter of dressing up and playing Indian. Many who are advanced far along this path never wear feathers or leather fringe. Medicine path never forgets its source in the original inhabitants of Turtle Island, but it has forms which are completely of today. Those who walk it use the powers of the elder times to create this special way.

This book is written because it is a part of Medicine Hawk's vision to bring the knowledge of his grandmothers and grandfathers to all the children of the Turtle Island that they may know the harmony of this land.

IS MEDICINE PATH FOR YOU?

You may have been drawn to this book for any number of reasons. Perhaps you simply wish to know more of a spiritual path currently being talked about. Perhaps you feel a need to relate your own religious/spiritual beliefs and practices to the land in which you live. Perhaps you feel strongly drawn to this journey and you hope that we will help you in your travel.

We write with all of you in mind. We hope we are informative, that your simple curiosity about these Native American religious practices will be satisfied. Perhaps it will lead you into even more study on the subject. We also hope that the philosophies, rituals, and attitudes presented here will be in a form through which you can relate your own philosophies and rituals to the grandmothers and grandfathers of Turtle Island. We do not feel that the intimate relationship of all things which is taught by medicine path is available only to those who follow its "doctrines" to the letter.

To those who feel the call to the medicine road, we hope that we can help you find your way along the first few inches. We have tried to be very clear about the ordinary physical aspects of this path. It probably isn't possible in any book to introduce you to the full understanding of the spiritual, emotional, mental, and life-encompassing aspects of the medicine path. Only you yourself can waken your mind and senses to hear the lessons in the wind.

WHAT CAN WE TEACH YOU?

All spiritual paths have as one of their goals, leading the individual to a realization of his spiritual and human potential. While each path may define these potentials differently, all aim at perfecting the individual following the path.

In medicine path, the perfection and growth of the individual is always seen in terms of his or her relationship to the land, this particular land, Turtle Island, and to the various beings, animal, vegetable, mineral, and non-material which live with and on this land. The wisdom of Owl is sought to guide one's steps, the fearlessness of Crow, and the healing powers of Bear for the courage to make one's journey.

Much of an individual's medicine path is just that—the individual's alone. The practice of Native American spirituality can be explained so that you, if you come to it with all your devotion, may walk in the footsteps of those who walked the land before the iron horses and the stone lodges covered it.

One criticism of this book may well be that we have treated the sacred philosophies of the Indian far too briefly and shallowly, that we haven't touched upon the totality of the Indian's world view nor communicated the true depth of his intense spirituality.

We have recommended a number of books which do the best that mere words may do to explain Indian spirituality. We do feel that the "secrets" of the Indian's beliefs may be found in the rocks and trees, the four-leggeds, the winged, the finned, and the creepers and crawlers of Turtle Island and that the totems will whisper to the serious seeker.

Those who approach the rituals, ceremonies, and practices taught by us in a serious and sacred manner will find the spirituality of

our land through their own visions.

The dilettantes, the "what's new this week" folks, those using our work only to become pretend experts will learn nothing from a million words of careful — even inspired — discussion. Those who will not learn cannot be taught. Those who will listen to the land must inevitably develop true understanding.

The need for the cleansing fumes of the smudging herbs is in no way reduced by the acid rain in our rivers, nor does the shower massage replace the sweat lodge in the purification of the whole person. The medicine wheel rolls down Interstate 75 just as meaningfully as it followed the buffalo trails. The spiraled smoke of the sacred pipe rises to the nostrils of Galunlati even through the murky air of our cities.

SOME STEPS ALONG THE PATH — WHERE WE CAN TAKE YOU

This book is intended only to help you find the first steps of the medicine path. Regardless of intent, this is all that it CAN do. The walking of the path is up to you.

The medicine path begins with learning meditation, the quietly concentrated state of mind basic to any accomplishment in spiritual matters. This does not mean that you cannot go on to further chapters before you have learned to meditate like a Zen Master! A good beginning and the decision to practice every day is more than enough.

We will teach the preparation and purification of mind and body in the next chapter so that you may perform the ceremoniies suggested in later chapters appropriately in a Wakan or Galunky'ti'yu manner. In the chapter fire we will share an important part of Native American culture, the concept of giving— giving to the earth and to your brothers and sisters. We will present a new idea of "ownership" and appropriate methods of expressing this.

The medicine wheel is a very useful tool to

those following the medicine path. Its design is traditional and is never twice the same. It brings the universe and all that is within it into your back yard or local park. Walking its stones can lead you great distances along the medicine path.

The sacred pipe is the gift of communication and participation. Not all are called to bear the pipe, but all may know its being and meaning. The pipe is universally revered among the Tribes and all respect its power and sanctity.

The sweat lodge is not solely a concept of the Native Americans. Many cultures have used similar devices for both physical and spiritual goals. It is a very powerful tool and entity, and lies close to the heart of Native American spiritual practice.

Vision questing also is found in many different cultures. It is the inescapable necessity of spiritual development regardless of the name of the path. A medicine path vision quest isn't necessarily that different from its cousins although its general focus on the finding of an animal totem spirit differs from some. In common with similar quests world-wide, the ultimate goal is the knowledge of one's self.

Medicine path is a group activity as well as an individual's seeking. At times of celebration and sorrow it has its own customs. Travellers on the medicine path must be concerned with their brothers and sisters when they need healing, celebration, or other help.

The Native Americans called the rocks, the trees, and the animals their brothers and sisters. They knew of their spirits and of their ways. In them they found great spiritual lessons and these may in part be passed on to you as story and legend. Before you go far on the medicine path, you will find your own personal spirits or totems. Through their traditional meanings and your own understanding of their communications, they will be your real guides on the path.

We will also offer you much lore on the making of your own sacred objects and tools which may aid you on your journey. You will be introduced to the concept of harmonizing modern urban life with the traditions of medicine path, and many specialized forms of the tradition will be presented as urban medicine.

Finally, we will try to help you find teachers, further information and encouragement on your journey.

WHAT CAN'T WE TEACH YOU HERE?

Books are great and wonderful things. They are the words of our ancestors. Our culture is based upon the written word. When computers became fairly common in the business world and it was obvious that the day of the "computer on every desk" was fast approaching, it was said that paper would become a thing of the past. Soon everyone would get all their information staring at a square screen. Actually, what has happened is that every office has more and more paper. We want to hold our words in our hand and have it "in black and white", not amber on a grey screen!

But not just every thing can be communicated by the written word. While not EVERYTHING can be communicated by the spoken word either, we are sure that when a grandfather wise in the ways of his people told one of the old stories to a child, he adjusted the story here and there to suit the times, the experiences, and the personality of that particular child.

We cannot teach you to think like an Indian, to relate to your environment like an Indian, to perceive the universe like an Indian. Only you can teach you that.

We cannot teach you "medicine power" for that must always be achieved by the individual him/herself. We cannot make you a "shaman" able to send one of your souls traveling to seek answers to problems.

CHAPTER 2

WINDS OF BLACK, WHITE, RED AND YELLOW

Who can follow a medicine path?

WHO IS AN INDIAN?

It would seem obvious that any individual who can trace her lineage to a Native American is qualified, more or less, to call herself an Indian. Not so to some Native Americans. Some groups deny the teachings of the medicine path to any not of full blood in a particular tribe (or group of tribes). Other groups require at least half-blood, or perhaps three-quarter blood, or some other specific proportion of Indian lineage. The Federal Government has specific percentage requirements for admission to residence on a reservation. There are groups of Native Americans who feel that no one not of full blood may teach or, indeed, even follow the ways of the medicine path.

What of others interested in this path who can point to no admixture of Indian blood in their family history? Are they ineligible, incapable even, of following this path? For those who protest the presumption of non-Indians (or part-Indians) stealing the Native American's religion(s) half understood, poorly learned and frivolously used. Shadowlight takes the position that these wayspeak to the native spiritual inhabitants of Turtle Island — the land upon which all of us live. These concepts, ideas and, yes, spirit beings are a part of THIS LAND and are not the exclusive possession of any group, whatever its lineage. We hope no one, blood, non-Indian, or mixed-blood, uses this information is a less than spiritual, serious, manner. As for "half understood, poorly learned, frivolous" practices — you don't have to be White to use these traditions badly.

Perhaps it is true that the fullest understanding of medicine path will always be reserved for genetic Indians who have been raised in Indian ways and who have from childhood spoken the language of the specific path which they follow. Certainly, no one who has not had the benefit of this near total immersion in the entirety of a culture will be able to fully understand the Old Ways.

Few can meet this criteria. Shadowlight feels that it is not intrinsically more difficult for a unega (person of European ethnic heritage) to become a medicine man/woman than for a full-blood raised in the predominant White American culture. We all must work toward the understandings which the Old Ones had, as we also work to become old ones ourselves, with an understanding of present day culture and life.

WOMEN - THE REAL STORY

Most of Indian history was written by white, Anglo-Saxon, Protestant men who owned land. Consequently the literary heritage of Native American women has been rather one-sided. We must examine such treatises with the objectivity due this double-standard.

Before "education" was provided by European settlers, most Indians treated both genders with equality. There were, of course, several hundred autonomous tribes on the continent. As each tribe was free to establish its own customs, inevitably these customs differed. It is likely that there were tribes in which women were clearly subordinate to men —, and tribes in which the obverse was equally true.

European males were not inclined to admire any of the social systems of the Indians, particularly those which allowed women to assume positions of leadership. "Deploring the Cherokee's practice of admitting women to their war councils and of giving them freedom ... Adair accused Cherokee men of living under petticoat government." [The Cherokee, Grace Woodward]

In the southern Floridian tribes, the female's matriarchal surname was taken by both parties in a marriage. Whomever was best qualified for a job got it. If the female was the best hunter of the two in a marriage arrangement, she hunted. If the male was the best cook, he cooked. If a female had proven her courage and bravery above all others, she became war chief.

Whoever proved to be the wisest elder of a southern tribe became Council Chief — male or female. These facts were suppressed by the European male settlers, fearful that their own women would desire more power in view of this example. It is theorized that the suppression of female power played as large a part in Cherokee removal as greed for land and (almost mythical) gold.

It is interesting to note here that Andrew Jackson, U. S. President at the time of removal, had a score to settle with Indian women. Jackson's troops had been soundly defeated by the guerrilla tactics of the Seminole in Florida. Contrary to written history, Seminole tradition insists that Osceola, War Chief of the Seminole, was a woman. Imagine the utter humiliation suffered by the hero of the Battle of New Orleans. His only defeat came at the hands of an Indian. Worse yet, at the hands of an Indian woman. Under a flag of truce, Osceola was treacherously taken into custody by General Thomas Jessup and perished from fever in a South Carolina prison.

The phobias exhibited by the oft-praised,
macho heroes of our nation's imperialistic history were well-founded. They had much to fear in their gender bigotry. Out of the same normalcy which had spawned equality of the sexes, came an imposing figure — the medicine woman. This behemoth spirit rocked the foundations of male-oriented society. She stood balanced with the powers of earth and spirit. She healed sickness, communicated fluently with the totem spirits, and showed the reasoning wisdom that comes only from a centered life.

More importantly, the medicine woman imparted this balance and understanding to both sexes. The only thing worse than enlightened women to the chauvinistic European settlers was men who understood this power. This was a threat to the settlers' prejudiced way of life. Thus came the systematic, premeditated genocide that postponed social gender-equality on this great Turtle Island for 150 years.

We do not discriminate against OR FOR women. We do teach that men and women are not the SAME; however, no conclusions as to superiority/inferiority are drawn therefrom. Men and women, after all, aren't "just the same". Shadowlight's policies in this matter have been fully set forth and appear in Appendix   of this volume.

MEDICINE PATH AND OTHER "MINORITIES"

Everyone is a "minority" with regard to someone else. In the 17 and 18 hundreds, the Europeans were a minority on Turtle Island compared with the AmerInds. Blacks as well as Jews, Irish, Polish, Slavs, Hungarians, etc., have a long history of being discriminated against in the United States. However, the whole concept of life held by the early tribes on Turtle Island was one of acceptance of all peoples, regardless of race. Blacks and Whites were accepted providing they pulled their own weight and did not force their beliefs upon those who did not wish to follow them.

The tribes welcomed run-away Black slaves and married with them, as they did with many Europeans. Indeed, it was only after Europeans found that Indians made lousy slaves that the import of Africans became profitable. There were half-black chiefs, medicine women, hunters and warriors, just as there were half-White privy cleaners and shamans.

The AmerInds did not expect everyone to be just the "same". They usually had traditional divisions of labor between the sexes, possibly amongst families or clans. However, the fact that these divisions were observed by most of the tribe was never taken to be the only way things might be done. Women were "allowed" to do men's work and men were allowed to do women's work.

Winktes were the gay folks, the homosexuals (usually) of the tribes. They were considered immensely powerful by all, including the chiefs, because they were one with their sexuality — the great power of the life force. Homosexuality was not uncommon. According to the account given in Hanto Yo by Ruth Beebe Hill, a chief performed fellatio on the tribal winkte to gain power for battle.

The winkte did everything anyone else did in the tribe, battle, cooking, skinning, hunting, etc. In some tribes he would dress in women's clothes and would at all times behave as a woman in others nothing obviously separated him from the other men.

The heyoka was a contrary — one who did everything backwards. When he/she wished to bathe, he threw dirt on himself. She rode horses backwards, etc. When one received a dream of the Thunderers (Ani-Hyuntikwalaski, Wudeligunyi, Sistsecom), it was a signal that he was to spend his life as an example for others "not to follow". The Thunderers protected heyokas and gave them powerful medicine.

The law of reciprocals is not one we can violate. For everything there must be an opposite. This holds the world in balance. Therefore, the heyokas and winktes of any race are integral parts of a healthy culture.

UTILITY OF ANCIENT WAYS IN THESE MODERN TIMES

The ways of the Native Americans were developed in response to a life lived in direct contact with "nature". For the most part, trees and plants grew by themselves wherever they found to grow. Animals ran their own lives without masters, herders, or professional butchers. Paths led around mountains and crossed rivers at narrow places. Miles weren't measured.

Obviously, most of us in this world of the late 20th century aren't in this sort of touch with our environment! Wait just a minute!! What exactly is your "environment"?

"Environ 1. To form a ring around; surround, encompass, or encircle. Environment 2. specifically, the aggregate of all the external conditions and influences affecting the life and development of an organism" [Webster's New Collegiate Dictionary]

Cities are environments too, for organisms live in them and are affected by them. And cities are not bare of Spirit. Perhaps because it is far easier to contact the spirit of a mountain way off from the noise of traffic and the ringing of the phone, we have lazily assumed that there is nothing to contact where we actually live. To live life in a Wakan manner, we must learn to live with our real environment, whatever that is. We must admit the spirits of our cities into ourselves, just as we must know that the rivers and the bears are our sisters.

This is not to say that we should not join the protests at the destructive excesses of our world. Our cities are being destroyed almost as much as our open lands. People in cities are being driven toward spiritual extinction as surely as the panda will die without his bamboo shoots. The follower of the medicine path can admit the spirit of the concrete mountains into her soul while working on all planes to prevent the destruction of beauty and even of life on earth. She works with the knowledge of what is as well as what has been and of what must be. Urban, suburban, exurban, small town, and back-to-the-land, we all have our path and our responsibilities to Grandmother Earth.

SOME RESIDENTS OF THE AMERINDIAN SPIRITUAL COSMOS

Galunlati, the Great Mysterious, is not merely a grand, abstract concept to the Amer-Ind. "Like one grain of sugar in a bowl of water, you can't see it, but you can taste it; that's how the Great Mystery speaks to you," Wallace Black Elk explains. It/He/She is reachable, hears, and may reply.

Many other supernatural beings inhabit the cosmology of the American Indian. To some extent, this Great Mysterious is identified with the sky and the sun. However the sky and sun were lesser, more visible evidences of this Mystery. Indeed, all which could be seen, felt, smelled, touched, heard, or imagined partook of the Great Mysterious.

Although White ethnologists, historians, anthropologists, and missionaries have often chosen to call the entities who populated the American Indian's spiritual cosmos "Gods" and "Goddesses"; these are not very accurate terms. While these beings share a number of the qualities found in European deity figures, the analogies are not good. The differences are not so much in kind or degree, but in the attitudes towards these supernatural figures.

The ceremonies and explanations given here, as well as any in further studying you may choose to do will help you understand more of the essences of these beings.

Many of these spirit beings are associated with natural phenomena such as the thunder, rain, the sun, and the moon. Some are associated with local landmarks, with the cycle of the seasons, or with the giving of life and/or death. Some take the faces of evil, catastrophic change, and unpredictability. Others are the grandmothers and grandfathers of the people, and the animals.

The sun, although most frequently appearing as male, was also seen as female. Sometimes the sun was captured or stolen by the "Hero". At other times, the sun attempted to destroy the people and/or the animals, and the "Hero" saved the world from him/her.

The moon, usually female, was often seen as a "night sun" and not distinctly separate from the "day sun".

The Sky was almost always seen as the male (generative) principal and was often called "Father" or "Grandfather". The Earth is the "Mother" and "Grandmother". She is the Mother of Four-Leggeds and the source of the corn and other vegetable foods of the people. But the Mother also doubles as the face of death and of the under/after world. She did not, however, first bring death to the people. They earned death themselves by violating the balance of life.

In the West (usually) lived "Thunder" or "The Thunderers", who generally displayed both "good" and "evil" qualities. Sometimes smaller Thunders lived in springs and caves. All these entities might have sons or daughters, frequently twins, a "light" twin and a "dark" twin. The "Hero" and after him or her, the medicine people and the tribespeople, could interact with these entities under certain conditions.

There also existed the Grandmothers and Grandfathers of the tribe and of the animals. These entities might appear in dreams and visions to teach the people and to help them when there was need.

Along with these generative elders there was the Hero figure, the Hercules of the tribe who preserved the tribe from destruction by another supernatural being. It may have been the Hero, who brought to the tribe the skills, knowledge, and sacred rites which made their life and existence possible. This Hero was not necessarily male - or even human.

A very important figure in this cosmology is the Trickster / Gambler / Magician / Fool. This figure is generally one of the chief teachers of the tribe's mythology, which express the principals of its social and religious system. He or she demonstrates, often negatively, the beliefs and behaviors which are valued.

Also, but never finally, there are the frightening figures, the "Boogers", the terrible monsters, dragons, "witches", and things that go bump in the night.

All these supernatural beings and many, many more appear in the myths and legends of the AmerInds. Their adventures helped make clear to child and adult alike the philosophical and religious beliefs of the people. These sacred stories were not static, ritualized "scriptures". They changed, grew, were explained, and re-explained as if Cinderella went back to her stepmother's house and lived forever sweeping ashes. Not even the "peaceful, natural world" of the pre-invasion AmerIndian was static and unchanging. Like good cosmic lore anywhere, the stories grew and changed to serve the needs of the people. These stories continue this process even today.

It is extremely important to keep firmly in mind during all your studies of American Indian spirituality and the medicine path that there is no way of knowing how the Indians before the invasion felt toward all these different spiritual entities. Attitudes, terminologies, and "superstitions" adopted by the Indians from the Europeans - and these same factors in the writings and interpretations by Europeans themselves - have affected all these traditions. The Cherokee did not originally call the Raven Mockers "witches"; this is a European word and concept. It may never be possible to really know how the Cherokee felt about these entities since they themselves seem to have adopted the White's concept of "witch". Since the European concept of witch is a product of a propaganda campaign begun in the middle ages rather than any accurate reflection of the individuals who were "witches", the result is a term with no solid meaning at all.

JUST TO GET SOME THINGS CLEAR

When teaching something new or different, one must take some pains to ensure that student and teacher are speaking the same language. There are a number of words linked to Native American beliefs and practices which have been widely used without care as to what, exactly, is meant by them. We will, therefore, set down definitions for some of these words for clarity of meaning. These definitions apply only to THIS BOOK and will not necessarily meet with wide agreement in the world at large.

Medicine is used to denote a sort of "spiritual power" which may be sought, increased, and used for many purposes including healing. A "medicine song" is to be understood as a song seeking or applying this spiritual power. A medicine man or a medicine woman is an individual who has successfully sought this power and has in some way demonstrated their possession of it to other individuals. A medicine wheel is a place possessing in itself spiritual power, and it is also a place to which one may go to gain or use this power.

Sacred. All that is a part of the Universe is imbued with Spirit and all is therefore sacred. However, objects, beings, people, places may through various means become particularly dedicated to the expression of this spirit and therefore may be specifically spoken of as sacred. A "sacred pipe" is made to become especially sacred and when complete, special ritual is performed in order to embue it with this special quality of particular sacredness. Some things are "made" sacred, other things are recognized as already being sacred.

Chanoopah is a Lakota word used by

Wallace Black Elk to mean a sacred ceremony, a sacred tool, and a "state of grace"; the present state of being sacred. Rather than being a static identification it is an "active" word implying that you are doing something.

Shaman (Which, by the way, has always been practiced by both males and females in most places where it has been identified.) "The Shaman, a mystical, priestly, and political figure...can be described not only as a specialist in the human soul but also as a generalist whose sacred and social functions can cover an extraordinarily wide range of activities. Shamans are healers, seers, and visionaries who have mastered death. They are in communication with the world of gods and spirits. Their bodies can be left behind while they fly to unearthly realms. They are poets and singers. They dance and create works of art. They are not only spiritual leaders but also judges and politicians, repositories of the knowledge of the culture's history, both sacred and secular. They are familiar with cosmic as well as physical geography; the ways of plants, animals, and the elements are known to them. They are psychologists, entertainers, and food finders. Above all, however, shamans are technicians of the sacred and masters of ecstasy." [Shamanic Voices, Joan Halifax]

Is a medicine woman/man a Shaman? In a sense, followers of the medicine path are all shamans when they have received their vision. They have communicated with the spirit world. In a more technical sense, "shaman" is the word used to denote a particular fashion of communication with the other world. Amerindian traditions rarely lead to this sort of "out-of-body" travel, particularly searches into the underworld.

It seems that in popular use and according to many authorities, a medicine man/woman can be called a shaman without distorting the word seriously. To be called either, the individual must be perceived by others to be learned, wise, and powerful.

Turtle Island is a translation of one Indian term for the North American continent.

Indians. we will use the terms "Native Americans", "American Indians", "Indians", "AmerIndians", and AmerInds" interchangeably to indicate the aboriginal or "native" population of the geographical area now known as north America. These terms are used as a convenience in identifying members of an otherwise disparate group and no derogatory meanings are attached to any of these words for us. We do not intend to explore the interesting subject of the origins of these peoples or visits to this continent by Europeans prior to 1492.

Blood, Half-Blood, and **Full-Blood** are terms applied to persons of Indian lineage. Full-bloods and Bloods claim to have no mixture of non-Indian ancestry. "Half-blood" generally refers to persons of any degree of mixture with Africans, Europeans, or Asians and does not refer to a precise percentage of descent.

Washichu, is a Sioux term for the invading Americans. It does not refer to skin color. We prefer using this term to "Whites" as we know very few people whose skin is "white".

Unega is the Cherokee word for "newcomer" and came to be applied generally to the European invaders.

SOME FINAL NOTES

On Turtle Island, which is now called North America, lived many, many peoples. There were several hundred mutually unintelligible languages. No one has any idea of how many different societies functioned in this land.

To add to this, Turtle Island had been populated for many, many thousands of years. Times change and customs, even those customs which involve what we call religion, change. It isn't possible to state that "the Indians did this" or that "the Indians never did that". What Indians? When?

Many tribes did not survive to the present

day. Many customs practiced 100, 200 or 300 years ago have been stamped out or forgotten. Many, of course, have survived - and these have survived changed by the changing environments in which those who guarded them have lived.

In some tribes the medicine rituals were considered secret and were not shared with those outside the tribe, or perhaps not outside a certain ritual group within the tribe. Other tribes, finding that the whites only made fun of all they were told, ceased to talk of their medicine. Sometimes they ceased to teach medicine ways to their own children. A few individuals have shared widely their medicine knowledge and therefore, many of the rituals and customs found among practitioners of the medicine path these days share in this knowledge. Black Elk, a Lakota (Sioux), was led by his vision to share his great knowledge with all who cared to take up a book. Because of his incalculably valuable legacy, few modern medicine people practice forms entirely free of materials he gave us. Lame Deer, H. Storm, and Sun Bear all have contributed from their stores of ancient teachings, from their hearts and souls that we may know of this path.

Perhaps this mixing of traditions once held strictly and exclusively by the various tribes is a necessary part of the forging of a medicine path which can bring the old blessings to those of new ways. Certainly we are not immune to this cross-fertilization. In this book we are using in most instances the Indian words used by the southeastern Cherokee. Names used by other groups and tribes, particularly when they are in frequent use by other traditions of medicine path, will be used on occasion and many of them appear in the Glossary.

Each follower of the path should consider the original (circa. 1700) residents of the land upon which they walk. We have found that we generally prefer to use the language used in older times in the area in which we are. That is,

in Florida to speak to the totems in Seminole, in Georgia to use Cherokee, etc.

Not all tribes used the sweat lodge, not all used a medicine wheel, not all used the sacred pipe — but the central meaning of these particular ceremonies was found among all the tribes. An individual from one tribe would rarely find it impossible to understand the meanings of these rites. These particular ceremonies are "accessible" to the minds and culture of persons not raised in the culture of an AmerIndian tribe — that is why these are the particular ceremonies included in this book. Each individual must go beyond this book to research her own area and to discover his own ceremonial desires and needs. This book is only a beginning.

PICKING AND CHOOSING

It is not a new thing that a non-Native American religion should use bits and pieces of the traditions of a local tribe. Early Christian missionaries, whether from honest interest and appreciation of the Indian forms of spirituality or for reasons of obtaining a greater volume of semi-converts, used one bit of tradition or another in their services. Currently a number of Christian churches incorporate various ceremonials or traditions in their rituals, many of them at the request of their Native American members. The essential similarity of the ceremony of the sacred pipe to the ceremony of communion has led to the substitution or addition of the pipe to this rite. The Native American Church has synthesized many Native American ceremonies, customs, and traditions with much of the Christian philosophy.

A large number of the religious groups which do not belong to the "big three" have incorporated some of the spirituality of Turtle Island into their own systems. "Indian chiefs" have frequently served as spirit guides to Spiritualists. Teepees are erected and vended at the Rainbow Gatherings of the Flower Children. Druids must cry for a vision, Wiccans become shamans, Pagans of various sorts practice some of the traditions of medicine path.

How is this mixture to be made? One man said to me, "I keep my Indian stuff and my Wiccan stuff separate". Shadowlight says that this cannot be done unless you really have neither sort of "stuff".

All the religious rituals of all residents of Turtle Island are done on the Grandmother beneath the eye of the Grandfather. The ways of the ancients are actually difficult to exclude. In order to more fully incorporate the spirits of this land into your work, you must take the time and effort to achieve some understanding of your relationship with this particular part of the universe. Calling the four quarters of the compass, a tradition shared by Wicca and medicine path, may be done with both the traditional words of the Wiccan and those of the Indian. As with Christianity, the sacred pipe expresses a relationship with the untouchable which many of these new or revived religions hold.

However, it is neither appropriate nor successful to mix undigested hunks of one sacred tradition with another. First you must see entirely through to the meaning of each. Then the specific details of exactly what and how to mix must be examined for harmony. In addition, you must be in "sympathy" with both, nothing may be jarring or undigestable. Finally, medicine path requires your full time, as does Wicca, Druidism, and other spiritual paths. Your mixture must be such as to foster your full-time devotion to one fully integrated tradition.

Whatever you may select from medicine path to make a part of your own religious life, be assured that you must live it all of the time not just when you feel like "Playing Indian". Calling on Artemis this week, on Oden last week, and on Galunlati next week is not a sign of religious sophistication, merely of ineffective dabbling at unchewed, unswallowed, untasted novelty.

GOING INTO THE SILENCE

Meditation

You may think of meditation as part of the Oriental religions. Indeed, most eastern religions and philosophies DO consider the teaching of meditation to be one of their most important disciplines. Meditation, however, is a part of every spiritual path, Oriental, European, African, Australian, and Amerindian. While many methods of practicing meditation have been taught by Gurus from India and the Orient, the Native Americans taught and practiced meditation long before the first Swami got on the lecture circuit.

Whether it is called meditation, going into the silence, sitting and thinking, or vision quest; meditation is a tool for the attainment of spirituality, self understanding, and communion with the spirit keepers, the totems, all of nature. It is important in controlling your restless mind, overcoming fear and illness, expanding knowledge and the development of your psychic abilities. Without some training in meditation, you cannot progress very far along the medicine path.

To understand meditation and its workings, you must understand your own make-up and realize that you are a spiritual as well as a physical being. It can be useful to visualize the self as having three facets of being: 1) your ordinary, everyday conscious mind. 2) your subconscious, a creature of habit and past programming. It is essentially a non reasoning, language free, and reactive facet. 3) Your higher consciousness. Your spiritual self, a telephone line to the universe and the Great Spirit. Remember that these divisions are merely a way of attempting to understand yourself. Actually, you and everyone else are actually one single, interactive, multi-layered unity.

Your spiritual and physical selves are united through physio-neurological centers which you may know by the Sanskrit term, chakras. In meditation, psychic energy flows between these centers in successive order from bottom to top. These centers gradually activate or open up. You develop a sense of peace and well-being. Your subconscious mind begins to clear of negativity. The undesired programming of the subconscious established over a life-time begins to modify. Continued practice brings a freer flow of these energies. One's perception of life and awareness of true reality begins to come into focus. It is through meditation that you gain control of a restless, materially oriented mind. You will reprogram your subconscious to enable yourself to function from your spiritually oriented super-consciousness or higher self.

To clear the pathway to your higher consciousness, you must apply self-discipline through meditative techniques. Not only must you be in control of your own consciousness, you must also conduct self-examinations to insure that you are indeed in concert with the spiritual.

There are five essential elements to clearing this pathway and opening yourself to the medicine:

1. Controlling the ordinary consciousness: In order to clear the channel to the higher consciousness, the conscious mind must remain quiet. This is only done through some variety of meditation.

2. Love: You must truly learn to love. You must learn to love not only humankind, the four-leggeds, the wingeds, the swimmers and

crawlers, but yourself as well. True love must be unselfish and undemanding. You must not only give love — you must BE love.

3. Rid yourself of strong emotionalism: Anger, fear, hate, and envy are quick and effective means of short-circuiting your own energy and blocking your own channels. You must be objective and free of unbalancing emotions.

4. Empathize, don't sympathize: One of the quickest ways to create trouble for yourself is to become part of another's problem. Certainly, you should be sensitive to the feelings and emotions of others, but remember to be objective. Someone else's problem is a part of his or her own path. They are where they need to be, whether you or I can see it. Understand, but do not meddle.

5. Self examination: As a follower of the medicine path you must continually examine yourself, your ideals, beliefs, and, most of all, motives. You must always ensure that you abide by an ethic of never causing deliberate harm to another. Remember, also, that no one has the right to judge another.

USING MEDITATION IN MEDICINE PATH

Meditation is important in medicine path, not only for its utility in bringing to you balance and serenity, but also for its many specific applications.

SEEKING OF THE TOTEMS

A totem meditation requires that you BECOME a plant, animal and/or mineral archetype through anthropomorphic imagery. There are a number of reasons for attempting to accomplish this goal. First of all, your identification with the totems which have CHOSEN YOU (see chapter 13) cannot become full and complete until you have participated in their existence. Although you may have only a few totems to whom you are committed, others may communicate much of value to you once you have learned to open yourself to their

messages. The medicine path means a walking with the Grandmother Earth and all her children. Through totem meditations, we become sisters and brothers in truth.

Everything in medicine path is interactive. You may receive your totems during your vision quest, or you may learn of some of them during meditation long before you are prepared for your quest. Certainly, many followers of the medicine path work with totem meditations before the time and place have come together for their quest.

CRYING FOR A VISION

Crying for a vision, or the vision quest absolutely requires that you have some abilities in meditation. Sitting outdoors all night worrying about every noise in the woods, thinking about the television shows you are missing, and worrying about what your significant other is doing is a sure way of NOT receiving your vision.

SOME METHODS OF MEDITATION

In all types of work with medicine power, concentration and vibrant imagery are needed. Healing, praising, and asking all require a clear and focused mind. There are, at the very least, dozens of methods of learning and doing meditation. Several are taught in weekend seminars in the larger towns and cities. These seminars vary widely in cost and most are at least reasonably effective. Many yoga classes teach a specialized form of meditation. Stress management courses may also teach it. Attending a class of this type may be best for you. We do recommend you avoid the trendy, high-cost ones.

You can learn meditation on your own, it isn't even particularly difficult. Just remember that however you decide to learn to meditate, you must devote time and effort to the project. There are a number of books on meditation which teach a variety of methods: staring at a candle, visualizing white numbers on a bl

RELAXATION AND MEDITATION ARE A PART OF THE MEDICINE PATH. (24)

background, simple and elaborate breath control, etc. Everyone meditates a little differently from everyone else. Each method is the very best one for someone.

We give here one method of learning to meditate which has proved quite successful with many people. If you find it difficult, persevere. If after sticking with it for a long time, you still don't feel comfortable with it, or just can't get it going, explore another method. All of them will take some time. And working alone may mean that it takes a little more time.

GENERAL PROCEDURE FOR MEDITATION

The reason that people often fail in their attempts at meditation is that they are using poor technique - or no technique. The main problem is that the conscious mind is busily dealing with the material world during every waking minute. In order to reorient yourself from the physical distraction, you must transcend your focus on the material world and become aware of the spirit.

During the waking state you are generally reaching out towards the horizon with your sight and other physical senses. You are focusing out into the physical world. When you are in a depressed mood, your eyes tend to be downcast and your are withdrawn from the physical world. The next time you find yourself in a depressed mood, lift your eyes upward. Focus your attention out and away, beyond the horizon. You will find that your mood will improve quite rapidly.

When you turn your eyes downward, you tend to relate to the subconscious. When you look straight away, you tend to relate to your conscious self and the physical world. When you look UP, you relate to your higher, spiritual consciousness and those realms beyond the physical. You tend to focus our attention in accordance with the focus of your eyes. You can take advantage of this characteristic to aid your spiritual development.

To open up to your higher self, focus your eyes upward and inward toward the third eye (Illustration 1). This is a spot about one inch above the line of the eyebrows and one inch INSIDE the surface of your forehead.

You must be comfortable and secure when you meditate. Your spine should be straight and your head up. If you are seated, your feet should be flat on the floor and together. An arm chair makes meditating when sitting safer. Lying down is an effective meditative position but carries the danger that you will go to sleep. We don't require that you sit cross-legged or in the lotus position unless you are comfortable in these positions. If they are uncomfortable, they can be a hindrance.

While there are ideal places to meditate: outdoors, in a very quiet place, perched on a rock high on a lonely mountain; these conditions are generally available to very few of us. Mostly we have to settle for a place which is fairly quiet and where we are unlikely to be disturbed. Arrange that the phone and the door will not bother you, that the children are somewhere else, and that everyone can get by on their own for those few minutes. You will probably choose your time for pragmatic reasons: when can you take the time to do it, when will the house be quiet, etc.

The most important thing to remember is that it has taken you a life-time to get your yammering consciousness into its present undisciplined condition. You are not going to change it into a well-oiled machine overnight. You must be patient and persistent. A few people achieve immediate results in meditation. Others may meditate for as long as six months before any noticeable success is achieved. Usually definite progress is noticed in two weeks or less. The key is to stay with it. Meditate each day, at the same time and place, for approximately 15 minutes. You will not achieve success in an on-again, off-again pattern.

It only takes one chapter to tell you about

meditation. To make it a real tool for your path, you must make it a part of your everyday life.

GUIDED MEDITATIONS

Guided meditations, in taped or written forms, are very popular and successful methods of meditation. You may wish to find one or two tapes of generic guided meditations to work with as you are learning to meditate. We suggest that those helping you form your own power place or visualized meditation spot will probably be of the most use in medicine path.

Guided meditation in print form is a bit harder to use but with a couple extra sessions, they will work. To use a printed meditation first read it through several times. If you have a tape recorder handy, record it yourself. You will probably do the recording over after a few experiments so you can get the pace just right for you.

After you are familiar with the words of the meditation, set up your meditation area and put the book handy (or the tape recorder). Get comfortable and begin letting your mind relax. One excellent method of relaxation begins with letting the muscles in your toes relax, then those in your feet, then your legs. You work upwards in this manner throughout your entire body. Once your body is relaxed, it is time to begin the guided meditation.

Open your eyes to glance at the words. Then close them again and let the first phrases repeat themselves silently inside you. LET your mind make pictures to go with the words. Don't actually work at this, don't try really hard. Just let the words go through your awareness.

After a few minutes with the first few phrases, steal a glance at the words again and do the same with the next bit. In this way, guide yourself through the entire meditation. Don't ever leave out the waking up part of the guided meditation as it actually is easy to lose yourself in a visualization. While this isn't particularly dangerous and you will eventually

come out of it; your friends and family may think you are acting a bit peculiar for a while.

BEGINNING MEDITATION

I am deeply relaxed. My mind is floating, floating.

I see a light in the distance. It is a pure, white light.

The light is changing. It changes into the rising sun.

The rising sun is lifting above the green trees.

The light falls upon a tiny clearing in the forest.

There are tall trees all around.

A small spring bubbles up in the center and a silver thread of water flows out of a tiny, mossy pool into the forest.

I sit beside the spring on a cool rock and listen to the quiet.

A bird sings and I see flashes of beautiful colors as the little songbirds fly around in the tree tops.

A tiny green frog croaks and jumps into the smooth pool. Rings of water flow outwards to lap against the shores.

I follow the rings of water through the air. I am flying above the tops of the forest. [Pause to look at the forest and the world.]

I fly back into my body. I feel my fingers and toes wake up. I feel my arms and legs wake up. I feel all my body wake up. I open my eyes and let myself come back to the everyday.

ADVANCED MEDITATION

After you have done the beginning meditation a number of times, you may add things which happen while you are sitting beside the spring. ....A bird sings and I see flashes of beautiful colors as the little songbirds fly around in the tree tops.

There is noise of something moving in the forest. I look that way and watch to see what is there. I am not afraid for nothing may harm me here.

I see a form at the edge of the trees. Does

it have feathers? Does it have fur? [give yourself time to watch your visitor and to see what it is and listen to see if it has anything to tell you.]

It is leaving. It returns to the forest. All is quiet again.

A tiny green frog croaks and jumps into the smooth pool. Rings of water flow outwards to lap against the shores......

RECORDING YOUR MEDITATION

I know, this sounds dull after you've been floating around on air currents being an eagle. There is agreement that keeping a diary of your experiences in meditation (and other activities related to your following the medicine path) is an important part of your progress. It does not merely allow you to measure your progress (although it probably will do that). The diary is an integral part of your journey.

But this diary can't be of the calendar pad type. You can't just note down, January 1, 1988, was an Eagle. You must really describe what happened. The following guidelines are not absolute. However, whatever changes you make, don't make them just to make the job shorter!

Your record should begin with the date, time of day and place of the meditation. Describe the physical feelings you had. Did you walk through the forest to get to the spring, or did you just float there? How did it feel to float over the forest when you left? What kinds of birds did you see. What was the animal which came out of the forest. What size was the rock you sat on. What color was it? How has this meditation affected you in your ordinary self? Do you see yourself differently? Physically? Emotionally? Mentally? Spiritually? Do you see the world immediately around you differently?

This is the sort of thing to make a note of in your record. Also record how you felt after the meditation was over. All this will help you realize what good progress you actually are

making in the medicine path. Also, as you progress on the path you may be able to go back to these early meditations and find messages you didn't understand at the time.

This amount of writing may seem excessive to you. It is! You may use a tape recorder if you like, but this is no excuse to skimp on the details. Following the medicine path is not playing Indian! You are responsible for your own learning and the methods by which you achieve it. Your mind and spirit contain a lot of cosmic waste. The methods you are learning will flush this toilet and replace it with the fluidity of a warrior. The medicine path is not for weekenders. It is Spartan, difficult. It requires you to change many preconceptions, and you must study the way. If you feel that this is too much work; then medicine path may not be your way. Only if your dedication is sufficient will you follow this to the end. Only then will you make a difference to Grandmother Earth and to yourself.

LOCATION OF THE THRID EYE

RIDING ON THE CLOUDS

Smudging and spirit bag

SMUDGING COMES TO THE SOUTHERN CHEROKEE

The European settlers brought many things to the Cherokee. One of these "gifts" was smallpox. It affected all the full-bloods and those whose blood was mixed with the Whites, killing with impunity. Only those whose blood had mixed with runaway slaves were spared. The Africans had brought a natural immunity with them from the tribes across the great waters.

One of these southern Black Indians, John Horse, vowed to bring the cure to his brothers. Off into the Okefenokee he hiked, seeking the heart of the swamp, the Great Mother of the medicine powers. The swamp became thicker with fog, the very essence of the marshes. Soon he sat wearily upon a cypress knee. Crying out to the Swamp Mother, he asked for the healing of his people. As he cried, head in hands, the mists moved with sound.

"Hear me, my son, the cure is all around you, the mists, the fog, the purifying smoke of the swamp. Use the gifts of the marshes: mix the sage, the sweetgrass, and the cedar with the sacred tsalu (tobacco). Burn this mixture in a shell and fan the smoke over the bodies of your sisters and brothers with a hawk wing. Then they will be cured. Good hunting, my son".

John Horse left the swamp and used this mixture to cure the southern Cherokee. The smudge is used to this day in purification before ceremonies and healings.

USES OF SMUDGING

Smudging is used by a great many of the tribes. It cleanses — it cleanses the area in which you are working; it cleanses the "vibrations", the psychic atmosphere around you; and it cleanses you of negative thoughts, actions, and attitudes. Use it to help bring you, your surroundings, your tools, and your mind into harmony with the spiritual. It is a little like the incense burned to remove the odors in a house and the incense burned in a church or other sacred area to make the deities more welcome. It is also like a ceremonial bath taken before stepping outside the ordinary world and entering the sacred world of religion, the place where humans may meet with the other spirits of our world.

In some ways, smudging is the heart of medicine path. It is taught very early to all students. Smudging others is usually one of the first jobs of a new apprentice. Smudging is an important part of healing ceremonies. It is used to cleanse sacred objects, the medicine wheel, the sacred pipe, the sweat lodge. It is used to empower, and to dedicate these sacred objects. In the dedication of the sacred pipe, the smoke of the smudge is the breath of the Great Spirit, Galunlati.

HERBS AND EQUIPMENT FOR SMUDGING

Almost any herb which smells good when burned is suitable for smudging. Smudging mixtures often include herbs particularly appropriate for an occasion. Availability is also a factor in arriving at a smudging mixture.

While the attributes of many plants are discussed later in this book. Some herbs appropriate for smudging mixtures are given here so that you may begin your study of medicine path without letting this important ritual wait. Rarely will a smudging mixture contain ALL of the following herbs. Frequently only 2 or 3 herbs are used.

Sage or Sagebrush, *Artemisia spp.*

Sweetgrass, *Hierochloe odorata*

Calamus, *Acorus calamus*

Red Willow Bark, Red Osier Dogwood, *Cornus amomum*

Dogwood bark, *Cornus floridum*

Cedar needles or bark, *Thuja, Chamaecyparis,* and *Juniperus spp.*

Tobacco, *Nicotiana tabacum* and *rustica*

Kinnik-Kinnik seems to be a name misused by early European botinists. Some sources identify it with dogwood, some with willow bark, and some with Bearberry *(Arctostaphylos uva-ursi).* It appears that the word meant something like "aromatic herb" and therefore, all the herbs above are "Kinnik-Kinnik".

The herbs used for smudging are usually cut or ground fairly finely. It is a very good idea to try burning a little of a smudging mixture to see how easy (or difficult) it is to light and to keep alight. Sometimes you may need to use a charcoal briquette especially made for burning incense to maintain your smudge. You need a lot of smoke so it should stay lit for several minutes.

A natural container of some sort is needed to contain the burning herbs. A shell, an earthenware bowl, or a hollowed rock are suggested containers. Worked metal is not recommended. You also need a "fan" of some sort to direct the smoke. A hawk wing is a highly prized fan. However, a simple fan of several feathers bound to a stick (see chapter 12) is more than satisfactory. Don't delay smudging until you obtain a fancy feather fan. Find an appropriate (preferably natural) object, one which will function, and worry about obtaining a wing or feather fan later. (Feathers

EQUIPMENT FOR SMUDGING

are   almost always available from Native American supply sources). Always have a lot of matches AND a lighter.

CLEANSING SELF AND SACRED SPACE

The most important use of smudging is to cleanse yourself and the area in which you are working. You may do this when you meditate; certainly most times you use your medicine wheel; and always when you offer the sacred pipe.

Mound a quantity of the smudging herbs in a dish. Facing west, light your smudging mixture. Offer the smoke, in order, to the west, north, east, and south in turn. Hold it up to offer it to the sky. With the bowl held high, draw the smoke (with your fan) over yourself, down your body to your feet, and offer it to Grandmother Earth. Draw the smoke to yourself again and raise the bowl up your body, ending at the heart. Pass your hands through the smoke (you may either put the bowl down at this point or change hands). The fan is used to keep the herbs lit and to direct the smoke.

That's it! You have cleansed both the area and yourself. You have also dedicated your smudge and your further work to the quarters and the spirits. So simple, to be such an integral part of the medicine path, yet as the aromatic herbal smoke rises through your body, it transforms you and makes you ready to enter the worlds of the spirit. Many people smudge their houses and workplaces regularly so that their everyday lives can also be cleansed and blessed. Smudge any place you are if it seems to have an unpleasant or negative atmosphere.

SMUDGING OTHERS

In medicine path, everyone who is going to participate in a ceremony is smudged. Well done, this is an extremely beautiful and uplifting experience. Our grandmothers and grandfathers did not try to use time as we do; they did not begrudge the minutes needed to make this a meaningful experience to all.

Usually one person smudges everyone in the group as well as the area in which it is to meet and work. This task is often assigned to a person young in the medicine path.

To smudge another person, fill your container well with smudging mixture, light it, and offer it to the four directions, the sky and the earth. (Always find out where the directions are as soon as you arrive at the location.) Cleanse yourself as directed above. Stand at the entrance to the sacred space with the fan and the smudge bowl. The other participants should come up to you one by one. Each one stands facing you. Often he will raise his arms.

Beginning at the feet, fan the smoke up her body to the top of the head. She may gather the smoke in her arms and "bury her face" in it. She will probably pass her hands through it.

When you have reached the head, the individual should turn his back to you. If he doesn't, quietly ask him to do so. Fan the smoke down his back, go to the feet, and to the ground. He should turn again to face you, signal his thanks, and walk into the sacred space. At this time, the next individual should walk up and you will repeat the above process.

The smoke of the smudge is IMPORTANT. Do not begrudge the time it takes to blow on the mixture or to fan it to increase the smoke. Relight it if it seems to have gone out. It is important that the smoke touch each of the participants and that they each feel it and smell it.

Do not suppose that because a person newly come to the medicine path is entrusted with this job, it is in any way unimportant! We have left the wisdom of our grandmothers and grandfathers; we forget that all that is, is sacred. For us, smudging brings us back to that time when all was known to be sacred, when the buffalo and the deer were thanked for their deaths that we might live, when the very plants were given offerings of tobacco before their fruits were harvested.

We are also reminded that each one comes to the medicine path as him/her self with his/her own vision. We do not have to seek blessings and enlightenment only from those who have received their vision: from leaders, important persons, or the wise old ones. The blessing of the Great Spirit is within us all.

THE USES OF SMUDGING IN MEDICINE PATH

Smudging is one of the basic ritual or ceremonial activities of medicine people. It is a very important part of ceremonies from the medicine wheel gathering, to the sweat lodge, to the vision quest. One's self, one's tools, materials, weapons, and the space to be occupied, all must receive the cleansing of the smoke. Use smudging to begin your meditations and to prepare the materials and objects to be included in your spirit bag. Smudging will be called for over and over as we discuss other activities you may perform in your journey along the medicine path. Practice it carefully and make its form a part of you.

THE SPIRIT BAG

In the days of our grandmothers and grandfathers, a child would be given a small leather bag by an elder. He or she might be given this when receiving his/her "baby name", the name used until a vision name was received. The elder, whether the child's own grandparent, the tribe or clan's medicine chief, or another individual, would seek the counsel of his or her totems and the Great Mystery to find the name of the child and to discover what should be placed in the child's spirit bag. This bag would be charged for a purpose, for protection and health. Frequently the purpose was the progress of spiritual awareness and its accompanying benefits. The individual would wear the bag around his or her neck or waist on a thong.

The spirit bag is carried as an extension and amplification of one's own inner being. It contains small objects which hold power for specific purposes. These may include stones, bones, crystals, seeds, dried plants, flowers, teeth, bits of hair, hide, or a plethora of assorted items. The guiding factor in selection is not value but rather personal significance, usually spiritual in nature. One's personal, individual spirit is represented by this bag.

The medicine bag IS its carrier on many different levels of reality. As a compass can tell you where north is, your medicine bag will tell you where HERE is. It may contain objects which are meaningful only to you. The bag's contents are not limited to NATURAL objects. We no longer live in a "natural" world. In many cases, modern spirit bags contain coins, pieces of glass and metal, nuts, bolts, nails, small gears, and numerous items of current urbania. Whatever the contents, the use remains the same.

The contents change, are added to and given away. The bag itself functions best in this state of flux, reflecting the changing of our lives.

Even a "half-way serious" follower of the medicine path should have a spirit bag. It serves as a constant reminder of your spiritual journeyings even while you are emeshed in the everyday world. In modern times the spirit bag is carried in the pocket or purse. Frequently one can be seen dangling from the rearview mirror of a steel pony as its engine carries the owner through the mutated stone paths of the concrete mountain range.

It also is your spirit world representative and may be used as a focus of meditation or to place on a moon or spirit keeper stone (as in a medicine wheel) to help focus your attention on the desired communication.

YOUR OWN SPIRIT BAG

Spirit bags are still made by medicine people. You may be able to obtain your bag in this traditional manner. Stores carrying Native American items may be able to put you in touch with someone to make your spirit bag. A number of mail order sources are listed at the end of this book.

The making and filling of a spirit bag for another person must be undertaken seriously and in a Galunku'ti'yu or Wakan manner. (Galunku'ti'yu, Cherokee and Wakan, Dakota, refer to the carrying through of an act in a prescribed and sacred manner). Each bag is different as each individual is different. Be sufficiently acquainted with this medicine person either by personal contact or reputation among people whose opinion you respect, so that you may be confident that your bag will be thoughtfully created.

You may also make and fill your own spirit bag.

MAKING A SPIRIT BAG

Spirit bags don't necessarily have to be made of leather, although this is the most common material. A simple cloth bag makes a perfectly good spirit bag. You can make it like this:

FABRIC BAG

Materials: Rectangle of material, usually about 3 inches by 4 inches (a bit more than twice the size of the finished bag), needle, strong thread.

Method:

1. Fold down one edge of the narrower side of the fabric about 3/4 of an inch. Sew a casing for the drawstring. Sew this down firmly but leave the ends unsewn so a string may be threaded through.

2. Fold the fabric in half the long way with the right sides together and sew across the bottom and up one side until you reach the casing. Knot the thread tightly and cut it.

3. Take a piece of thin cord or yarn and knot one end. Put a very small safety pin through it behind the knot or thread it through a blunt needle with a large eye. Work the cord through the casing. Remove the safety pin or needle. Cut the cord or yarn to a convenient

length and knot the end. You may wish to tie a feather to this drawstring or string beads on it.

LEATHER BAG, WITHOUT FRINGE

Materials: Leather working needle - an "S" shaped needle is the best sort. A leather needle has two or three knife-like edges which cut the leather rather than forcing a large hole into it which may tear the leather. Very soft suede may be worked with a large sewing needle. You will need sinew thread or very heavy cotton thread and a piece of fairly soft leather at least twice the size of the finished bag. You may want to add beads, feathers, etc.

Method:

1. Practice for a few stitches in a spare piece of leather to learn how to handle the needle. Work with a knot in one end of the sinew and a short end coming through the needle.

2. Cut a rectangle of leather about 4 by 6 inches, or twice the size you want the finished bag to be plus about 1/2 inch each way for the seams.

3. Fold the leather in half the long way with the side you want to show in the finished bag on the inside.

4. Starting at one corner beside the fold, draw your threaded needle through the leather and pull the knot tight. If it comes all the way through the leather, you need to double the knot.

5. Sew to the next corner and up the side.

6. Now it is time to make the drawstring without cutting the thread. When you have stitched up to the third corner, stitch all the way around the top through one layer of the leather only. You may crimp the leather to make it go faster. Test to see if you can draw the top closed and open it back up.

7. Turn the bag right-side out and straighten it to cover the stitching.

FRINGED LEATHER SPIRIT BAG

Materials: Same as for leather bag above

Method:

1. Cut a piece of leather in an "L" shape.

2. With the right sides folded to the inside, fold one end of the "L" over. Then fold the remaining side of the "L" over, making a three-layer sandwich. The leather which will become the fringe is the "filling" in the sandwich.

3. Starting at the corner where the two folded over portions meet at their folded edges (there is only one such point), stitch all the way through ALL THREE LAYERS to the next corner. Try this first with a piece of paper and it will be easier to figure out.

4. Sew only to the corner. not around it. Lift up the top layer of the sandwich. Fold the "filling" of the sandwich into a triangle to get it out of the way of the next seam. Smooth the top layer (the bread) back down to meet the edge of the bottom layer (other piece of bread).

5. Going through TWO layers only, sew to the top edge of the bag, holding the folded-in triangle of the inner piece in place with your fingers.

6. Sew in the drawstring as in the leather bag without fringe. Turn the bag right-side out and pull the inside piece (the sandwich filling) out. Cut the fringe, being careful not to cut into the bag or the seam.

FILLING YOUR SPIRIT BAG

Your spirit bag, whether you make it yourself or it is given to you by a medicine person, is not a static thing. You will give away some of the items which fill it. You will certainly add others as you continue your journey on the medicine path. When a spirit bag was created for a new person by the tribe's shaman or medicine man/woman, he or she sought directions from the spirit keepers and the totems for the contents of the bag. You can do the same.

Perhaps the symbols of the totems of your birth moon can begin the filling of your medicine bag, or the symbols of the moon in which you began medicine path, or the present moon. Perhaps you already feel particularly drawn or chosen by a particular plant, mineral, and/or animal totem. If you have been practicing your meditations and have kept notes of the results, you may have some very good ideas of things to place in your medicine bag.

Stones have always played an important part in the filling of spirit bags. As a small child, you probably knew that stones were special. You may always have arrived home from a visit to a new place with your pockets full of rocks

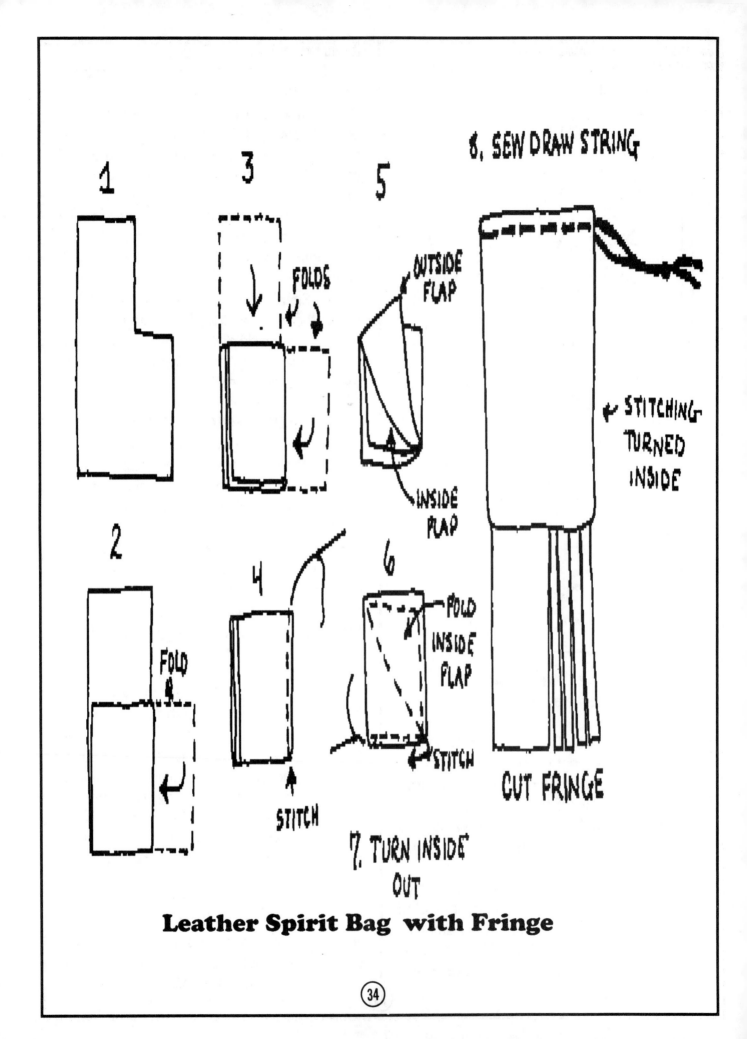

Leather Spirit Bag with Fringe

34

you had picked up.

Stones are an extremely important part of the medicine path, both common stones such as driveway gravel, beach pebbles, stones from especially beautiful and/or sacred places and semi-precious and precious stones, rock crystal points, cut, polished or tumbled stones of intrinsic beauty, symbolism and power. In chapter 16 we shall discuss many of the attributes of mineral totems.

For your spirit bag, either stones chosen for their traditional significances or through your own intuition, which you are increasing with your work with meditation, are appropriate additions.

There aren't any rules governing what goes into a medicine bag. While things symbolic of your personal totems are generally in it, or added as you are chosen by them, frequently these would never be recognized by anyone else.

A piece of money, old, new, or merely handy, is frequently included for prosperity and a bead is a traditional inclusion for luck. An object from an ancient American Indian archeological site can be a powerful link to the Path you are following. These objects, however, should come from sites which were not burials and which are connected with "ordinary" living, and not rare sites of the grandfathers of the Indians. Many people say that we amateurs should never, ever remove any object from an Indian site of any sort. While theoretically each of these sites, carefully excavated by trained and conscientious archeologists, might add valuable knowledge to our understanding of early AmerIndian cultures; actually no such thing generally happens. While occasionally a major site is carefully and respectfully excavated, this is by far the exception. It is our strongly held belief that our ancestors would prefer us to quietly share in medicine power they have left for us and would not wish to have their bones or possessions displayed disrespectfully to the gaze of the ignorant, or worse yet, lying forgotten in a museum basement.

Feathers are particularly sacred as birds are the link, the messengers between earth and the spirit realm. There are three sisters of the vegetable world: beans, corn and squash. These plants were grown in one field and composed the staple diet of many AmerInd peoples. Acorns are another important food for many Indians.

The selection of items for your spirit bag need not follow any identifiable "logic". If you feel that something should be in it, put it in! Usually you will take objects out as you add new ones. It should never be packed full and overflowing; you can't concentrate on too many things at one time.

Your spirit bag is a part of the story of your life, your spiritual life. Selecting the items to be included - and eventually understanding why some of them are there — is also a part of your journey on the medicine path.

The spirit bag is held while crying for a vision and is carried on your person to act as a focus for prayer and spiritual energies. May your spirit soar.

FABRIC SPIRIT BAG

FABRIC SPIRIT BAG

REACHING OUT TO THE WORLD

Giving to Man, Nature, and the Spirits

THE SHREW GIVES AWAY

Long ago in the lush Piedmont Plains, Siyu, the shrew, scurried through the underbrush. She came upon Tsistu, the Rabbit, the great trickster of the Piedmont.

"Siyu, little sister", spoke Tsistu, "It is time for your journey."

"What journey, Brother Rabbit? I go in search of my dinner," answered Siyu.

"Ahead lies your vision, little sister. You must seek your vision on the great Stone Mountain. You will find what you desire there," explained Tsistu.

Siyu shrugged her shoulders and walked away toward Stone Mountain. At the edge of the plain she paused, observing the open area. Tlanuwa, the red-tailed hawk, circled overhead. At this point Siyu heard a sobbing voice behind her. It was Kagu, the Crow, wings drawn over her eyes.

"What is the trouble, my sister?" asked Siyu.

Kagu withdrew her wings and stared back at Siyu from vacant sockets. "I have lost my eyes, little sister," sobbed Kagu. "I can no longer see."

"I have two eyes, Sister Kagu. You may have one that you may once again view the earth," spoke Siyu. Immediately one of Siyu's eyes flew out of her head and into that of Kagu.

"I can see! I can see!" shouted Kagu. "Thank you, my sister! Now I shall fly above you so that Tlanuwa will not see you. Follow me, little sister." Kagu flapped her wings and rose into the air above Siyu.

Across the Piedmont Plain they travelled, safe from Tlanuwa. Soon Siyu reached the other side and hid in the covering boxwoods. "Thank-you my sister!" shouted Siyu, as Kagu flew away in the direction they had come.

Siyu was soon at the base of Stone Mountain, and began the gradual climb up the granite monolith.

"Siyu, little sister," spoke a voice from the pines.

Siyu looked toward the voice with her one eye. A furry face with two pointed ears stared back at her. It was Wesa, the Cat. This alarmed Siyu, because she was Wesa's prey.

"Do not fear, little sister. I will not harm you, for I am blind. My eyes are gone. I see nothing," spoke Wesa. "If you will give me your eye I will guide you to the summit of the mountain."

Siyu eyed Wesa warily. "If you can see me, will you not hunt me, my brother? With no eye, I will be blind and helpless."

"You must trust me little sister. I have told you I will not harm you," replied Wesa.

"My eye is yours, my brother," spoke Siyu. At that moment, Siyu's remaining eye flew from her head into Wesa's eye socket.

"Follow me to the summit, little sister," instructed Wesa. "Listen for my foot-steps."

Siyu scurried along behind Wesa, ever climbing the granite stones. Higher, higher they climbed until they reached the summit of the great Stone Mountain.

"I must leave you now in the keeping of my brother, Walasi the Frog." Wesa gave his leave, thanking Siyu for her eye.

"Greetings, sister Siyu," croaked Walasi. "How do I look?"

"I cannot see, my brother," answered Siyu. "I have given away my eyes."

"But only by giving away all you have can you receive your vision," said Walasi. "Now look at your true self."

Siyu strained and strained but could see nothing. Suddenly Siyu began to see with her spirit. She felt as if she were becoming lighter. She seemed to fly.

"I can see! I can see!" shouted Siyu. "I can see all of the plain down below me! I am flying!"

"You have a new name, little sister. You are no longer bound to the earth. From this day forward you will be known by your new name," spoke Walasi. "Behold your new name, Hawk."

THE GIVEAWAY - WAPANI

This particular style of giveaway originated (in the strictest Native American sense) with the Lakota Sioux. The general idea then and now is to devalue the material aspects of life while at the same time exalting the spiritual values of giving. At a time which seemed right one would give horses, pipes, leggings, moccasins, tipis, etc., to others in the tribe. On special occasions, such as a naming or a vision quest, the family, relatives or friends would giveaway in the name of the person doing the rite. Often these gifts were given to the needy of the tribe (old, infirm, blind). At special times some individuals in the tribe would giveaway everything they owned, right down to their breechclouts.

The object of the Wapani is to give something away. You may give away to anyone: someone you don't know, a relative, a friend. Perhaps you will experience the highest form of giveaway: forgiveness. Forgive an arch-enemy or foe. Perhaps you will giveaway love to someone you consider unloveable.

In a material sense, you may give away something that means quite a bit to you. Perhaps you will giveaway something you make yourself with a special blessing. Perhaps you will giveaway something in your spirit bag. Whatever you giveaway it must be meaningful, at least to you!

To giveaway in a Galunky'ti'yu manner, you must giveaway thoughtfully and with caring. Should you giveaway an item used in a sacred manner be sure it has been smudged. This will cleanse it of any possible misuse or handling by an unclean person before you hand it on to another.

The person receiving your wapani need not know of the significance of the gift. You should not demand great thanks or appreciation. The giveaway is the purpose, not thanks.

In your meditations for a few days after practicing wapani, be alert to recognize the effects this giveaway has had upon you and your progress upon your journey. The giveaway must not be practiced only once and then forgotten. You should giveaway to mark all special milestones upon your path.

It is not wrong to possess material items. However, excessive attachment to material things will impede your progress upon the medicine path.

SPIRITUAL SEED COMES TO THE CHEROKEE

Long ago in the Okeefenokee Swamp a grandmother lived in a log lodge with the two grandchildren. One day the children sat upon the stoop, sharpening their weapons, and complained loudly about the fare they had for dinner.

"Always venison and rabbit — night after night", spoke Little Hawk, the younger.

"We can but hunt my brother. It is the way of our grandmothers," answered Dancing Fire, as she tested her bow.

"Perhaps my grandchildren will be pleasantly surprised this evening. When you return from your hunting and Geyaguga, the midnight sun, has risen, I will cook the meat for you in a new way," Grandmother beamed at the young hunters.

Greatly excited in anticipation of the evening's meal the two ventured into the boskages and thickets of the Great Swamp. Later that evening when the hunters returned, they carried a small buck and two rabbits. As they approached the lodge a new cooking smell reached their nostrils. It was a new aroma which they had never known. The two rushed to the lodge.

Grandmother took the deer and rabbits, cutting the meat into stew. As the meat simmered it blended with the new ingredient. The young hunters' mouths watered as it cooked. Finally, Grandmother placed the steaming bowls before them, bidding them "eat". The stew was magnificent — the finest they had ever tasted. It filled them as the meat alone had never before done. As they reclined, resting from the evening meal, the elder spoke to her grandmother.

"Ah, mother of my mother, from whence came this wonderful food? Never before have I tasted such a meat!"

"It is not meat, my granddaughter," she replied. "It is the fruit of our Earth Mother, Agisaegwa."

This puzzled Dancing Fire as she drifted off to sleep beneath the South Georgia moon. Upon the morrow she roused her brother early.

"Let us hide in the boxwoods until our grandmother rises. Then we will see where she goes to hunt this special new food," she whispered.

Rubbing the sleep from his eyes Little Hawk followed his sister into the boxwoods that surrounded the lodge clearing. They waited patiently until the lamp was lit inside the lodge. Soon their grandmother emerged and strode to the middle of the clearing. She spread her colorful robe upon the ground and stepped to the middle of it. Grandmother began to change. Her arms extended to the ground and her back straightened out parallel with it. Short fur grew from her entire body as her face grew longer — elongating into a muzzle. Grandmother was now a doe. She shook, as deer shake — as if to get water droplets off her body. But no droplets but yellow nuggets fell from her body onto the robe. They gathered in little golden piles wherever they fell. Shortly grandmother changed back into an old woman. She gathered the robe by the corners and carried it into the house.

Little Hawk stared at Dancing Fire, open-mouthed. "Our grandmother is Agisaegwa, the great female four-legged!" he exclaimed. Together they rushed into the lodge.

"Grandmother! Why have we never known?!" shouted Dancing Fire.

Her grandmother stared at them with a look of utter dismay. She collapsed into a log chair and began to weep — wailing in a high, keening voice.

"Grandmother — why do you weep so? What have we done?" cried Little Hawk.

Grandmother looked up, the tears streaming down her wrinkled face.

"You know my secret — Oh, if only you hadn't spied! Now I must go away to the Cave at the World's End! I must return to the Canyon of Clouds."

She began to weep again. Finally she stood up, drying her eyes, and spoke: "The golden nuggets are called Selu (corn). It is hokshichankiya, the spiritual seed. It will always be with you. You must plant it wherever you live; wherever the People live. It cannot benefit you unless you give it away to the earth. As the great green stalks grow toward the sun, they will bear fruit for you to eat and plant. Plant the selu and remember me."

With that Grandmother changed back into a doe and scampered away in the direction of the Canyon of Clouds.

Each year the two young hunters planted and reaped the a harvest. They saved some of the seed to plant for the following years. The seed multiplied, blessing all it touched. And so it is unto this day among the South Georgia

Cherokee.

HOKSHICHANKIYA means "spiritual influence or seed" in Oglala Sioux. This belief concerns the passing of power from one individual to another. The passing of power is the highest form of medicine. The Shadowlight Clan practices hokshichankiya as husband/women to the three kingdoms: plant, animal and mineral. This is accomplished by the transfer of seeds, stones, animal totem objects (and in some cases, actual animals) to new environments. Such a transfer has a fourfold significance: survival, spirituality, genetic vigor and new vistas of development.

Speaking in survival terms, it is painfully evident to all that great masses of animals, plants, and stones are being destroyed daily on Grandmother Earth, turning Mother Maka into a vast concrete mountain range. Someone must intervene for the sake of morality, if not survival. Planting seed insures the survival of plant life. Transference of stones and animals to safer places insures their survival as well.

Spiritually, the medicine path teaches that the Nunahe, the spirit beings, live in all things. Many spiritual paths find deity in all things, Peter Caddy and the Findhorn group maintain constant communication with these nature spirits which they call the Devas. These spirits must have homes in which to live and manifest themselves. In taking seeds away to be planted deeply in the earth we improve the housing situation for such spirits. This can have enormous impact in a variety of situations.

When Shadowlight moved to a quiet Atlanta suburb the property bordered a large wooded area. Not two weeks later the rapacious earth-moving machines rolled in, laying waste to the greater part of this forest. Communication with the totem spirits and megadeva of this area revealed the lamentations of these displaced nature spirits. Many were invited over the fence into the protection of the Shadowlight medicine wheel. The wheel

and garden housed many (literally) uprooted spirits, but still more floated about having lost their homes forever. Acorns from the area were planted in cast-off soft drink containers. Once sprouted they provided new homes for the despondent Nunahe.

Most plants have the opportunity to develop and grow only in the immediate environment of the mother plant. Exceptions are subject to chance, the attachment of their shells or pods to clothing, animals, automobiles, trains, the blowing of the wind, or the flow of water. The greatest bulk of plant species remain for generation after generation in the same environment with no new opportunities for development. At this point the husbandman/woman must intervene to insure the survival of the species. In times when hundred-year-old trees can be destroyed in a matter of minutes, we must provide new opportunities for the species ourselves. Providing new environments for the development of seeds alters the genetic structure of the specie. The specie itself becomes stronger through evolutionary development.

We know the mineral kingdom functions in much the same manner. Mineral spirits are equally valid although they vibrate at a lower level than plants and animals. Small animals, insects, arachnids, reptiles, amphibians, and even smaller forms of mammals can be transferred from overpopulated or unsafe areas to environments more conducive to their life and development.

Think of the implications of hokshichankiya: Mother Nihoestsan is threatened, as are all of her children. We have within our grasp the ability to save a portion of nature. We have the opportunity to fill the gap caused by the destructive acts of our kind. This is not tampering with nature, it is the act of stewardship. With an eye for taking for transference only a few (those needed for survival and development) the opportunities for all of nature may be expanded. What greater work could there be.

Hokshichankiya, as taught by Shadowlight Clan, has spread to Mexico, Canada, West Germany, Yugoslavia, and the Soviet Union. Participation in this gift to the totem spirits is a matter of more than just your own journey on the medicine path!

MATERIALS FOR HOKSHICHANKIYA

You will need seeds, small plants, rocks, insects, and/or animals, whatever NEEDS a new environment. Have also some small feathers and a bag of sacred tobacco.

To make tobacco sacred, put a small quantity of loose tobacco (pipe tobacco, uncut tobacco obtained from a farmer or Native American supplier, any other type of loose tobacco — tear apart a cigarette) in a bowl or other container. Smudge the bowl and tobacco in the way you have learned. Offer the tobacco to the four directions, the sky, and the earth, the ancestors, and the nature spirits. Place the bowl in the center of your sacred area and invite the Great Spirit Galunlati to infuse the tobacco with his breath. Smudge the bowl again and put the tobacco in a bag (which you have also smudged).

CEREMONY FOR THE HOKSHICHANKIYA

Take your seeds, feathers and tobacco to the area which you wish to plant. If possible smudge the area, yourself, and the hokshichankiya materials as you have learned to do. If you know that the place is too public for this, do the smudging before you leave home. Offer the seeds, feathers, and tobacco to the four directions, the sky, the earth, the ancestors and nunahe. Place or bury pinches of the sacred tobacco at the four directions and in the center of the area. Plant the seeds with the feathers and small amounts of the tobacco. Sit a time and tune-in to the nature spirits in the place. Accept their thanks for your gift.

TOBACCO TIES

Long ago the People gave very special gifts to the spirits and the land. They traveled great distances to gather the precious colored earths of Agisegua. These were the paints. The People used the paint to draw sacred symbols and beautiful designs upon their homes and tools. These symbols are part of a system of communication which exists between the People and the unseen. The sacred paints mark the bodies of the People when they perform sacred actions. These paints are also offered to the powers as a part of the ceremonies of the People. The paints, as dust, may be released upon the wind, or buried softly in the earth of the Mother. They can be given to the long man of the river, or daubed upon the earth. One of the clans of the Cherokee is named Paint for the sacred gifts to and from the earth.

When the unega came, they brought something only a few of the People had ever before seen. They brought woven cloth dyed in beautiful colors. They also cultivated the tsalu, the sacred tobacco which became much more easily available. With the unega also came the destruction of the trade routes which the People had used to exchange the beautiful paints. So it happened that the beautiful cloth was taken in the place of the sacred paint. Should an individual wish healing from a medicine woman, he/she might bring a length of cloth in one of the beautiful new colors as a gift to the wise one. And the wise one might make of this material, tiny bags filled with the sacred tsalu to be given to the spirits.

Strings of these brightly colored tobacco ties are now an important part of many of the ceremonies of the medicine path. A medicine man might request that 50 ties of each of the colors of the winds be made for a ceremony. A Lakota altar for an eagle ceremony might be ringed with four hundred and five tobacco ties. Strings of 50, 100, 110, or many more might deck a sweat lodge ceremony. Five red ties in a string may be made and carried to request that a wish be granted.

There are no absolute rules about the

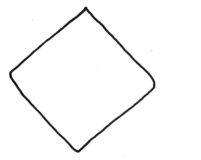 

colors and numbers of tobacco ties needed for a ceremony. Each medicine person receives instruction from his/her totem spirits in this. Perhaps more ties are needed for an important ritual, or for a difficult request — perhaps not. Here the wayfarer must listen to his/her intuition.

There is one rule about tobacco ties, they must be given to the earth when the ceremony is over. Or in the case of the five red ties made for a wish, when the wish is granted. At this time the ties must be buried in the earth. Occasionally they are burned instead. They must be buried as they are; do not put them into a plastic bag, wrap them up in something, or put them in a box. The cloth and tobacco must be placed bare in the earth that they may return to the substance of the earth.

We make tobacco ties for much of the work we do in medicine path. You can make a tie, or a string of ties, for all tobacco offerings mentioned in this book. As they are very decorative, they are a very good addition to any ceremony you do. Make ties in an appropriate color(s) and just the right length to go around your altar when doing a sweat. Or hang them inside the sweat lodge. You can place them around the central stone in the medicine wheel — or around each of the spirit keeper stones. Make and offer tobacco ties any time you contact a spirit keeper or totem to aid you in your medicine.

HOW TO MAKE TOBACCO TIES

The most common colors to use for tobacco ties are clear, primary colors. The colors of the four winds, Black, White, Red and Yellow are good. Adding Blue for the sky and Green for the earth gives a beautiful palate of colors. Buy a yard or so of cotton broadcloth in each of these colors and you will be prepared for most occasions. This is not to imply that other colors are unacceptable. You will soon be able to consult the totems and your own intuition to learn what

colors to use. You will also need a roll of lightweight string and a quantity of loose tobacco. Any form of tobacco will work.

For your first tobacco ties cut squares of fabric 2 to 3 inches on a side. Later you may wish to learn to make smaller ties, but this size is far easier while you are learning. Take one square of fabric and place a pinch of tobacco in the center. Lift up two diagonal corners of the fabric square and hold between finger and thumb of your left hand. Then lift up the other two corners and hold in the same hand.

Pinch the tobacco into a small ball in the center of the fabric. Hold the corners of the fabric firmly. Hold the cord with the 3rd or 4th finger of the left hand letting the long end lie up beside the tobacco tie. With your right hand make a loop of a single crossing of the string. Put the loop over the ball of tobacco. Pull the end gently to draw the loop up to the fabric.

Now make exactly the same sort of loop again being sure to turn your hand exactly the same way as you did for the first loop. Put this loop over the ball of tobacco. Pull both ends of the string to tie the knot tightly around the tobacco. This completes one tobacco tie. DO NOT CUT THE STRING!

Fill the second square of cloth in the same way as the first one. Hold the first tie in the palm of your left hand. Hold the long end of the cord against the new tie which you have grasped between your thumb and first finger. Make loops in the cord exactly as you did for the first tie and draw the knot tight. Now you have two tobacco ties firmly tied and attached to the same piece of string. Continue this process until you have made a string of as many ties as you want. Usually each string has ties all of one color. However, as many different strings of different colors as you want may be made.

As wapani is the giving of gifts to other people and hokshichankiya is a gift to the earth and the totems, tobacco ties are your gift to Galunlati, the Great Mysterious.

A MAP OF THE COSMOS

Construction of the medicine wheel

THE MEDICINE WHEEL COMES TO THE SOUTHERN CHEROKEE

The medicine wheel came to white people who lived across the great waters upon the Island of the Lion. Called Stonehenge, the shamans of the tribes caused it to be. To the south, the Zulu and Bantu tribes built their medicine wheels upon the Dark Island. Our dark brothers and sisters worked their wheels in prayer and reverence. Many of these dark ones later mixed with the blood of the People when the unega brought them to this great Turtle Island as slaves. The black brothers escaped to the villages of their red sisters and brothers, recognizing them as the same tribes they had left on the Dark Island. These settlements of red and black peoples became known as "maroons".

Here the agriculture and ceremony of the Dark Island mixed with that of Turtle Island. The tribes from the Dark Island recognized their own medicine wheel in the center of the council lodges. The stones represented the twelve moons, the four directions and the great roads. In the center, where the dark sisters remembered the lion or leopard skull, they now saw the buffalo skull and smiled. For they knew that it represented "Ubaba ungulu", grandfather, whom their red sisters called Galunlati, Great Spirit. They turned and travelled the wheel in the same spirit. Thus it stood, nothing changed. The earth, water, fire and air returned as they had to the Celtic and Druid sisters and brothers of the Island of the Lion, far across the waters.

In the ancient days the wheel had come to the yellow brothers of the Dragon Islands. Many red brothers went there in the unega's war to kill the yellow man. They came upon the ruins of the great wheels upon the Dragon Islands. When they returned to Turtle Island, they too recognized the universality of the wheel. And so the directions returned to the People again. The races of all the People: red, white, yellow and black were the directions. They all had the wheel.

PHILOSOPHY OF THE MEDICINE WHEEL

The medicine wheel is a spiritual sending and receiving device. It is used to establish a living energy circuit between individual and group souls and the total universe, or Miaheyyun. It is a transcendental teaching and learning instrument which can become the universe to you, the seeker. It helps you find universal truths however elusive they may be. The governing factor in the effectiveness of this interdimensional altar is your willingness to reachout and touch these truths. If you are willing to let go of everyday consciousness and see reality from a new perspective, the wheel can open these truths to you. The medicine wheel teaches balance and harmony as all-important cosmic realities. Once you have opened yourself to giving and receiving these sacred teachings, you will begin your journey around the medicine wheel.

You entered life in flesh on this planet at a particular date, and through this you fall under the influence of a particular moon upon the wheel. You begin your earth-walk with the strengths, lessons, and challenges of the moon under which you were born. You were equipped with the powers of its totems. As you continue your journey you may come to realize that the qualities ascribed to your birth moon no longer apply to you. This means that you have moved on to new lessons under the rulership of a different moon. We are all constantly travelling. We are regularly presented with new challenges and new opportunities for spiritual growth. The only way to stop this process is to cling to the strengths of one moon and refuse to let go.

WHAT IS A MEDICINE WHEEL?

The medicine wheel is a directionalized circle of stones with four spokes and a center. The outer circle is made up of sixteen stones, one for each of the twelve moons, and one for each of the four spirit keepers. The central stone is surrounded by seven smaller stones. From this configuration four paths of three stones radiate out toward each cardinal direction. At the north, south, east and west a stone is placed to represent the spirit keeper of the direction. These spirit keeper stones are connected to the central stones by paths of three stones each

In time correspondence, the twelve moon stones of the outer circle begin with the Icicle Moon stone approximating December 22. The moonstones proceed around the circle, interrupted at intervals of three by the spirit keeper stones. Eventually they return, moving clockwise around the wheel, to the Icicle Moon stone.

The medicine wheel exists in chante ishta, the one, true eye of the heart. It becomes three dimensional reaching into the earth and sky, surrounding you with its sacred space. As you work with it, it becomes multi-dimensional; crossing and pulsating simultaneously in and out of all levels of reality affected by your existence. It sanctions the area you are in so that you may perform your tasks there in a gracious manner.

MEDICINE WHEEL AT MEDICINE HAWK'S HOME

SELECTING A SITE FOR YOUR WHEEL

The size of your medicine wheel will depend upon a number of factors. The size of the stones you have located, the available site and the number of people you aniticipate working with you at any one time will all affect your plans. There is no right size for a medicine wheel. A six to twelve foot diameter seems to be convenient for personal wheels. a six-foot wheel allows plenty of room for one person and can be used by as many as four — unless the stones are very large.

If three or more individuals will frequently participate in working within the wheel, a larger diameter is recommended. A large group can participate at ceremonies at a small wheel by standing outside the moon-stone circle. This in no way invalidates the work you may do at the wheel.

Once you have determined the size of your wheel, you must find a site for it. You don't need to locate your wheel in the depth of the country. Medicine Hawk's wheel is in an urban backyard within a few feet of an 8-lane highway. In at least one case, the stones of a medicine wheel have been carefully placed in holes and turf replaced over them thus making an invisible although entirely physical medicine wheel.

If you must place your medicine wheel in a public park or on the grounds of an apartment building or complex, we suggest that you use very small, unnoticeable stones. Or you can bury the wheel as suggested above. Be sure not to damage the vegetation in the area. Your medicine wheel site should have at least the illusion of privacy. It also should not interfere with the uses and expectations of any others who share the land, whether family members, fellow tenants, or all the residents of a city. After meeting these criteria, further selection should be made by meditating in each possible site and opening yourself to the wishes of the land itself.

STONES FOR YOUR MEDICINE WHEEL

If you live more or less in the country you won't have trouble finding stones although color availability will differ. You may not find truly red or black stones for the paths. But you will be able to symbolize the red and black paths with the stones you do find.

If you live in the city you may have to use considerable ingenuity in finding stones. Construction sites, road building and friends with gardens are possible sources. Generally it is illegal to remove stones — or anything much else — from any sort of public park.

You will need 6 medium sized red stones — or six stones of a color or quality which will set them apart from the other stones of the wheel. Six black or dark stones of similar size will also be needed. One fairly large stone should be chosen for the center. A flat-topped, rounded stone is good. Seven fairly small stones will be needed to place around the central stone and four medium sized stones for the four directions are also necessary. Finally you will need 12 medium to small stones for the moons of the year.

THE LAYOUT OF THE WHEEL AND MEANINGS OF EACH STONE

Each individual stone in the medicine wheel has its own particular meaning. The relationships of the stones to each other are also rich with meanings and messages. It is not possible to explore these messages completely here. You will find much meaning for yourself in your work with the wheel. We can only suggest the most generally agreed upon messages which are suitable for public ceremonies and for your beginning work with the wheel.

THE CENTRAL STONE

The central stone is the first one you will place. Be sure that it is in the center of the area you have chosen so that there will be enough room to lay out the remainder of the wheel.

The central stone is the abode of the Great Spirit, Galunlati. It demonstrates the unity of all things. It is also a messenger to Galunlati for the People's prayers and FROM Galunlati to the People.

THE SEVEN SURROUNDING STONES

Lay the seven smallest stones equidistant from each other AND from the central stone. You may need to dig slightly to make secure beds for these stones so they will stay as you have placed them.

These seven stones are the universe. They are the seven sacred streams: life, matter, energy, dimension, time, motion (movement), and spirit. All that exists is formed of one or more of the seven streams.

"...To come to a knowledge of the Seven Streams, is to see the power and the glory of all creation, this is the (Great) Spirit...the Seven Streams are representative of Life Universal and Life Individual. They contain all the magic of the universe. The Warrior could study, walk any path until his days were old and his sight was faltering and he would still know nothing of how life works until he comes to the Sacred Streams. With this knowledge, he would find himself. Thus, the Universe, the Great Spirit, and ourselves are found in the Quest for the Seven Streams, for these are our life, our dance, our dream, this is what we have, it's a good way..." Sequoyah, Chief of the Cherokee

At the entrance of a Cherokee lodge are the seven sacred stones with an eighth stone forming an entrance into the lodge.

The number seven is an important mystical number world wide. In AmerIndian traditions, it is one of the two particularly revered numbers (the other being four). To the Seneca it is the seven stones: the bloodstone, fertility stone, sun stone, blossoming stone, water stone, charity stone, and healing stone. (Brad Steiger, American Indian Magic) To the Sioux, it is the seven arrows of the seven directions:

west, north, east, south, sky, earth and spirit (center). Seven is also the number of the chakras (the powers of the human body): the base, the sex, the solar plexus, the heart, the throat, the third eye and the crown. Often AmerIndians were part of organizations of seven tribes — or frequently seven clans made up the tribe.

THE FOUR STONES OF THE SPIRIT KEEPERS

Unless you are very, very sure of the directions at your site use a compass, placed on a level surface, to determine the placement of the four stones marking the prime directions: west, north, east and south. These four stones should be placed in that order. Each is dedicated to one of the spirit keepers.

The spirit keepers rule the four prime directions. Long ago the Great Spirit set the spirit keepers to watch over and guard the sacred powers of the four directions, the four winds. These spirit keepers travel to and from the abode of the Great Spirit in the center of the medicine wheel, along the paths and roads laid out for them to follow. They work constantly for the healing and evolution of Grandmother Earth and all her children. They are always ready to guide, inspire and protect those who would aid them in their tasks.

These stones also represent the four seasons (renewal); the four sacred ceremonies held at the changes of season. They represent the sacred powers of the four directions and the four sacred elements which are the source of all things. They are the "last four"; the four worlds of the dream on Grandmother Earth; the minerals, plants, animals and humans.

The west stone is Yanu, the bear, and its color is black. It is usunhiy, where it is always growing dark; wudeligunyi, where it [the sun] sets; wusuhihunyi, there where they stay overnight. Here is the dwelling of the thunders.

The north stone is Yunsu, the buffalo and its color is white. In the north lies the cave of

CENTER STONE AND SEVEN SURROUNDING STONES

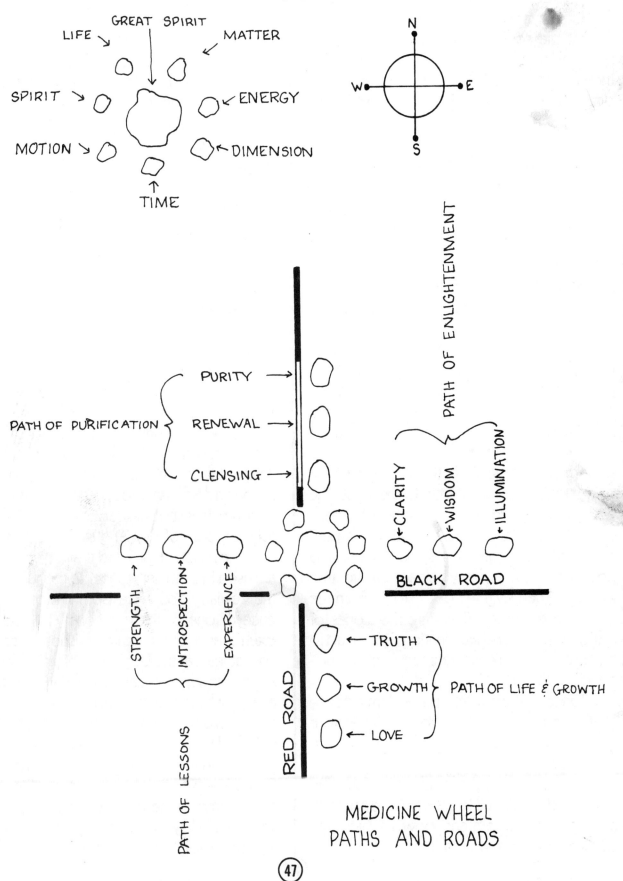

LIFE
GREAT SPIRIT
MATTER
SPIRIT
ENERGY
MOTION
DIMENSION
TIME

N
W
E
S

PATH OF PURIFICATION
PURITY
RENEWAL
CLENSING

PATH OF ENLIGHTENMENT
CLARITY
WISDOM
ILLUMINATION

STRENGTH
INTROSPECTION
EXPERIENCE

BLACK ROAD

TRUTH
GROWTH
LOVE
PATH OF LIFE & GROWTH

RED ROAD

PATH OF LESSONS

MEDICINE WHEEL PATHS AND ROADS

the great white giant who breathes out the cleansing wind.

The east stone is Awahili, the eagle and its color is red. It is nundagunyi, the sun land; digalungunyi, where it comes up.

At the south is the stone of Tsistu, the rabbit and its color is green. Tsistu is the trickster who teaches by opposites and is the direction which the People are always facing.

THE PATHS AND ROADS

The paths which lead from the center to the spirit keeper stones each has its own special lesson. The red paths are placed first. Lay three of your red stones equidistantly from the center and from each other in a line to the south spirit keeper stone. These are the stones of trust, growth, and love on the path of life and growth.

Next lay the remaining three red stones from the center to the north. The north path, made up of the red stones of cleansing, renewal, and purity, holds purification of the heart and mind both physically and spiritually.

The black paths are now laid in much the same manner as the red paths. First place three black stones from the center to the west, The west path is made up of the stones of experience, introspection, and strength. This path holds the force of lessons, hard work and possible pain which may be necessary for true learning. Then lay three black stones from the center to the east. These are the stones of clarity, wisdom, and illumination which lead to the east and hold enlightenment and the substance of lessons.

Together the two red paths form a north-south road; the good red road. This is your spiritual path, the one where you will be happiest.

East and west, the black paths form the black road of difficult lessons and the achievement of the wisdom and power which age and experience may confer.

THE MOON STONES

At the last, you place the 12 moon stones. The moon stones have very rich associations. They demonstrate the turning of the seasons and the cyclic nature of life. Each moon has its own animal, plant and mineral totems.

Three moon stones are put between each of the spirit keeper stones together forming the outer ring of the medicine wheel.

To place the moon stones, begin at the west stone. Place a stone for the Birds Fly Moon 1/4 of the way between the west stone and the north stone. Next place the Woodchuck Moon stone about halfway and the Long Sleep Moon stone 3/4 of the way: almost to the north spirit keeper stone. These stones represent the moon of the months of October, November, and December.

In the same manner stones are placed between the north and east stones for the Icicle Moon, Frost Moon, and Thawing Moon. These are the moons of the months January, February, and March. Between the east and south stones are placed the Flower Moon stone, the Mockingbird Moon, and Dogwood Moon stones: April, May and June moons. And last place the Red Hawk Moon, Sassafras Moon and Squirrel Moon stones between the south and west spirit keeper stones. These are for the moons of July, August, and September.

The moon stones and their characteristics are used in a similiar manner to the sun signs of the zodiac. You were born under the influence of one of these moons. Its strengths, totems and other characteristics described you, at least at the beginning of your life/path. As you grow; physically, mentally, and spiritually; your path may lead you around the ring of the moons many times. Perhaps eventually it will lead you spiralling into the center.

Within the stones of the medicine wheel lie many ways of perceiving yourself and your relationship to the earth, the sky and the universe. It is a key to your growth in understanding and in spirit. It will aid you to travel along

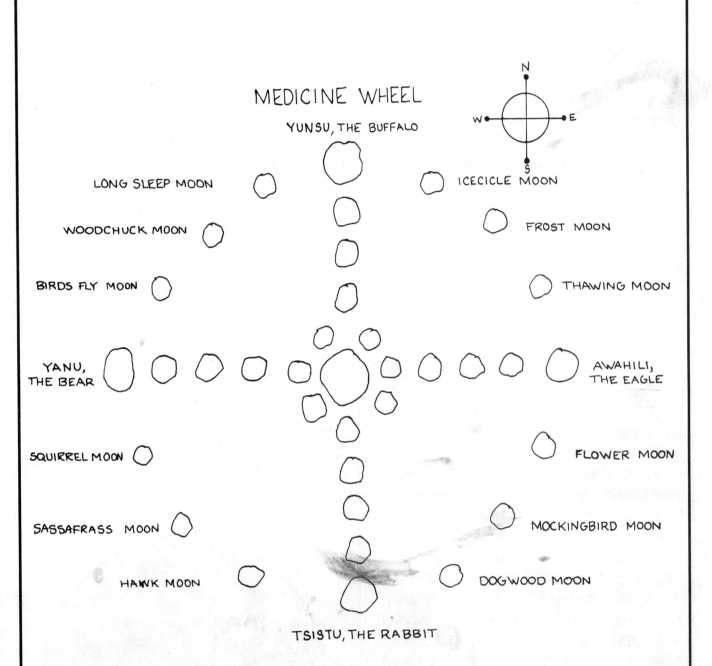

MEDICINE WHEEL

YUNSU, THE BUFFALO

LONG SLEEP MOON

WOODCHUCK MOON

BIRDS FLY MOON

YANU, THE BEAR

SQUIRREL MOON

SASSAFRASS MOON

HAWK MOON

ICECICLE MOON

FROST MOON

THAWING MOON

AWAHILI, THE EAGLE

FLOWER MOON

MOCKINGBIRD MOON

DOGWOOD MOON

TSISTU, THE RABBIT

WEST: YANU, THE BEAR, "WHERE THE SUN LIES DOWN AND DIES"

NORTH: YUNSU, THE BUFFALO, "THE HOME OF THE GREAT, WHITE GIANT"

EAST: AWAHILI, THE EAGLE, "WHERE THE SUN SHINES CONTIUALLY"

SOUTH: TSISTU, THE RABBIT, "THE DIRECTION IN WHICH WE ARE ALWAYS FACING"

THE MEDICINE WHEEL COMPLETED

the medicine path in a galunky'ti'yu manner.

Please always remember that these identifications—names, languages and totems we give for the separate stones of the medicine wheel—are from one specific native tradition. You need not use the animal, plant and mineral totems which we have named here. Many medicine people seek these designations through meditations, channelling. They receive their own individual plant, animal, and mineral totem spirits for each moon. Remember the basic powers of each direction and proceed accordingly. If you have a good memory, your own designations can add intense personal power to your sacred space.

The medicine wheel we describe here was developed from the traditions of the Southeastern Cherokee . This tradition is different from those described in some sources such as Mooney. [See Bibliography]

THE PORTABLE MEDICINE WHEEL

Medicine wheels need not be large stone constructions set outdoors. An excellent way to work with the medicine wheel is to make a small wheel on a piece of cardboard or wood. Or you might set one up on a table or shelf in your house. Many people use carefully selected semi-precious stones to make a miniature medicine wheel. It can be very interesting and enlightening to work with stones of various carefully chosen colors.

Medicine wheels don't have to be fancy. You can go out right now and grab a handful of stones from the driveway and set up a wheel as you re-read this chapter. Everything we have said will mean a lot more with an actual wheel growing in front of you.

A medicine wheel can also be portable. You will need five sticks or dowels. These can be from 1/2 to 1 inch in diameter and about 5 inches long. An old broomstick would make a good set. We suggest that you paint four of them in the colors traditional for each direction. That is, black for west, white for north,

red for east, and green for south. The fifth may be left unpainted or might be painted blue. With these five sticks you can set up a medicine wheel wherever you go. Just tuck them into your pocket, perhaps with a compass, and take off.

When you wish to set up your wheel, determine the directions from the sun or a compass. The center stick is placed first. From the center to the west take a certain number of steps and place the black stick. Call to Yanu the bear as you set the stick in the ground. Return to the center and take the same number of steps to the north. Calling upon Yunsu the buffalo, place the white stick. In the same way set the red east stick calling upon Awahili the eagle and the green stick in the south calling upon Tsistu.

Once you have some experience working with the wheel, these five sticks will give you sufficient guidance to work with the wheel when you cannot be within a fully set out stone wheel.

Of course, five special stones or other tokens might be substituted for the five sticks. They are an aid to assist you in the visualization of the complete wheel.

MONTH	MOON	ANIMAL	CHEROKEE NAME	MINERAL	PLANT	CHEROKEE NAME	QUALITIES
January	Icicle	Screech Owl	Wahaunu	Granite	Pine	Natsi	Purification, grounding, rest, introspection
February	Frost	Cat	Wesa	Quartz	Poplar	Tsiyu	Vision, emotion, romance, humanist
March	Thawing	Crow	Kagu	Turquoise	Plantain		Healing, hunting, spiritualism, sincerity
April	Flower	Rat	Tisdetsi	Opal	Dandelion		Hope, energy, foresight, enthusiasm
May	Mockingbird	Beaver	Dayi	Chrysoprase	Thistle	Tsitsi	Growth, alteration, change, engineering, building
June	Dogwood	Deer	Awi	Moonstone	Dogwood	Kanvsita	Grace, sensitivity, expression, intuition
July	Red Hawk	Hawk	Tlanuwa	Agate	Yarrow		Mysticism, perception, individuality, friendship
August	Sassafras	Turtle	Saligugi, Ulanawa	Garnet	Sassafras	Kanasdatsi	Leadership, inner strength, courage, dominance
September	Squirrel	Squirrel	Salili	Copper	Mullein	Tsaliyusti	Cheer, good nature, curiosity, reason
October	Birds Fly	Dog	Gili	Jasper	Cedar	Atsina	Duality, paradox, adaptability, wariness
November	Woodchuck	Woodchuck		Obsidian	Oak	Ataya	Balance, sexuality, transformation, harmony
December	Long Sleep	Blacksnake	Gulegi	Amethyst	Sage		Stateliness, steadfastness, practicality

Yanu is the Spirit Keeper of the Moons of January, February &
Awahili is the Spirit Keeper of July, August, and September.

March. Yunsu is the Spirit Keeper of April, May, and June.
Tsistu is the Spirit Keeper of October, November, and December.

MOONS OF THE MEDICINE WHEEL

GRANDMOTHER'S CIRCLET, GRANDFATHER'S HOOP

Using the Medicine Wheel

In the late twilight of a summer evening, street lights cast deep shadows under the overgrown privet. Across the dusty hedge, cars are zipping, 8 deep, from mall to bar, to grocery, and home.

Light flashes out a door and across a small yard as four shapes walk silently across the patio and up a step to a circle of glimmering limestone rocks. Wisps of fragrant smoke are fanned into the air with a dusky wing and the noise of traffic fades within the ring of stone. A bulky figure, face hidden below hawk's wings, chants words in an old language. Around the edge of the stones the shades of the ancestors, the spirits of the totems, gather to watch and assist in the work of the evening. The alto of a woman's voice takes up the chant and the aromatic smell of tobacco rises to the sky propelled by the heartbeat of a drum.

Within the sacred space of the medicine wheel, the city has ceased to exist. The wheel comprises there, in the nexus of earth and sky, past and future, a sphere wherein the power of the medicine person is given and taken. In a time which cannot be measured on a liquid quartz display, four ordinary human beings have become a part of the energy rivers of the Cosmos.

WHAT IS A MEDICINE WHEEL?

The medicine wheel is a physical representation of sacred space and of the Earth and the Universe. It is used as a meditational tool to aid the seeker in learning the lessons which life has to teach. It is a way of reaching outside the seeker's own life into strange worlds and places where man cannot walk in his flesh (or woman either). The medicine wheel teaches you to change and grow; to be open to life and to all of your relatives on the earth. As you travel around the wheel, you learn about many of the totems.

When you learn to keep your own life in constant change, you keep the life force high. Every totem has a gift for you which will enlarge and enrich your life. The wheel enables you to experience many manifestations of human nature. We all contain these manifestations within ourselves but we have to place ourselves in different positions and experiences in order to feel them. The essence of the medicine wheel is movement and change.

The medicine wheel is also the ceremonial center for medicine path people. Here we practice our healing. Here we look into the past, the present, and the future for knowledge and guidance. Here we come to pledge our lives in marriage or to celebrate a new life beginning its travel on the wheel. This might be a newborn child or it can be an older individual beginning his/her journey in/on the medicine path.

We come to the wheel, alone and in groups, to celebrate the turning of the seasons, the changing faces of the moon. We meet here to formalize giveaways, wapani, to energize and dedicate seeds and offerings for hokshichankiya. We come to refresh our energy in touching the turning of the wheel and to build our strength for our journey. We come, one or many, to work for unity of purpose and to build our medicine. We come to the medicine wheel to honor the spirits by passing the water bowl; making offerings to the earth, the spirit keepers, the moon and the totems. We celebrate our communion with the universe and each other with the sacred pipe and the talking stick.

Work with the medicine wheel may take many different forms. Each begins in much the same way. The wheel is tidied, if necessary. It is thoroughly smudged. Each person participating in the activity is smudged before taking his/her place at the wheel. An offering is made to the spirit keepers of the four directions, usually either by smoking the sacred pipe or by offering tobacco.

The pipe or tobacco offering is begun at the west and continued through the north, east and south. The sky, the mother of four-leggeds, the ancestors and the spirits of nature are also offered smoke or tobacco.

The words following are those used by Medicine Hawk and include words in several languages. These are not the only acceptable words. Grey Cat uses the Cherokee language because she works on Cherokee land. You may begin with these words. As you proceed along the path, perhaps you will find others.

[West] Mudjekeewis, Yanu, Paksikwoyi, Kyaiyo, "Where the sun lies down and dies", Home of Thunders.

[North] Waboose, Tetanal, Yanash, Yenasa, Yanasi, Strong Heart Country, White Mountain Standing.

[East] Wabun, Quanah, Awahili, Wanbli, Galeshka, Dark Horizontal Mountain, Red Eastern Mountain.

[South] Shawnodese, Saynday, Agawela, The Spirit of Corn, Turtle Mountain, Atsila the Fire.

[Sky] Wakan Tanka, Father Sky, Great Spirit Ma'hpi'ya.

[Earth] Cha'ko, Mother Earth, Maka Ina, womb of all things.

[Ancestors] Ancestors (name names if desired)

[spirits] spirit guardians and allies, totems (Name those whom you wish to particularly address).

It is a very good idea to memorize this or your own words of your offerings to the spirit keepers.

Once the wheel and all participants have been smudged and your offerings have been made, you are ready to begin your use of the medicine wheel.

INDIVIDUAL USES OF THE MEDICINE WHEEL

A medicine wheel is often the best place to follow the disciplines of your own personal medicine path. It is an excellent place for meditation. Ask there for direction or guidance, or to refresh and restore your energy. It is also the best place to

work to build your own personal medicine.

There are infinite ways to use the medicine wheel in your personal search for harmony, knowledge, and power. Movement around the wheel helps you learn the lessons that life has to teach. This is what the totems (and the wheel) are all about.

USING THE WHEEL TO REFRESH AND RESTORE ENERGY

After smudging yourself and the wheel use the meditative techniques outlined in Chapter 3 to ground and center yourself. Release all the cares of your everyday life and reach out to the protection and balance of the medicine wheel, the spirit keepers, the totems and moons. This is an appropriate time to offer a sacred pipe (Chapter 9) and/ or to make offerings of tobacco or corn meal to the earth or your totem spirit(s). Give yourself as much time as possible within the wheel to restore physical, nervous and spiritual energy.

USING THE WHEEL FOR PERSONAL GROWTH OR INFORMATION

Smudge yourself and the wheel and offer a pipe or tobacco to the spirit keepers. Place your spirit bag (See Chapter 3) or other object with a strong personal meaning to you, on the moon or quarter stone which rules the totemic powers with which you wish to commune. This establishes a link between you and the totem. As you stand (in a spiritual sense) at that moon and in the presence of that totem, make your prayers and ask for the teachings of the totem(s). You must use meditative techniques to ground and center yourself. You may offer prayers, tobacco, smoke, etc. to the totem spirits you wish to honor. You must release your daily life and enter a receptive state of mind so that you will be able to hear their messages in return.

Occasionally messages and/or visions will come with great clarity and be easy to understand and apply to your own actions. Generally, they come cloaked with symbolism from your own inner, wordless self or obscured in the traditional symbolisms which have gathered over the ages around that totem concept. (See Chapters 14, 15, and 16) Reach out with courage for the messages of these spirit keepers and totems for they are the gift of the wheel.

USING THE WHEEL FOR BUILDING PERSONAL MEDICINE

Take with you to the wheel any materials needed to physically construct the medicine object you have in mind. Smudge yourself, the wheel, and the materials you have brought. Offer a pipe or tobacco to the spirit keepers. Using your spirit bag and/or any appropriate physical objects, make a connection with the spirit keepers, moons and totems you wish to lend power to your medicine working. Choose the appropriate path or direction for your work. Place yourself and your materials near or on them. Open yourself to the inflow of power from these spirits. Carefully and with utmost concentration construct the medicine object.

When the object is completed - or you have finished work for the day - smudge the object and offer thanks to those who assisted your work. When practical, leave an uncompleted medicine object within the wheel until you can complete it. Otherwise, it should be wrapped up carefully with the unused materials and stored.

SOME GROUP USES OF THE MEDICINE WHEEL

There are numerous occasions for a group to use a medicine wheel. The wheel is an ideal place to commemorate important happenings within the group or to individual members. Births, marriages, dedication to the medicine path, and the leaving of this life are all suitable occasions. The wheel is used to observe the turning of the seasons, usually at the Solstices and Equinoxes. The full, new or other days of the moon are also marked at the wheel.

The wheel is also used as a tool for group psychic bonding. Such ceremonies as giveaways, joint sacrifices, the passing of the water bowl, or the talking stick work to mold individuals into a working group. It is also used to focus medicine working by the group when there is a joint purpose, whether public or private. The commonest of these is probably healing.

GROUP CEREMONIES FOR THE MEDICINE WHEEL

All group workings with the wheel begin as do personal workings with smudging the wheel and the participants. Usually one person undertakes the offering of tobacco or the pipe. The special focus of the meeting is often expressed as a part of the calling to the spirits and keepers. A Cherokee-based Winter Solstice ritual for filling the pipe follows:

[West] Yanu, the Bear, Spirit Keeper of the West where the sun lies down and dies, Home of Thunders, Come and be welcome this day of the Long Night.

[North] Yunsu, the Buffalo, Spirit Keeper of the North; Strong Heart Country, White Mountain Standing, Home of the great white giant from whose mouth streams the cleansing wind. Come and be welcome; guard us during your cold time.

[East] Awahili, the Eagle, Spirit Keeper of the East where the sun does ever shine. Red Eastern Mountain, Come and be welcome; keep the sun safe until his day of returning.

[South] Tsistu, the Rabbit, Spirit Keeper of the South. Trickster of the People. Spirit of Corn, Turtle Mountain, Atsila the Fire, come and be welcome, bring us your heat for our life and comfort.

[Sky] Galunlati, Father Sky, Great Spirit Ma-hpi-ya, let your eyes see us.

[Earth] Agisaegwa, Mother of Four-Leggeds, Grandmother Earth, Maka Ina, womb of all things, the cold year readies the seed of your green time.

[Ancestors] Ancestors, Old Ones, Wise Spirits, Agayunli (name names if desired). We seek your counsel in the long cold.

[spirits] Spirit Guardians and Allies, Totems, Spirits of Nature, Nunahe (Name those whom you wish to particularly address); visit us in the time of the long sleep.

Other seasonal celebrations are treated in a similar manner: Spring Equinox is the time of the coming of spring and growth, Summer Solstice is the opening of summer and the time or early ripening; Fall Equinox, the time of harvest and preparation for the hunt. For the moon celebrations, the special qualities of each moon may be remembered.

Most of us live far from the country and maybe

we have some difficulty even seeing the moon. We have allowed modern life to insulate us far too much from the rhythms and cycles of Turtle Island. Though you may have to look up the dates on a calendar, making a formal observance of these turnings of the great medicine wheel will slowly but surely create stronger links between you and our land.

BIRTHS, MARRIAGES, DEDICATIONS TO THE MEDICINE PATH, THE LEAVING OF THIS LIFE

In ceremonies celebrating these milestones in life, the spirit keepers would be called to witness the occasion in appropriate terms. Frequently, the qualities of the moon time can be tied into this calling. A sacred pipe or special offering may then be made for the commemoration and formalization of the occasion. Remember that weddings must be performed by someone acceptable to the state of residence in order to be legal. The spiritual qualities are binding regardless of the legal aspects.

OTHER GROUP RITUALS

Most group celebrations at the medicine wheel have as their primary purpose the enjoyment and spiritual expression of the participants. At the same time, groups actually need not meet at the medicine wheel, council lodge or whatever, in order to enjoy the benefits of group ceremonial observances.

As this book is written primarily with the individual traveler on the medicine path in mind, we will not detail the numerous ceremonies suitable for group work. The needs and inclinations of the group itself and the study and imagination of the individuals will surely suggest appropriate methods of group expression. You and members of your group are the very best sources of ritual and ceremonial practices.

PASSING THE TALKING STICK is an ancient practice and may be in itself a ceremony or it may be just a part of a more ambitious observance. It is extremely easy to do and is of great assistance for group interactions. To pass the talking stick, first find a stick. This may be any small stick which happens to be handy, or may be a finished and decorated prayer stick (see Chapter 12).

Everyone taking part in the ceremony makes themselves comfortable. Someone begins by holding the stick. This individual may then talk about whatever is on his/her mind. Only the person holding the stick may talk. After speaking, the first person passes the stick on to a person near.

Slowly the stick makes its way to everyone present. Everyone has the opportunity to say what they wish without interruption or rebuttal. It may be that your group will wish to pass the stick several times around.

Some of the benefits of the talking stick are to allow the quieter individuals of the group an opportunity to let everyone know what is on their mind. This can also be a good way to begin the consideration of a decision the group needs to make. It does prevent the noisy interruptive argument which can accompany the making of a group decision.

THE CORNMEAL OFFERING ceremony is just about as easy to do as the talking stick. Cornmeal is the most appropriate substance to offer in this way as it is the important grain of the AmerIndian.

A bowl of cornmeal is set in the center of the group or passed from one person to another. Each one takes a pinch of the cornmeal out of the bowl. Holding the cornmeal each individual either expresses thanks for some benefit recently received or asks the granting of a wish. They need not speak aloud if they do not wish to. The individual then tastes of the cornmeal and scatters the meal on the ground It is customary for the entire group to consent to each thank you or request by saying "Ho". For an indoor ritual a bowl of dirt should be used to receive the cornmeal. This dirt should later be ceremonially buried or burned outdoors.

After the activity of the ceremony is ended, it is appropriate to sit and meditate a few minutes before all leave the ritual area and return to normal socializing. Courtesy requires that all who share in the ceremony help clean up the wheel. All should also help to return any materials used to their places.

BLOOD AND BONES OF THE PEOPLE

The Sacred Pipe

THE PIPE COMES TO THE PEOPLE

Many say that the pipe came to the Plains tribes first through White Buffalo Calf Woman. The sequence of the pipe gifts to the many tribes is inconsequential. The significant point is that the pipe came to save the people — to bring them closer to Galunlati, the Great Spirit.

The pipe came to the Southern Cherokee from Atagahi, the enchanted lake. A hunter named Sadayi, 'Arrow Annie', sat down to rest on the bank of Atagahi one day. She noticed an unusual ripple in the waters. A great water serpent, Uktena, raised its head above the surface. In its mouth was a tubular object with a crooked end. Uktena swam closer to Annie — right up to the bank. She stood her ground as all courageous warriors do. The serpent laid the object at her feet and spoke:

"This is the sacred altar which your people must carry everywhere they travel. Place the sacred tsalu (tobacco) within it. In this manner you place yourselves into the altar. When it is lit and the smoke billows forth it is your prayers going up to the Great Spirit, Galunlati. When you draw the smoke into your body it is the breath of the Great Spirit coming in to cleanse and heal you. The bowl is the blood of the people: it is of the mineral kingdom and it is Woman. The stem is the bones of the people: it is of the plant kingdom and it is Man. The skins and feathers are of the animal kingdom. Smoke the kanunnawu (pipe) that the People may live."

With that the Uktena returned to the lake's depths leaving the kanunnawu on the bank. Annie returned to her people with the sacred pipe.

THE PHILOSOPHY OF THE KANUNNAWU

The medicine pipe, sacred pipe or peace pipe, may be the most readily recognized Indian ceremony. We have seen travesties in horse opera westerns, and well documented, seriously reenacted pipe ceremonies in films and on TV. If you have attended a sweat, pow wow, medicine wheel gathering, or other public occasion led by a follower of the medicine path, you have doubtless seen a pipe ceremony.

Even in the most sloppily thrown together caricature of a pipe ceremony, done for the least historically accurate of movies, it is clear that something serious, important, **SACRED**, is happening for the participants. The pipe is not a **SYMBOL** of sacred things: it is in itself **SACRED!** It becomes, after it is consecrated, the embodiment of the Grandmother and Grandfather; Earth and Sky. It becomes the Great Spirit Galunlati.

Many people think of the pipe as a **SYMBOL** of the sacred. Indeed, it is much more than that; it is the sacred in reality. For this reason not everyone, not even every follower of the medicine path, is called to bear a pipe. It is a heavy responsibility to be burdened with the care and preservation of the consecrate nature of the pipe. The pipe bearer assumes a responsibility to all his or her brothers and sisters, to the clan, the tribe, the country, and, indeed, the world. He/she does not own the pipe but only has it in his/her care for a time. The pipe bearer is the caretaker of a means of direct communication with beings of the spirit. He/She is responsible for its preservation and for using it honorably, well, and when needed. It is clear from James Mooney, Black Elk, and many other sources, that women, equally with men, were pipe bearers.

If a pipe is misused or not cared for properly it will cease to work. Should a pipe bearer be dishonorable, a liar or a coward, the pipe will repossess its power from that person. It will refuse to work.

You should give very careful thought as to whether or not a pipe calls to you as bearer. Be sure you understand its meaning and that you have a healthy respect for this embodiment of the sacred Be prepared to have IT make demands on YOU!

The bowl of the pipe is the Earth Mother, the stones, the mother of the four-leggeds. The stem is Grandfather Sky, the tree which reaches from the earth to the above. The fire and the sun live in the bowl; all are one family within the sacred pipe.

When the bowl and the stem of the pipe are connected, The pipe is **AWAKE**. Remember that the pipe is not a symbol of the sacred — it is the sacred: not symbol — reality.

WHAT IS A MEDICINE PIPE?

In one sense, any smoke producing, herb burning object can be a kanunnawu. A perfectly ordinary purchased pipe, even a cigarette, may be used as a sacred pipe. For some individuals it may be appropriate to fully consecrate an ordinary pipe as your medicine pipe. You will know when/ if this is the case.

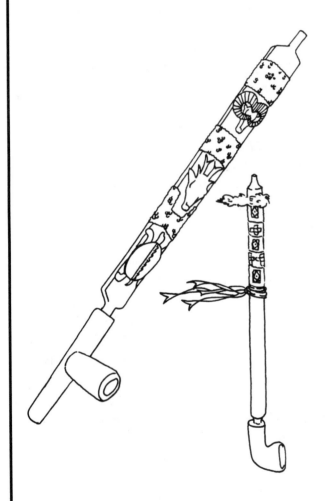

THE SACRED PIPES

Traditionally, the Native American sacred pipe is made in two distinct parts, the bowl and the stem. The bowl is made of a number of different materials: wood, stone, antler, bone, or clay. In the modern medicine path the bowl most frequently is carved from one of a number of soapstone type stones. Catlinite or red pipe stone is favored. Plains pipes most commonly were red. In the eastern woodlands red pipes were smoked at times of war and white pipes were used at peaceful ceremonies.

The stem of the traditional sacred pipe is usually longer than the stem of ordinary pipes. It can be as short as 8 or 10 inches though stems of 20 to 30 inches are not unknown. It may be intricately carved or quite simple. There must be a small hole drilled entirely through the stem. Wood, including commercial dowels, is the commonest material used to make the stem these days, although many other materials are used.

The bowl of the pipe has an upright portion which contains the tobacco (the bowl) and a right angled portion (the shank) which connects with the stem. Bowls come in a large variety of designs reflecting different tribes. Pipe makers and bearers may make a distinction in the design of the bowl of a sacred pipe to be borne by a woman. It may have a plain heel (where the bowl joins the shank) while one to be borne by a man is made in a "T" shape. Other tribes make no distinction.

If you feel particularly connected with one particular tribe of Native Americans attempt to find or make a pipe which follows their traditional design. For many of us, our pipe so soon becomes our own personal expression that any lack of specific tribal identification may be unimportant.

OBTAINING YOUR PIPE

There are a number of sources where you may purchase finished or partially finished pipes. (See Chapter 19) You may decorate them according to your own vision. You may wish to have a pipe made especially for you. Inquiries at local shops carrying Native American items may lead you to someone who can do this.

PIPE KITS

Pipe kits generally consist of a bowl and stem which you must work on to fit them together. Your pipe kit will probably come with instructions but here are a few hints. Carve the stem to fit into the shank of the bowl - not the bowl to fit the stem. Don't attempt too tight a fit as most of the stone bowls are not particularly strong. Should the bowl break at this point, it can be carefully glued with something like Duco Cement, wound with sinew or heavy, strong thread, and covered with suede - which should then be dyed red or white.) A little beeswax rubbed on the stem will ease the fitting. Except when testing the fit of bowl and stem the two pieces of the pipe should never be joined except when the pipe is being smoked in a ceremony.

The stem of the pipe is frequently covered or banded with fur. Rabbit is quite common and appropriate. Ribbons, feathers, shells, and almost any other desired decoration may be attached. Do keep in mind that you need to be able to handle the pipe after all the decoration has been added. Don't make working with the pipe too awkward. Beading, quill work, inlay, and carving are other ways of decorating the stem of a sacred pipe. The decorations added to the pipe will help connect with your totems, with the spirit keepers, or with any other natural forces you feel led to.

The bowl and stem of the pipe are stored in separate bags. These may be made of leather or other material you find appropriate. You will also need a small bag for a store of old or consecrated tobacco or herbal mixture and a bag for new tobacco or herbs. You will also need a bowl in which to mix the new and old smoking mixtures. Many people have a large bag or basket in which they can keep and carry the pipe and all the other necessary items for a pipe ceremony.

WHAT TO SMOKE IN THE PIPE

There are almost as many smoking mixtures as there are people bearing the sacred pipe. While tobacco is the base of many of these it is not necessary to use it at all. Some other herbs frequently used as part of a smoking mixture include:

Bear berry (Arctostaphylos uva-ursi)
Inner bark of the red willow, red osier dogwood (Cornus amomum)
Mugwort (Atremisia vulgaris)
Mint (Mentha spp.)

Damiana** (Turnera diffusa)
Skullcap** (Scutellaria galericulata)
Wormwood** (Artemisia absinthium)
Chamomile (Anthemis nobilis)
Borage (Borago officinalis)
Passion flower (Passiflora incarnata)
Lobelia** (Lobelia inflata)
Chaparral (Larrea tridentata)
Jimson weed** (Datura spp.)
Lungwort, Mullein (Verbascum thapus)
Southern red sage
Wild lettuce (Lactuca spp.)
Amaranth (Amaranthus hypochondriacus)
Muscadine (Vitis spp.)

Most of these herbs have a definite effect when smoked, both physical and psychic. Some can be extremely dangerous. We recommend against using the starred (**) herbs although they have traditionally been used in smoking mixtures. They have been included here only in the interest of historical accuracy.

Herbs, though natural, are drugs! Misused they are just as dangerous as anything produced by modern medical science or sold on the street by pushers. Those who wish to follow the medicine path must be responsible. They must inform themselves before using any of the gifts of the Great Spirit or the Earth Mother as these gifts contain great power for good **AND** ill. Tobacco, of course, contains a highly addictive drug and all the herbs listed contain chemicals which can be dangerous if misused.

Any tobacco may be used. It is possible to purchase leaf tobacco which has not undergone any commercial processing. While this sort of tobacco is desirable, any tobacco is suitable. In an emergency tearing apart a cigarette is acceptable. Loose pipe tobacco is widely available and any one which you find appealing is fine. Chewing tobacco not only won't burn, it has sugar added which burns with a lot of nasty carbon compounds you don't want in your smoke.

Tobacco should be stored in an airtight container, whether a jar or a bag. It is supposed to be just slightly moist. Other herbs should also be stored air tight. In general herbs other than tobacco should be as dry as possible. One reason for using tobacco in your smoking mixture is that it smolders better than most herbs. This may mean you don't have to re-light your pipe quite so often. Tobacco IS traditionally at least a part of the mixture smoked in the sacred pipe.

EQUIPMENT FOR A PIPE CEREMONY

SACRED TOBACCO

Mentioned above was a pouch of old or sacred tobacco. This is an important part of the sacred pipe ceremony. Before you first smoke your pipe you should consecrate a special bag of tobacco. If you have been presented with tobacco or other appropriate herbs in the past, some of them may be included in your bag of sacred tobacco.

Take your bag and a quantity of smoking mixture, including any gift tobacco and/or herbs, to your medicine wheel, altar, or other sacred space. After smudging and making offerings to the spirit keepers, smudge the bag and the mixture. Fill the bag and offer it for the blessings of the powers. Close the bag carefully and keep it with your pipe.

CONSECRATING YOUR SACRED PIPE

You may consecrate your pipe in your medicine wheel, at an altar, or in any other place which seems right to you. You will need a smudging mixture, your pipe, old and new smoking mixture, and lots of matches or a lighter. The traditional mixture for use in smudging the pipe consists of sage, western sage, sweetgrass, calamus, bear berry, or the dried inner bark of red willow (red osier dogwood). Other herbs you may use include cedar and tobacco. (See Chapter 4 for more information on smudging.)

Mound your smudging mixture in a clay bowl, shell or other container made of natural materials. Finely cut herbs will probably burn on their own. Test a little before-hand. Use special charcoal incense briquettes if it doesn't burn well.

Face west and light your mixture. Offer it to the spirit keepers of the four directions, beginning in the west, to the sky, and the earth. Using a feather fan, a wing, or other appropriate tool, draw the smoke over yourself in cleansing and to indicate a change in your consciousness. Set the smudging bowl down. Pass the bowl of the pipe over the smudge fanning the smoke over and around it. Do the same with the stem. Pass your hands through the smoke. Lifting the bowl of the pipe in your left hand and the stem in your right hand, join them. This is the joining of the male and female, the heavens and the earth, the mundane and the spiritual. When they are joined the pipe is awake.

Pass the pipe through the smoke fanning it well. Hold the pipe over the smudging bowl and allow it to fill with smoke. The Great Spirit Galunlati smokes first!

If you do not plan to smoke the pipe at this time you should offer it to the spirit keepers, the sky, the earth, the ancestors, and the spirits before you take it apart and put it away. The pipe is never put away with the bowl and the stem joined.

SMOKING THE SACRED PIPE

Take out your bags of old and new tobacco or smoking mixture and your mixing bowl. Make a guess (the first time) of how much your pipe will hold and take that much out of EACH of the bags. Put both into the mixing bowl. Offer this mixture as you did the smudging herbs. Return half of it to the pouch containing your sacred tobacco that it may never be empty. The rest of the mixed tobacco is to be packed into your pipe.

Hold your pipe bowl in your left hand. Join the bowl and the stem if you have not done so earlier. If your are left-handed, reverse these directions. Let the stem lean against your left shoulder. Packing the pipe may be a quick matter of just placing the tobacco in the bowl and tamping it down lightly. More frequently the bowl is packed pinch by pinch. Dedicate each tiny pinch to the spirit keepers in turn, the moon(s), and/or the totems. You will learn to judge the amounts so that, when the pipe is packed, there is no mixture left in your bowl. Should there be a little left it can be disposed of later along with any unconsumed tobacco and the ashes in the bowl of the pipe.

When the bowl is packed face west, hold the bowl in your left hand, and the match or lighter in your right. Put the stem in your mouth and light the pipe. Unless you are used to smoking don't inhale the smoke, particularly when you are lighting the pipe. The longer the stem of the pipe, the harder you must draw on it. Extend the stem to the west, holding the bowl in your left hand and the stem in your right, and say:

"Yanu, the bear, spirit keeper of the west. Thunder-beings, Wakan-yantanka. Come smoke with me/us and share the blessings of the sacred pipe."

Take a puff (relight the pipe as often as necessary throughout the ceremony) and blow the smoke to the west. Turn to the north, extend the stem to the north and say:

"Yunsu, the buffalo, spirit keeper of the north. Waziuh, great white giant, from whose mouth streams the cleansing wind. Come, smoke with me/us and share the blessings of the sacred pipe."

Take a puff and blow the smoke to the north. Turn to the east, extend the stem to the east, and say:

"Awahili the eagle, spirit keeper of the east where the sun shines continually. Father Wi. Come, smoke with me/us and share the blessings of the sacred pipe." Take a puff and blow the smoke to the east. Face south, extend the stem to the south and say:

"Tsistu, the rabbit, spirit keeper of the south, the direction we are always facing. Wopay. Come smoke with me/us and share the blessings of the sacred pipe." Take a puff and blow the smoke to the south. Face west again, extend the stem towards the sky and say:

"Galunlati, Father Sky; Great Spirit Ma-hpi-ya. Come smoke with me/us and share the blessings of the sacred pipe." Take a puff and blow the smoke towards the sky. Extend the stem towards the earth and say:

"Agisegwa, mother of all four-leggeds, Chako, Mother Earth; Maka Ina, womb of all things. Come smoke with me/us and share the blessings of the sacred pipe." Take a puff and blow the smoke towards the earth. Extend the stem over the left and then the right shoulder and say:

"Ancestors, Agayunli" (name names if you desire) Revolve the stem in a circle before you and say:

"Nunahe, spirit guardians and allies, totems," etc. (name the appropriate names) "Come smoke with me/us and share the blessings of the sacred pipe." Take a puff and blow the smoke into the air.

PASSING THE PIPE

When others are to smoke the pipe, each participant should pass his/her hands through the smoke of the mixture. The pipe is held with the bowl in the left hand and the stem in the right hand. It is passed around the group in clockwise fashion (to the person on the left). Each person takes the pipe in both hands (bowl in left, stem in right). At all times the pipe is held with one hand on the bowl and one on the stem. It is wise to pass a lighter or matches with the pipe — first hand on the pipe then tuck the lighter or matches into the other person's hand.

When the pipe is passed to an individual he/she usually points the stem to the four directions, the sky, the earth, and over each shoulder. The exact manner of handling the pipe isn't particularly important so long as the pipe is offered and also held securely. Generally the fit between the bowl and the stem usually isn't really tight in order to preserve the bowl of the pipe. Even if this is not the case, it is appropriate to hold the earth and the sky with respect and care. If there are more than a few people the pipe may be puffed only once, after the gestured offering, by each participant.

In any case, after the offering(s) the pipe should be smoked until it goes out. It is not at all necessary to inhale the smoke from the pipe. You may draw the smoke in, hold it in your mouth as if it were water, and blow out the puff. It is perfectly permissible when sharing a pipe to bring the pipe to your chest, placing it flat over your heart in token of smoking it. However, to be a pipe bearer you must smoke the pipe! Whether or not you inhale is up to you.

When the pipe has finally gone out separate the bowl and the stem. The ashes may be placed in your smudging bowl and the whole relit if necessary until all has been burned. The ashes may be scattered on the earth or buried at the end of the ceremony. These ashes remain sacred and must be reverently treated.

Before the pipe is truly put away it must be cleaned, either before leaving the ceremony, or a short time later. A straightened-out coat hanger wire is usually of a good size for cleaning the stem. It may be clamped in a variable speed drill and, running it slowly, pushed from one end of the stem to the other. The bowl must also be cleaned out carefully. The bowl and shank should be wiped out with pipe cleaners. Some people suggest heating the wire red hot and burning out the stem as well as anything left in the bowl of the pipe. Keep in mind that the pipe is itself a sacred object. Treat it as such.

As your vision grows and changes so will your pipe ceremony. This is as it should be. Little Hawk has said that, "It has been shown time after time that the pipe will itself teach you how to use it properly. All you need do is listen."

Remember that the pipe, the spirit keepers, all the names on which you call, are not symbols — they are real. May you come to know this for yourself; may the Great Spirit guide you always, that you work wisely and well. Hetchetu Welo (it is done)

THE OFFERING OF A PIPE

ALL MY RELATIONS

The Sweat Lodge

In the ancient days the people began to sicken and die. Even the most powerful medicine women were powerless to stop the feverish demise of many of the People. At last Yanu, the bear, came down from the north Georgia mountain bearing her name. She spoke to the people: "You are dying because you are polluted. You are no longer pure. You must return to the womb of Agisegwa, the Great Earth Mother, whom the unega call by many names: Isis, Astarte, Diana, Hecate, Demeter, Kali, Rhiannon, Mary. Come, come to my den where tunkayatakapakah, the ancient stones and peta owihankeshni, the sacred fire, will cleanse and heal you."

The people followed, some supported by others, so weak were they from their illness. Far up into the mountains they travelled, following Yanu to the foot of Mt. Yonah (near present-day Gainesville, GA). There they came upon Yanu's den. A low doorway led into the dark heart of the mountain. Yanu sat before her den. She passed the sacred pipe, calling upon the spirit keepers.

"Enter the lodge as equals - men and women alike," Bear spoke.

"As you enter say, 'All my relations', that we may be as one within the lodge."

With that Yanu entered and the people followed. They circled around the lodge clockwise. In the center of the lodge was a pit containing heated rocks which made it very warm. The people began to sweat and the impurities of their beings were given to the stones. After four quarters they emerged, purified, and renewed.

To this day the people enter the sacred asi (sweat lodge) to purify themselves in the womb of the earth.

The sweat lodge ceremony is the Native American custom which has found the greatest acceptance in the NeoPagan, New Age, and other alternative cultures of this country. Any time a half a dozen or so of them come together they hunt for someone to lead a sweat.

Black Elk's description of Inipi, the Lakota rite of purification [The Sacred Pipe, Joseph Epes Brown; University of Oklahoma Press, Norman, OK; 1953] is an extremely moving and forceful account of this ritual. However, the sweat lodge is found in virtually all American Indian cultures. Among the Cherokee a sweat lodge or asi was a permanent structure. Usually there was one near each family house. It was "... a small hut of logs plastered over with clay, with a shed roof, and just tall enough to permit a sitting or reclining, but not a standing, position inside. It is used for sweat-bath purposes, and as it is tight and warm, and a fire is usually kept smoldering within, it is a favorite sleeping place for the old people in cold weather." [Myths and Legends of the Cherokee; Mooney.]

The asi, particularly when combined with one or more pipe ceremonies (as it generally is), is firmly rooted in the four elements, the four prime directions, the spirit keepers, and the four paths of the medicine wheel. Everything used in the asi ceremony has it own rich tapestry of spiritual meanings, from the young trees used to build the lodge, to the placement of the fire.

The asi cleanses the body of physical impurities and from its ties to its common concerns. It is a form of the death and rebirth mythology of the vision quest and of initiation. It cleanses the spirit with its focus on the harmony of the elements with man's own spirit as the center. It releases the spirit fully for participation in important projects, for the asi may be only the preparation for a ceremony! In Native American tradition the asi is undertaken only for a specific PURPOSE. People didn't run in and out of it all week just to sit, sweat, and induce multiple visions and/or hallucinations.

The Cherokees were a non-migratory people with permanent dwellings. For them it apparently was a somewhat more ordinary occupation than for their nomadic brothers to the west. "... the myth-keepers and priests were accustomed to meet together at night in the asi... to recite the traditions and discuss their secret knowledge.". [op.cit.] Those who wished to learn of the ways of the medicine path would meet the medicine man/woman in the asi and spend the night there, lighted by a small fire. At daybreak they would leave the building and, after a ceremonial scratching, would dip seven times under the water of the (usually) nearby stream.

A sweat lodge absolutely must be led by someone who really knows what they are doing. Sweat lodge leaders need first to take part in quite a number of sweats led by qualified persons. They must receive special instruction on how to lead a sweat. This book **WILL NOT TEACH YOU TO LEAD A SWEAT!** We will attempt only to explain many of the meanings of the asi and the customs, tools, and materials used in it. We will also introduce a very modified asi ceremony suitable for any not having access to a properly led sweat. This gentle asi is designed especially for people who, for medical/physical reasons, cannot participate in a full-fledged sweat lodge.

BUILDING THE ASI; WHERE TO PUT IT

The ideal site for a sweat lodge is beside a perfectly clean, clear-running stream. It should be placed at a spot on the bank where you can walk or jump into the water. You don't have a lovely, pure stream in your backyard? A lake, swimming pool, outdoor shower, or even a garden hose will do the job. Build a lodge in a hidden part of your back yard and bring water in a bucket. Many people aren't able to build a sweat lodge in their own yard. This explains much of the eagerness to participate in a sweat at gatherings and workshops on Native American traditions.

You will also need quite a number of good, rounded rocks. Never use rocks which have been in water. Such rocks have water within their crystalline structure. When they are heated they may burst and spray razor sharp stone chips around the fire or asi. It is best to get your rocks from high on a hillside.

BUILDING AN ASI

The traditional plains sweat lodge is made of very small saplings of willow or other very flexible tree covered with buffalo hide. Most modern sweat lodges are constructed of available saplings covered with quilts, blankets, canvass, or tarpaulin. Buffalo hides that big have become very hard to come by! Beware of black plastic, it may melt and drip down into the asi.

The asi should be just a hair too small for the number of people expected to take part. 4, 8, 12 or 16 flexible sticks are used to build the framework. The first four sticks should be placed in the four prime directions. The door should face one of the prime directions. East is perhaps the most common although west doors aren't at all unusual. Offset that stick a little bit to one side to allow for the doorway.

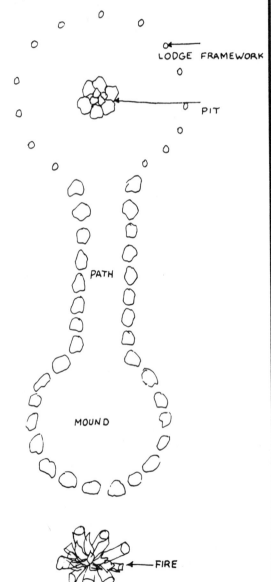

LODGE FRAMEWORK

PIT

PATH

MOUND

FIRE

DESIGN FOR CONSTRUCTING A PATH

The framework is tied together with string or cord. Don't use plastic rope as it may melt. The covering is arranged over this framework and tied securely. Black plastic may be used over other coverings in order to fully exclude light. Be sure that there is a generous flap to draw across the door. The inside should be completely dark when the door flap is closed.

The floor of the sweat lodge MUST be bare earth. Using a small round tent is acceptable, however, the floor of the tent must be cut out. In the first place, hot rocks would ruin it. In the second, contact with Grandmother Earth is a primary requirement. One other problem with a tent such as this is it may let in too much light.

The lodge is at one and the same time the entire physical universe and the dwelling place of all the spirits, the totems, the spirit keepers, the ancestors, the Great Spirit, Grandfather Sky, Grandmother Earth, and all of human kind. When the door flap is closed it is the underworld, the abode of death and rebirth, the womb of the Mother, Maka Ina.

The darkness of the asi during the quarters is the darkness of our own souls and spirits as we prepare for the light. The light when the flap is thrown open is the knowledge and assistance given us by the spirit beings, the Great Spirit.

THE ALTAR

In addition to building the asi itself, a number of other building projects are required. The center of the asi contains the heated rocks. This area becomes an altar. First sweep the central area clean of leaves, twigs, gravel, etc. Push a small stick into the earth at the center of the asi. This is the center of the universe. Draw a circle 2 to 3 feet in diameter from this center point. Dig this area out to make a place for the rocks. Save this earth, it will be used later. The four points of the compass should be marked at the edge of this circle. Herbs, particularly sage or cedar, may be strewn around the lodge.

The cleared space at the center of the lodge is the altar. The hole at its center is the center of the earth and the universe. It is the abode of Galunlati and the heart of the Grandmother. At the edges of this altar mark the four quarters. These are the abodes of the spirit keepers. This altar is, in effect, a miniature medicine wheel. Offer pinches of tobacco at these points to acknowledge the presence of these spirit beings. The first five rocks are placed at these points to invite the participation of these spirits.

THE PATH

A path is built with some of the earth removed from the center of the asi. It leads from the altar, directly through the door, to a point eight to ten yards away from the lodge. This marks the sacred path. Rocks for the sweat will be brought beside this path. If the pipe is to be used it also will be carried beside this path. It is the path of the Grandmother which leads to the Great Spirit. You should try never to step on or over this path. Walk around the mound should you need to go to the other side.

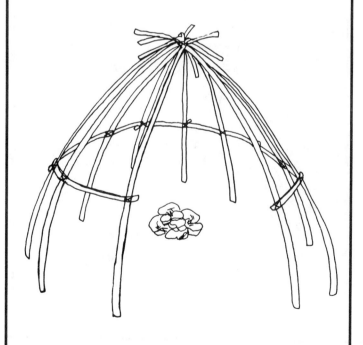

FRAMEWORK OF THE SWEAT LODGE

THE MOUND

At the end of the path a small mound is constructed. It is a reflection of the hollow inside the lodge. The sacred pipe may be leaned against this mound between uses. The bowl is pointed towards the direction from which the pipe will be started. The stem points to the sky. When the pipe is passed out of the lodge, it is repacked and placed again against the mound. The stem will slant towards the direction to be next addressed. Other objects may be placed on the mound by the leader. Sometimes a small framework of sticks is built for the pipe. This framework resembles the racks built to dry meat.

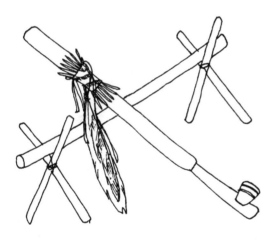

RACK WITH PIPE

THE FIRE

Beyond the mound - or to one side of it - the fire is laid. The rocks should be piled nearby. The fire for heating these rocks is built in a special way. Begin with four sticks laid east to west. Cross with four sticks laid north to south. (Illustration 4) Above these a good deal of wood is piled teepee fashion. When the fire has been lit and fallen into itself a little, pile rocks on it for heating. It takes one to two hours to heat the rocks properly.

This fireplace is the spiritual energy of the Great Spirit and all the keepers and totems. The fire is lighted from the east where the sun first touches. This fire is considered flame of the sacred fire which has no end. It is ever burning and as eternal as the sun.

A garden rake, a potato or hay fork, and a shovel are suggested tools to help remove rocks from the fire. They should be shaken free of ashes and carried into the lodge. Skilled fire tenders use the traditional forked stick, or two sticks for this. Long practice is required to accomplish this successfully.

TOBACCO TIES

Tobacco ties are frequently a part of a sweat lodge. The number and color of the ties may be determined ahead of time by the leader. Frequently 50 black and 50 red ties are made and hung in the asi. Other colors and other numbers are used depending upon the nature of the sweat being done. The ties look beautiful in the lodge when the curtain is drawn at the quarters.

Another form of tobacco tie, called a robe, may be used in an asi. It is made from a long narrow piece of cloth with a large ball of tobacco tied at one end. The robes are hung at the appropriate quarters. Both ties and robes carry your thanks to the spirits when the lodge is over. As with all uses of the ties, they must be buried carefully in the ground after the ceremony.

PERSONAL PREPARATION FOR AN ASI

An asi is not generally a one-person activity. Even if only one individual is actually doing the sweat for personal cleansing (as before a vision quest), several people are needed to provide support services. An asi needs an experienced leader, even though he or she may leave the lodge. A fire tender is also required. This person does a great deal more than just keeping the fire burning. The fire tender carries rocks into the lodge; the sacred pipe in and out of the lodge, repacking it between uses; and beats a drum at the direction of the leader. Since the first five rocks carried in must be placed to represent the center and four quarters, a fire tender needs to be sensitive to the rocks themselves. The fire tender is also part of the protective safety net watching over any inexperienced participants.

As one taking the first steps on the medicine path your responsibility is your own spiritual and physical preparation. Be sure that you have no physical debilities which would make it dangerous for you to take part in this ceremony. Individuals with heart disease; very low or high blood pressure; bronchial or lung problems; blood sugar disorders; or other similarly limiting conditions may find a full asi inadvisable. At the end of this chapter we present a modified version developed especially for those for whom high heat and restricted oxygen are dangerous or undesirable.

Customarily an individual who has suffered a recent death among friends or family does not take part in a sweat for several weeks after the death. Menustrating women should check with the sweat leader before taking part in an asi. This is because a woman's power is very great at this time. It may inhibit the power of the leader.

You should spend all day preparing for an asi. Find out the purpose of the sweat. If the leader looks at you and wonders what you mean by that, perhaps he/she isn't the leader you want to work with! Many sweats have as their purpose the spiritual needs of all the individual participants. This is an acceptable purpose, so long as everyone knows what it is.

Think about your reasons for doing the asi and the purpose for which it is being held. During the time before it begins you should initiate the process of cleansing. Prepare to direct your spirit self into the universe which will be created. Meditation, silence, ordinary forms of cleansing, and even fasting are appropriate ways of spending this preparation period.

You should arrive at the lodge site at least an hour before the time the lodge is to begin. Laying of the fire; purifying the lodge and participants by smudging; prayers, chants, and invocations of the spirit keepers and totems; may take place during this time. You must also help in laying the fire and carrying firewood and rocks. These are the responsibility of everyone taking part in the ceremony. If you don't have time to help, you probably don't really have the time or the need to participate in the asi.

Sweat lodge leaders often use some of this time for teaching; story telling; pipe ceremonies; smudging; chanting and/or drumming; etc. During this time find the space to meditate. Begin to build a silence within (and without) you. Aimless chatter with friends does not belong here.

ENTERING THE SWEAT LODGE

When the rocks are hot and all is ready the leader will enter the lodge alone to complete its purification. Then he/she will come out and make it known that it is time for all participants to enter. A special note here: Often many participants in an asi are completely naked. While this may well be desirable, it should not be a general rule. If you will be unhappy or uncomfortable unclothed wear a bathing suit or underwear. You should wear as little as convenient. However, there doesn't seem to be any strongly held custom of total undress enforced in older times.

Lodges may be all male, all female, or may be carefully balanced with men and women alternating. Shadowlight usually holds co-ed lodges. There are, however, occasions when special ceremonial aims make the holding of a male or female sweat appropriate. This does not imply a discrimination against EITHER sex but a recognition that the ritual needs of each sex can be, on occasion, different.

The doorway into the sweat lodge is low. Upon entering bow low and say "For all my relations", "We are all one family", or words to that effect. The leader will probably already be seated. Move around sunwise (that is, to your left) and behind the leader. Fill the lodge completely from the door all the way around. When you reach your place, sit down.

From this point sweat lodge ceremonies differ according to their purpose, the tradition, and inspiration of the leader. In general the ceremony is performed in four parts, the quarters. At the end of each quarter the door flap will be thrown open. Usually water to drink or pour over your body will be passed at the quarters. Should you be feeling unwell this is a good time to say "for all my relations" and step outside. If you feel able to return before the door is reclosed, enter reverently and return to your place.

If the sacred pipe is to be smoked during the sweat, the fire tender will bring it in at the beginning or end of the quarter(s). Water is poured over the rocks at intervals and often aromatic herbs are thrown upon them.

The quarters (there may be more than four) may be dedicated to four directions. They also may be divided in a number of ways such as using one round for the calling of the spirit keepers and totems; one for the conveying of group and/or individual needs to them; one to allow the participants time to express themselves; and the last devoted to thanksgivings. All this is determined, usually in advance, by the leader or leaders of the asi.

LEAVING THE ASI

It is always permissible to leave an asi ceremony if the heat, oxygen deprivation, or emotional/spiritual intensity become more than you can handle. You should leave as quietly as possible, being sure to move sunwise (to your left). While the best time to leave is at the end of a quarter when the door is already open; do not wait if you are feeling truly unable to continue. The fire tender should be alert for anyone attempting to open the door. Please do not make any noise once you are outside the lodge.

When all the quarters are complete the leader will indicate that it is time to leave the asi. The fire tender may bring a smudge to the entrance for you to step through. As soon as you leave the asi, douse yourself with cold water. Again, those with heart conditions should consider the wisdom of a truly cold shock. Adjust the shock in accordance with your own needs.

You should pause to savor the fellowship and kinship created by this ceremony. A feast may

follow the asi. Often though, the asi is a prelude to another ceremony. When this is the case do not loose the spiritual focus which the asi is designed to create.

HERBS FOR AN ASI

The Lakota use sage over the floor of a sweat lodge. They may burn sweetgrass before or during the sweat to cleanse and scent the lodge. Various groups use a great variety of herbs both on the floor of the sweat and thrown on the hot rocks. Many aromatic herbs are appropriate. Do be very careful: some herbs may release chemicals which have poisonous or mind altering qualities. We advise using mints, cedar, sage, or sweetgrass.

THE BLACK DRINK

There seems to be a lot of information and mis-information available about the black drink used particularly by the southern Indians. This drink was made from a species of holly, (*Ilex vomitoria*), which contains caffeine. While it is true that drinking a good deal of a decoction of this holly will cause vomiting. actually it was the caffeine which was the poi,t of the ceremony.

As in the restricted and ceremonial uses of tobacco, caffeine was used in a ceremonial manner. It was drunk on an empty stomach and in small quantities. However, after some hours of sitting around, drinking caffeine; smoking strong tobacco; and fasting, the effects were quite potent. Caffeine is used to heighten psychic participation in ceremony. It allows ceremonies to go on longer than would be very easy without its stimulation. Individuals may easily have more of the drink than their systems can endure; vomiting would not be an unusual result. However, it does not seem to have been the whole point although some writers in the past have been of that opinion.

THE GENTLE ASI

This is Grey Cat's contribution to western civilization. She feels that few things can make you more unpopular faster than to throw up on hot rocks. This form of asi is for those of us to whom, for **WHATEVER REASON,** participation within the dark, crowded, hot, hot, steamy, herbal sweat lodge is not recommended. It is also suitable for solitary individuals who do not have access to a qualified sweat lodge leader. What follows is a cleansing and focusing ceremony. It is closely based upon the principals of the asi with the dangerous or too-uncomfortable elements subdued.

Build an asi following the instructions above. If you are building it just for yourself make it quite, quite small. Create the altar space in the center and make the sacred path and the small mound of Grandmother Earth leading to the fire area. If you are a pipe carrier use your pipe for this rite. We have found, however, that it is wise to keep all smoke out of a gentle asi done for a group. In this case do the pipe at the quarters when the door is open. An alternative is to do it outside the lodge before or after doing the sweat. If you will not use a pipe you should have smudging materials and some sacred tobacco for offerings.

Prepare a smallish fire as described above. Have at least five rocks, one for the center and one for each prime direction. These should not be very small rocks but they don't need to be much larger than a fist. We find that 10 or even 20 rocks may not be too many for a gentle asi.

We smudge the lodge long before anyone is to enter so that the smoke will have dissipated. It is wise to omit throwing aromatic herbs on the rocks inside the lodge also. We even greatly reduce the amount of steam in the lodge. For a gentle asi we throw water on the rocks at the end of the first interval and a large amount at the very end of the lodge.

Begin by settling your mind and approaching your meditative state. Seriously and quietly light the fire, calling to the spirit of the fire and to the Great Spirit, Galunlati. Place the rocks on the fire calling to the Grandmother Earth, Agisegua.

Enter your lodge; create an altar by placing pinches of sacred tobacco at the center, calling upon Grandfather Sky and Grandmother Earth. Place more tobacco at each of the four directions calling upon the spirit keepers.

Allow at least an hour for the rocks to heat. Once they are hot, bring them in one at a time. Begin with the center rock; then bring one for each of the four quarters starting with the west. A pinch of smudge or tobacco should be dropped on each rock — outside the lodge — to consecrate it.

You have created within your lodge all of the universe, the four elements, the spirits of the keepers and totems, the Great Spirit, the Earth, and yourself. You now do the same spiritual cleansing which takes place in a regular asi.

Observe the pattern of the four or more separate quarters wherein the periods of the primal darkness are broken by the bright light of the universe. Offerings of tobacco and/or smudging may be used as substitutes for (or in addition to) the sacred pipe.

When you leave the lodge pour some water over you to at least symbolize the usual cold immersion. This asi should include most of the events of a regular sweat except for the heat, smoke, and steam. It may take more concentration and more spiritual dedication to make this ceremony as powerful as a full asi. The benefits of the cleansing and dedication of the sweat lodge are not be denied those who cannot participate due to physical limitations or solitariness.

As you work with the gentle asi you may find that the reduction of smoke and steam will enable you to develop quite a lot of heat. Find your personal limits or the limits of the group. Careful experimentation will let you tailor the asi to your exact needs.

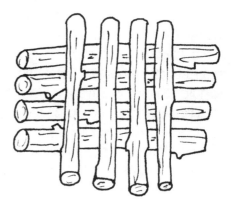

LAYING FIRE

(69)

ALONE WITH EARTH AND SKY

Crying for a Vision

Pressed deeply into the breast of Grand-mother Earth are the footprints of a youth. They lead far away from the villages of her people, far into the mountains. There she will sit upon the rock of the Mother and cry aloud to the universe for her name and for the vision which will direct the path of her life.

In the pathless snows of the northlands a young candidate for shaman loses his life to the universe in order to return with a vision. He seeks knowledge that he may bring healing and direction to his people. In the deserts of the west and the silent forests of the east, medicine men must leave their work to receive power at the hands of lone-liness, danger, and silence. From this death and rebirth the shaman returns to work with new strength and understanding. These must be obtained to guide the people in the ways of the spirit.

A medicine vision is not given to you just for yourself. You are given a vision only because there is work for you to do for all your relations. That is why one says, when crying for a vision, "Not for myself do I ask this, but that the people may live". [Brooke Medicine Eagle, Shamanic Visions].

WHY DO WE CRY FOR A VISION?

The vision quest is one form of the symbolic death and re-birth experience which most reli-gious and spiritual disciplines find necessary for true achievement of spiritual understanding. We try not to use progress-oriented words to describe

spiritual development. We feel that the concept of progress has been mistreated by our culture. For most of us the concept of progress includes value judgements of better/worse, more/less, etc. The enlightened spirit, while changed, is not necessar-ily better or worse than any other person.

Crying for your vision is a specific instance of a life-long process. Visions are received in many other ways. Important, life-changing visions (not necessarily accompanied by visual phenomena) may come to you at any time and place! The vision quest is a time set apart for you to seek a special vision to fill a need you perceive within yourself. You may need to find your own name, your totem spirit, or the direction for the initial dedication of your life. You may be returning to the silence to seek further help, power, clarity, or inspiration.

If you are newly beginning your spiritual jour-ney a vision quest may tell you the type of work you will do with your training. This may not be your occupation, the way you earn money. It is the particular direction your medicine will take in your individual commitment to the earth. A balance must always be kept between medicine work and bread-winning. All true medicine people also have regular jobs, yet all are true medicine people.

There are many, many reasons for making a formal vision quest. You may be seeking a name, a totem spirit, a direction for your life, or the medicine power to enable you to do the work you are being called to. Later you may make quests to seek specific answers to questions, to increase your abilities as a medicine person, to complete transitions in your life, or to prepare yourself for the end of your personal cycle.

WHAT IS A VISION QUEST?

A vision quest consists of three components. First is to leave behind your everyday life and all the things which you hold tightly around you to make yourself feel safe. Second, it is a sort of death. You must stay with your quest long enough and seri-ously enough to allow all your physical and spiri-tual centers to open to the universe. For a few minutes outside of time you should be completely a part of the universe and not yourself at all. Thirdly, you must re-birth yourself into the common life of the world you live in. You must carry the illumina-tion and knowledge of those timeless moments

BEAR TOTEM

MISCELLANEOUS DETAILS

The difficulty of the physical challenges of your vision quest are really up to you. Frequently questers fast. So long as you drink sufficient water fasting for a few days won't hurt most people. Fasting on a quest is found so universally that it probably works. If you decide not to fast, or to fast only part of the time, take very basic foods. Eating should not be allowed to break your concentration. In other words, eat but try not to enjoy it.

Mind altering drugs are not an acceptable part of a serious vision quest. These drugs are extremely dangerous, illegal, and damaging to your brain. They will alter your perceptions of the environment thus interfering with the entire purpose of your quest!

WHAT DO I DO WHILE ON A VISION QUEST?

Well, you get quiet within yourself and wait for the universe, or a fox, or the wind to talk to you!

In a more practical vein, you get settled in your place. You'll probably want to mark the prime directions. Perhaps you will decide to build a stone circle or a medicine wheel. You can offer your pipe or tobacco once or several times. Drumming, singing, and talking to yourself are good. Build a small fire and think about all the things it means to you. Watch the sun go down, come up. Keep a journal. Write down the things you see, hear, and think. No one else ever needs to read it so write down silly things too. We are a civilization not only literate but dependent upon the written word. Things are realer to us when they are written down. This journal will be a help to you the rest of your life.

If you know your quest is over and you've only been out one day, or only five days, go on in. When you know you're through, you are through! Give yourself some time before plunging back into your job, family, whatever. You need some time to come back to life.

HOW DO I UNDERSTAND THE VISION I RECEIVED?

Many medicine people have needed years to entirely accept and understand their visions. Sometimes an individual doesn't want to do what the vision indicated. They may spend a lot of time fighting against its power. Other times a vision seems clear and relatively simple to understand. In the course of the years a deeper understanding often grows. In the end the vision is perceived differently from that first impression.

Your vision may not be clear. Hopefully you will know someone who has more experience than you with the medicine path. They may give you some ideas for interpreting your experience. Your vision will not be completely undecipherable. If it seems that way to you, it's probably because you don't want to understand it.

WHAT IF I DIDN'T RECEIVE A VISION AT ALL?

Failing to receive a vision is a not uncommon occurrence. While most people find it difficult to admit that they spent all this time and effort crying for a vision and nothing came; many do not receive a vision the first time.

The only thing to do is to try again when the time seems right. In the end EVERYONE can receive a vision. There are a number of mental attitudes which will get in the way of receiving a vision. These include a purely self-seeking attitude, ambition for personal status, sloppy preparation, mental unpreparedness, and hurry. Perhaps you just had too strong a notion of what was supposed to happen which caused you to fail to notice what actually did occur!

Examine your attitudes, make your preparations seriously and in a galunky'ti'yu manner, and make another quest. There is an answer.

FINDING YOUR NAME

The name you were given at birth may not apply to the person you are now. A new name may express many things. When it is chosen, knowingly and voluntarily by you, it expresses where you are now or where you are going. It more closely defines your new relationship with the universe.

Sometimes on a vision quest you are told your name. You may be told it's a secret name to be given to no other. You may find your name in ordinary occurrences you observe on your quest. You must be alert to all that happens. There may be messages in the least noticeable thing. If you are paying attention, at some point, your intuition, if not your knowledge, will tell you that this is it.

Occasionally a name is sought through other agencies than the quest. Divination of many sorts may be used for this. I know of one name which appeared on a scrabble draw. As your ability to listen to yourself grows, you will know how to recognize such an occasion.

LIVING YOUR VISION

This is something we cannot tell you much about. Each vision is a personal vision and it applies to you alone. You must find the way to keep your vision fresh and alive in your mind. You must consult yourself, your totem spirits, the spirit keepers, and all other resources to aid you in carrying it through.

Part of the wisdom of the medicine man/ woman is the learning which accompanies following a vision. They begin to know the feeling of rightness when they are in step with their vision. They recognize the malaise which results from losing the path.

A vision quest is an extremely serious undertaking. Once undertaken it must be followed through to its end. Denying your vision cannot lead elsewhere than to unhappiness and dissatisfaction with your life. Do not start this process unless you are convinced you are willing to follow it through!

WHAT ABOUT A NON-TRADITIONAL VISION QUEST?

We said something earlier about locking yourself in one room of your apartment to make a vision quest. This was not a recommendation but a recognition of the fact that sometimes the time for the vision has come and it will wait upon no arrangements, nor upon the weather, or convenience.

It certainly is not unknown for a vision to suddenly descend upon an individual who had made no preparations for such a thing, who was, in fact, doing something quite different at the time!

It is more difficult to cry for a vision outside of the traditional frameworks. Traditions exist for the very good reason that they generally work very well indeed. This isn't to say that a vision experienced under non-traditional conditions is less authentic than any other. It may not be easy, not at all dependable, to attempt a vision quest Friday evening after work and be back in time to cook Saturday breakfast; but it is not impossible!

Certainly it is advisable to follow what traditions are possible regardless of the exact form of your vision quest. Should a vision descend upon you entirely unexpectedly, when it is over, offer your thanks with the pipe, tobacco, or smudge. Make detailed notes in your journal. Carefully monitor your re-entry into your regular life. No vision quest is safe regardless of the physical conditions. You will be in touch with another whole world or universe from that of everyday life. You should always attempt to have a safety net in place.

SETTING FORTH ON A VISION QUEST

THE THUNDERS AND THE WIND

Dancing, Drumming, Songs, and Healing

Next to the image of the peace pipe and the one of the Indian attackers appearing on the crest of a hill; one of the most pervasive images of Indians in movies is the war dance. Hypnotic drumming, shuffling dance steps, and songs in weird, wailing keys not known to the European are a part of our folk heritage.

Of course, the Indians did many dances besides the war dance and the weatherman's favorite joke, the rain dance. There were sacred dances marking seasons of celebration. There were the dances which re-told sacred myths. There were simple story-telling dances, relating history or personal exploits. There were victory dances and dances demonstrating skill in dancing. There were dances held just for fun and dances dedicated to particular totem animals.

It is not our purpose to help you learn any specific traditional dance. You may want to search for someone qualified to teach you the dances of a particular tribe. Many followers of the medicine path wish to express themselves in dance, drumming, and/or song in the idiom of today.

Medicine path dancing may be done as an individual expression, as a part of a group ceremony, or as a carefully choreographed and rehearsed group performance. If you wish to add dancing, drumming, and/or song to your journey on the medicine path a few words on the generalized traditions should allow you to express your own personal visions in these forms.

DANCE

The footwork is not the most important part of medicine path dancing. Those taking part in a group dance usually move their feet in the same pattern. The dances depend upon costume, mime, and body-language for their communication. Coordination of this style of dance puts a heavy responsibility upon the drummer(s). S/he, through the beat and emphasis, helps direct the course of the dance.

The easiest of the commonly used steps of Indian dancing is called the toe-heel step. It is done to a two stroke drum beat with the first stroke the emphasized (or louder) one. On the first stroke the toe of one foot is touched to the ground in front of the dancer. On the second (softer) stroke, the heel of that foot is brought sharply down in a small stomp. On the next beat (a loud one again) the other toe is extended and on the next, that heel brought down.

A second step can be called the drag step. In this one the drum also does a two stroke beat. However the emphasis is on the second beat rather than on the first. To dance this step extend the toe of one foot to the ground in front of you. This time, as soon as it touches, slide that foot back across the ground towards you. On the second, softer, beat bring your heel down hard. If you wear moccasins do the drag gently as it can wear them out very quickly.

The toe-heel step can adapt to a four beat on the drum by simply repeating it for the other foot on the third and fourth beats. The drag step adapts to a three beat. After the drag on beat one and the stomp on beat two, bring the other foot up parallel on beat three. After you have used these two simple steps for a little while you will find it possible to invent other steps suitable for the dance and drum rhythm you choose.

TOTEM DANCES

The totem dance is probably the most popular type of dancing in modern medicine path. It frequently features the totem of the particular moon as part of a new or full moon ceremony. Once a group (or individual) has figured out a step and a beat, dances for the totems may be done. If, for instance, you or the group want to dance at a full moon ritual in June it would be appropriate to dance the deer totem dance. First you must think about how deer behave in the wild. Think of the alert head watching for danger all around. Picture the deer reaching down to nibble grass; reaching up to strip bark off a small tree. See her freezing at the first sign of danger and then running like the wind to escape. This is the essence of a deer totem dance.

The dance might begin with the deer grazing. You bend over slightly as if pulling grass from the ground. Circle around reaching up to eat leaves or bark. Suddenly you hear something. The drum beat quickens. You look around to try to sight the danger. Quickly the danger is located. You freeze. The drum beat stops for a long second. Then the beat becomes fast. You flee from the hunter. Used as a part of a ceremony this dance need not last very long.

At another time, your group may wish each to dance his/her own totem animal. Participants should consider very carefully what the natural movements of the animal is. Such dances are an excellent way to improve identification with totem animals. They will draw the medicine power of the totem spirit into whatever you do.

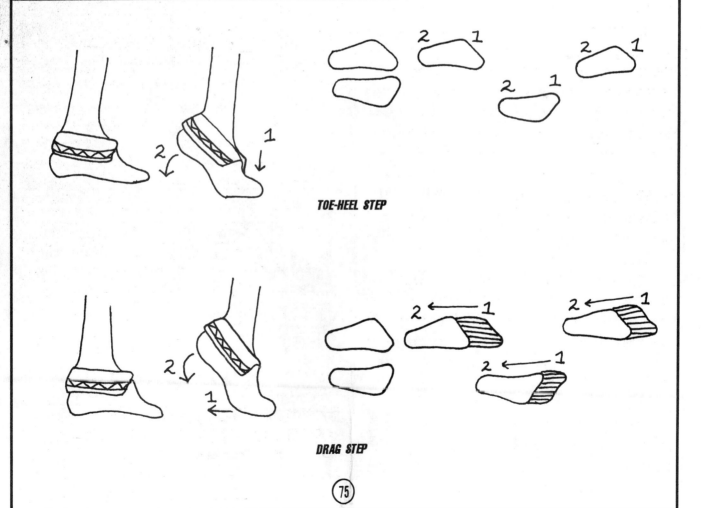

TOE-HEEL STEP

DRAG STEP

In addition to these short totem dances, many tribes had longer dances for particular animal spirits. The Lakota have a horse dance. Many of the plains tribes dance the buffalo dance. Practically all the tribes had a version of the eagle dance. Usually an eagle dance begins with the free flight of the eagle. It continues with a hunter finding and killing him. Killing an eagle is an important story in medicine path because eagle feathers are so important as sacred objects.

CEREMONIAL DANCES

The various tribes each had a variety of religious or ceremonial dances. The Green Corn Dance was the most important celebration of the Cherokee. The various components of this dance took most of a day and a night to perform. Portions were danced by the men alone, by the women alone, and by both together. The Sun Dance and the Horse Dance of the Sioux, the Katchina dances of the southwest Indians, the Devil Dance of the Apache, and the False Face Dance of the Indians of the woodlands are all important spiritual expressions of these peoples. The Ghost Dance was part of an extremely important rallying of the western tribes. It provided the final excuse for their conquest by the unega. All these dances must be done in a sacred manner and should be learned only from those who are their true heirs.

FUN DANCES

Probably most of the tribes had a collection of dances appropriate just for fun - for the focus of a party. Some of these dances were designed to allow the young people to flirt or court. Others required specific skills from the dancers and were competitions.

The feather dance is one of the latter. In it a large quill is stuck upright in the ground in the center of the dance area. Each participant has a chance to dance alone into the center and circle the feather. At some point s/he attempts to bend low enough to pick up the feather in his/her teeth — without ever losing step. It is a version of the limbo.

The Cherokee Booger Dance is a fun dance although there are serious overtones. A portion of the dancers are chosen to be boogers. Each of them must construct a mask, the funnier or more horrifying the better. The dance begins with the regular dancers, men and women, dancing in two lines around the center of the dance floor. At some point the boogers come into the dance area screaming and capering. The dance leader appoints someone to be translator. boogers do not speak the language of humans. The translator asks each booger his/her name. The booger whispers the name and the translator shouts it out. In the original these names are mildly obscene and usually pretty funny.

After his name is announced each booger dances alone with maximum clumsiness and clowning. Then the translator asks the boogers what they want. They roar women, food, skins, or whatever. They then run after the other dancers, grabbing at them. After a short time of noisy play the other dancers chase the boogers from the dance area. The boogers remove their masks and join in the rest of the dance, the party, and other dances which follow.

In the original, as recorded at the end of the 18th century, the boogers were the unega. The strangers were in this way made objects of ridicule. The Cherokee had found an excellent way of decreasing the culture shock from the changes brought by the unega. It is easy to think of appropriate boogers for our own booger dance.

DRUMS AND DRUMMING

Justifiably we connect drums, tom-toms, with Indians. It would be difficult to hold an Indian dance without a drum to set and keep the rhythm. Drums also make an especially powerful background to ceremonies.

There are literally dozens of styles of drums, not to mention rattles and other percussion noisemakers, found amongst the tribes. We are not including any instructions for the making of drums. That standby of the Boy Scout, the wooden cheese box, has completely disappeared from the general store. There now seems to be no easy way to make a drum. Anyone who has skill working with wood can easily find instructions for building a drum. The rest of us must turn to commercial sources for our drums.

In the sources listed in chapter 19 are a number who sell drums suitable for medicine path work. Actually, we're not sure that there is an UNSUITABLE drum. Hawk uses a basket drum and Grey Cat has a drum of Celtic design. We think that a drum should be chosen for your reaction to its sound. If you like the way a drum sounds, whether it is English, African, authentic AmerInd, or liberated from a marching band, shouldn't make much difference. You probably have preferences as to size, portability, etc.

Drums are painted and often are decorated with red flannel, bead or quill embroidery, fur, and feathers.

PLAYING A DRUM

Perhaps somewhere there is someone who can really teach drumming in a book. I fear that we are not so talented! We can give you just a few pointers and perhaps help you get started.

The drum is extremely important in both dance and ritual. It is the heartbeat of the Earth Mother, Maka Ina. This is so strongly believed that in some tribes women do not play drums. It is felt that they are already sufficiently tuned to this rhythm. The rhythm set by the drummer gives everyone else their cue. If there is more than one drummer, one should be acknowledged the lead drummer. All other drummers should take their cadence from him or her. A

good drummer pays a great deal of attention to what is going on in the dance or ritual. He or she adjusts the beat and time to help keep the entire group together. S/he helps the leader guide the group from one phase to the next. A drummer playing for a group should never go off into the clouds of personal communication with/through the drum.

A beginning drummer should learn one or two basic beats. Keep working with these beats at different speeds until you can keep in the beat while speeding up, slowing down, stopping, and beginning again. Use a drum stick or your hands as you prefer. Sit, stand, or join the dance if you have an appropriate style of drum. All these things are far less important than being able to stick to the beat.

We taught two dance steps using a 1 - 2 beat so those might be the best beats to begin with. The first of these requires two very even drum beats. The first beat is louder than the second. This can be written X-x-X-x-. The "X" stands for the loud beat, the "x", the soft beat. The "-" indicates that there is an even time between all the beats.

Another two beat is the above reversed: x-X-x-X-. This is the beat used for the drag step. Of course, by varying the intervals between the beats, you can get such beats as Xx—Xx—. That is, a hard beat, a soft beat and a slight pause.

There are two other common and easy beats for dancing. The first is a three-beat played: X-x-x-X-x-x. That is: a hard beat and two soft ones. The familiar four-beat is played: X-x-x-x-X-x-x-x-. This is the THUMP, thump, thump, thump; THUMP, thump, thump, thump with which we are so familiar.

Drums are quite effective not only for dancing but also for the quiet portions of a ceremony. Drumming is appropriate while the pipe is being passed or during the preparations for an asi . A good drummer can contribute greatly to the offering of the tobacco or smudge to the seven directions. With the beat

spirits.

THE BEATING OF THE DRUM

DANCE IS PART OF THE CEREMONY

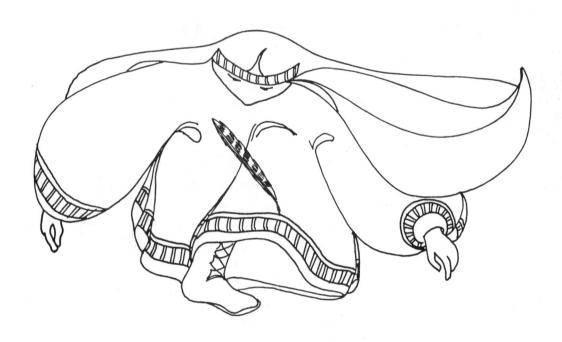

RATTLES

As an additional accompaniment to dancing, AmerInds fully developed the rattle. Hand held rattles are made of a very wide variety of materials. Rattles and bells are worn on the wrists, ankles, and knees. An expert can select times to prevent the rattles on ankles or knees from sounding even while dancing!

Hand held rattles are easily made from almost any hollow object tied securely to a stick. Turtle shells make very powerful medicine rattles — but aren't very easy to get hold of. Rattles are also made of gourds and cow horns. Practically any hollow object which can be sealed and attached to a handle may be used to make a rattle. Rattles have small pebbles, beans, and/or dried corn inside to make noise when they are shaken.

Other rattles are made by hanging a number of objects in a bunch. They make noise when they strike each other. Deer hooves, dew claws, small bones — quite a number of natural objects — will make pleasant sounds when shaken against each other.

Make your first rattle out of whatever you can find handy. A small plastic margarine cup, yogurt container, or large pill bottle can be the basis of quite a nice rattle. Find a handful of small rocks, dried beans, or popcorn. Get a stick about one inch in diameter at the large end and smooth it carefully. Cut holes through the cup or gourd so the stick will just fit all the way through. The right size stick will fit like a cork in the top of a pill bottle. Let 1/2 to 1 inch of the stick come out at the top of a margarine or yogurt cup. (Illustration 5) Put the cup on the stick, the stones inside, and the top on it. Use hot glue or a good clear glue to securely attach the cup to the stick and the lid to the cup. We suggest that you cover it with cloth or leather. Feathers, bells, animal tails, beads, and other decorations may be hung from above and below the body of the rattle.

The hand held rattle is generally played to whatever beat the drum is using. Practice a bit to get the hang of it so you can keep time with the drummer through the tempo and beat changes.

Leg and wrist rattles were made by stringing together objects like deer hooves, turtle shells, bits of shell, and/or metal. After the coming of the unega, metal bells became popular. These are pretty easily made by sewing the bells to a small leather strap; soft, easily tied leather band; or a piece of elastic. If you dance in step your rattles or bells will sound in time with the drums.

SONGS

Many of the traditional dances of the tribes had songs which went with them. These seem on paper to be rather repetitious and full of nonsense syllables; but so do many of the folk and dance songs of European tradition. Think of Old MacDonald and all the Eei, Eei, Oh's. Recordings of these songs are fairly widely available. Quite a number of the suppliers in Chapter 19 carry records and tapes.

There is another sort of song which is more important to the followers of the medicine path. These are the songs you may bring back from your vision. In some ways these songs resemble the dance songs. They are repetitive and use nonsense syllables. These songs are power songs, medicine songs. There is medicine in the words and there is medicine in the very sounds.

In translation many of these are very brief statements of a truth sensed as a part of a vision. They evoke something of the wonder and enlightenment of a single moment of transformation or a particular understanding. By singing your own song you can recreate yourself as you were at that moment. You may then use this power to heal, to teach, or to reaffirm your understanding of your vision.

Listen in your quest for a vision and during your totem meditations. You may find that you are given a song to be an aid to you on the medicine path. If your primary language is English your song will probably be in English. Your own song(s) may be for healing, for offering the pipe, or for other sacred activities to which your vision leads you. Listen for your song. If you are given one remember it and use it in accordance with your vision.

HEALING

Using the medicine you have received for healing is one of the most important uses to which you may put it. This is one of the primary reasons that this path is called medicine. It is one of the ways in which you return your thanks for the insight and power to which this journey leads you.

Healing may be done on an individual or a group basis. You will eventually be shown your own methods of personal healing. However, many of the practices you have already learned are excellent healing methods.

SMUDGING

The smudge was given to the people by the swamp mother for the healing of illness. Any time a friend or family member is ill, smudge them carefully. Speak to the spirit keepers and all the seven directions. Ask them to help the person overcome his/her illness. Smudge the person carefully while directing the smoke to carry away all the disease organisms and to leave healing strength. Smudge yourself any time you feel unwell. It's remarkable how well this can work.

SACRED PIPE

We may offer a sacred pipe with the intention of obtaining healing for someone. As with the healing smudge, offer the pipe in much the usual way. Remember to request healing of the powers.

MEDICINE WHEEL HEALING

You may combine the work of healing with any ceremony you do as a group. One way is to write the names of the individuals seeking healing on slips of paper. Place these names in the center of the group. A pipe is smoked, smudging is done, a chant or dance is offered. Request that the powers extend healing energy to those individuals. If the individual in need of healing is present place that person in or near the center of the group. The group may then focus their thoughts and hopes on that person's better health.

OTHER HEALING METHODS OF MEDICINE PATH

There is no room in this book to offer a detailed discussion of the numerous methods of healing within the medicine path. The sweat lodge is a primary healing tool. A sweat may be conducted solely for someone ill. Of course be conservative about how much heat and cold you use. It is also possible to dedicate a sweat to the healing of one or more individuals who are not able to be present.

As your relationship with the totems and the spirits grows you will find your own methods of healing. These will be expressions of your individual vision. You must be aware as you meditate and work within the medicine, path in order to recognize your own healing gifts as they are given to you.

FEATHER HEALING

According to Cat Dancing, "A part of an animal connects you to the whole animal and its totem spirit." Each animal has inherent totem powers. Examples are: bear - healing; buffalo - strength; eagle - enlightenment and spirituality; rabbit - learning and lessons.

Each feather from a bird species carries with it the totem power of that particular species: pigeon - survival; robin - hope and fertility; hawk - farsightedness; owl - wisdom; crow - interpretation and discernment; jay - transformation and displacement; chickens and turkeys - grounding of energy; macaws and parrots - communication; woodpeckers and flickers - removing obstacles.

Birds fly and are closer to the Great Spirit than other animals. They have special power to connect us to higher energies. Feathers are a physical liaison of this connection. We use feathers for healing, enlightenment, and to effect change in the physical sphere.

We can divide the powers of feathers in ways other than by the medicine powers of the birds themselves. One of these ways is by color as it relates to the human body systems

White — the color of bones (skeletal system)

Yellow - the color of bile (digestive and glandular systems)

Brown - color of feces (excretory system)

Red - Color of blood (circulatory system)

Purple/lavender/violet - calm colors (nervous system)

Light brown - color of skin (epithelial system)

Another method of classification of feather power is to match feather color with traditional chakra centers:

Red - root chakra - genitals - survival and manifestation

Orange - abdomen - navel or just below - emotional center, childhood

Yellow - solar plexus - midriff - intellectual center, fear

Green - heart - center of chest - higher self, feelings

Blue - throat - neck - communications, self-expression

Purple - third eye - mid forehead - psychic, personal visualization

White - crown - top of head - energy portal of all enlightenment.

If a particular color feather is not available to match the chakra on which you wish to work, match the quality of the chakra with the medicine power of a bird from whom you do have a feather.

METHOD

A. Diagnosis: If the particular dysfunction of the person you are working with is not known or is doubt, you should scan with a diagnosis feather (crow or owl). This will give you insight as to the area of dysfunction. Place the feather on the third eye and scan the chakra centers. You should see a slight vibrational wave in the affected area(s).

Another method is meticulous, but gives good results:

1) Put your hand over your left eye, leaving the right eye open.

2) Hold the feather directly in front of the right eye, lining it up between you and the body.

3) Moving the feather in a clockwise arc, turn it very slowly until the top of the feather disappears. That means there is a psychic blind spot there. When the feather is on the invisible spot the medicine power is transferred to the body and identifies trouble spots. Look for the top of the disappeared feather on the body areas that are troubled.

Remember that each persons dysfunction(s) is not necessarily entirely physical. It may overlap into mental, emotional, and spiritual areas. Watch the chakras for further information.

You do not need to have vast knowledge of the human body to do this diagnoses. Instinctively/psychically identify the trouble spots. Once you know where they, are begin the healing.

B. The cutting:

Use the appropriate feather(s) relative to chakra center and/or body system. Center it on the trouble spot. Make a downward cut with the side (blade) of the feather which is closest to the midrib (thinnest from outer edge to midrib). Then make a cross-cut across the first cut. This opens the aura around that trouble spot.

C. The Fanning

As if the feather were a magnet draw the negativity out of the trouble area. You may do this in sweeps or spirals. Consciously direct this energy into transformation. Send it back to the earth by touching the feather to the floor or ground.

D. The Sealing

Using the thicker part of the feather (the part where the edge is furthest from the mid-rib) retrace the cuts. This seals them closed.

E. Optional:

Smudging may now be performed as an all-encompassing energy ritual. The burning mixture helps to ground and settle all the energies you worked with during the healing process. Smudging is also recommended to purify the feathers afterward.

SWEEPING THE AURA

Sweeping the aura is performed by using the feather as a broom. Sweep it over the entire body about one inch from the skin. Intuition is the key here. Sweep the aura as if you were smoothing out a surface of fine sand.

SPECIAL AURA WORK

Prosperity: To clear the aura for the blessings of prosperity work on the first chakra with a red feather or use a survival medicine feather such as a pigeon feather. Image what you desire strongly.

Relationships: To draw the desired types of relationships work on the heart chakra with a green feather or a love medicine feather such as a robin feather. You must strongly image what you desire.

Use your discernment and imagination. Think of groups of birds - raptors (birds of prey) are helpful in drawing out things which are unwanted. Woodpeckers and flickers are helpful in shattering blocks much in the same way they peck holes into trees. Jays transform energy in much the same way as they take over another bird's nest. The birds who mate for life, hawks, lovebirds, some ducks, are help in draw lasting relationships to you. Some birds bring the power of endurance and stick-to-itiveness. These are the birds who do not migrate such as hawks, cardinals, and jays. Create new ways to work medicine energy with feathers. Your intuition can be your greatest teacher.

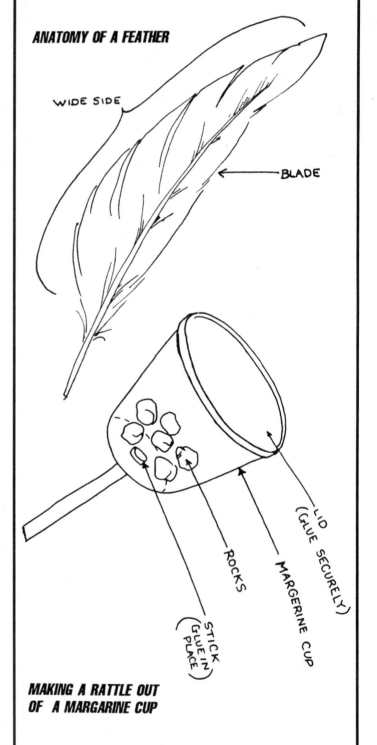

ANATOMY OF A FEATHER

WIDE SIDE

BLADE

LID (GLUE SECURELY)

MARGERINE CUP

ROCKS

STICK (GLUE IN PLACE)

MAKING A RATTLE OUT OF A MARGARINE CUP

FROM MY HANDS IT IS SACRED

Construction of Tools

In a way the American Indians do not have special methods for constructing sacred tools. It is difficult for anyone raised in current society to understand their attitudes toward possessions. All their tools, clothing, weapons, tents, houses, etc. are hand made. Usually anything which the individual does not make for him/herself is made by someone he/she know.

Before the coming of the unega there was no value placed on time. Nor was there really any value placed on the possessions themselves. Each object was made with care and love. Whatever amount of time needed to make the object well and beautiful was devoted to its making. The object was then either used by the individual who made it, given to someone else to use, or perhaps traded for food or some other object which the craftsman couldn't make for him/herself.

It is extremely important to keep several principles in mind. Possessions are rather often given away without thought of thanks. Virtually everything an Indian makes is made slowly, carefully, and without measuring the time taken or the value of the object itself.

Because the religious life of the Indian permeates all of his/her life all objects he/she makes are sacred. All are made with care and love. All are used with respect. None are possessed in the way we think we possess objects. A cooking pot is sacred in exactly the same way that a smudging bowl is sacred. A bow is as holy as a dance rattle.

To construct objects useful in your study of the medicine path it is necessary that you learn to slow down. You must take your time and make them carefully and beautifully.

We usually smudge ourselves, our tools, and materials before beginning the construction of a ceremonial object. We also suggest you consecrate the finished object much as the pipe is consecrated (Chapter 8).

SOME USEFUL TECHNIQUES

Cleaning and preserving feathers

It is illegal to have any part of a wild bird, including abandoned nests and egg shells, without a permit from the Department of the Interior. There are special regulations covering owl, hawk and eagle feathers absolutely restricting their use to a few American Indians. These permits are never issued to anyone who has previously been found in violation of the regulations. If you plan to work with feathers, apply for the permit now. The U. S. Fish and Wildlife Service has the necessary forms. Most feathers you can buy are from domestic birds: chickens, guineas, and turkeys. Often these have been dyed or painted so they will look like wild bird feathers.

CLEANING FEATHERS

Really dirty feathers should be soaked in cold water for up to two days. Use your fingers to work off the dirt. DO NOT USE A BRUSH. The feathers should then be very, very gently patted in luke-warm water with a mild soap until the dirt and stains are removed. Rinse the feathers twice in clean lukewarm water.

After washing in water, really dirty feathers may be further cleaned in white gasoline (Coleman fuel, marine gas). Please do this outside as the fumes are dangerous. This washing will lesson the possibility of moths getting into the feathers.

After soaking and swishing the feathers, pour off as much of the gas as possible. Cover the feathers with dry plaster of paris or HARDWOOD sawdust. Soft-wood sawdust contains resins which will dissolve in the gas and get on the feathers. After a few minutes, the moisture will be absorbed. Brush the feathers carefully with a very soft paintbrush. Fluffs (the short, puffy feathers) may be cleaned the same way. They may be blow-dried with a fan or hair dryer (no heat).

After cleaning the feathers, they must be re-oiled. Put a very little unsalted lard or other unsalted animal fat on your hands. Stroke it on the feather very lightly with the finger tips. Feathers may be straightened by running the shaft (only the shaft) over a 200 watt light bulb.

PREPARING THE FEATHERS FOR USE

It is often helpful to have a loop on a feather. A loop helps you to attach the feather to a bag, pipestem, or headdress. There are several ways of attaching loops. One way is to wrap the whole quill end with colored thread. Fold the wrapping thread in half. Let the folded loop hang past the end of the quill. Bring the thread up the length of the bare quill and glue it to the base of the veins. Hot glue, super glue, or a good clear glue all will work. Wrap the thread in a spiral to the end of the quill and glue the ends. A traditional and decorative addition is to place one or two fluffs at the top of the wrapping.

If the quill is very short or broken whittle a wooden match or round toothpick to the right size. Slip it into the quill before wrapping.

For a large feather you can make a loop from the quill itself. Soak the base of the quill in hot water for a few minutes and cut it as shown in . You will need to use a very sharp knife to do a neat job. While the quill is still soft put a drop of glue on the end. Tuck the end up into the hollow of the quill at the top of the cutout. When the glue is dry wrap the quill from the bottom up with tape or glued thread. Fluffs may be tucked in at the top of the quill. If tape you use wrap the feather with a bit of fabric, usually red felt or flannel. Tie the fabric on with embroidery thread.

Feathers provided with hanging loops in one of these ways can be attached to a pipe stem, spirit bag, or even a war bonnet.

FUR, CLAWS, TEETH, AND BONES

Environmentally aware utilization of animal parts — or — "there's a dead skunk in the middle of the road". Indians attempt to live in a balanced relationship with the various animals; the four-

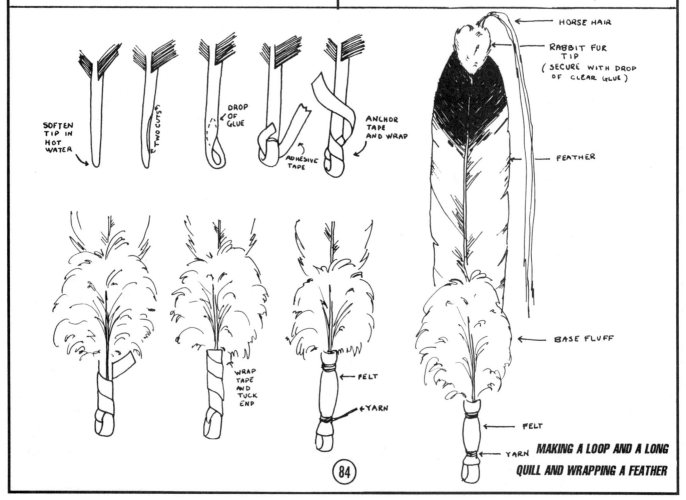

SOFTEN TIP IN HOT WATER

TWO CUTS

DROP OF GLUE

ADHESIVE TAPE

ANCHOR TAPE AND WRAP

WRAP TAPE AND TUCK END

FELT

YARN

HORSE HAIR

RABBIT FUR TIP (SECURE WITH DROP OF CLEAR GLUE)

FEATHER

BASE FLUFF

FELT

YARN

MAKING A LOOP AND A LONG QUILL AND WRAPPING A FEATHER

84

leggeds, the wingeds, the finned and the creepy crawlies of Turtle Island. Most medicine path people eat meat. All medicine path people respect their food sources whether plant or animal. Animals not only to provide meat, eggs, or occasionally milk. Animals also provide clothing, containers, and decoration. Certain parts of animals are used to call in the medicine powers of the respective species. Animals are treated with respect. They are rarely killed unnecessarily. Little is wasted.

In modern medicine path we use fur and feathers on our pipes, in our spirit bags, and in specialized totem bags. We frequently make leather bags to contain various ceremonial objects. The claws, teeth, small bones, feathers, scales and many other parts of animals form a part of our medicine. A great many modern medicine people have found that road kills provide an excellent source of these items. This ceremonial usage gives dignity to at least a few of these deaths.

Anyone who regularly drives a car can probably find most of the animals he or she wishes to work with by watching the roadsides. We do suggest that you attempt to work only with fairly fresh kills. Not only are older ones unpleasant to the utmost degree, they generally aren't usable once the critter has been squashed flat. Keep a couple of garbage bags and a small shovel in the trunk of your car. This will reduce a distasteful task to an acceptable routine. Any time you are unable to deal with a carcass immediately we suggest you wrap it up tightly and store it in the freezer. Even when you freeze the carcass it is always wise to complete this task as quickly as possible.

Skin the animal by cutting a straight incision beginning just above the genitals, up the abdomen and chest, to the chin. Please be careful to cut only through the skin. If you puncture the insides you'll be sorry. Cut around the tail (unless you want to save it), all four legs, and the neck. Make a cut out from your central incision to the cuts at the legs.

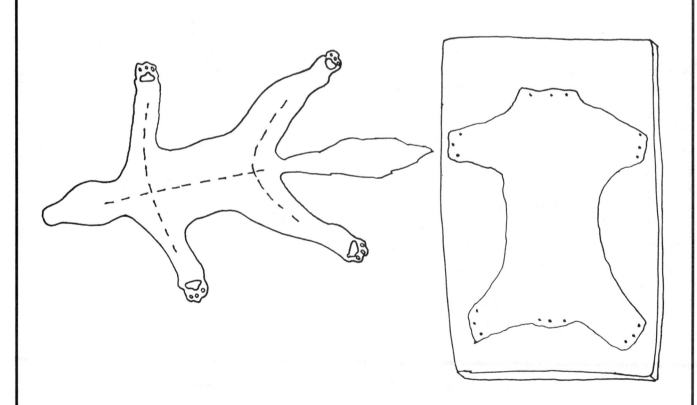

TAKING SKIN OFF AN ANIMAL AND STRETCHING IT OUT ON A BOARD

Peel the skin away from the body. If it is difficult to peel, pull with one hand and snip the connective tissues with kitchen scissors.

Take a piece of board or plywood a bit larger than the skin and stretch it fur side down. Staple the edges of the skin to the board. Salt the skin heavily and leave in a safe place for a couple days until it is dry. Be sure that it is out of the reach of any cats and dogs.

When the skin is reasonably dry and free of excess flesh, tan by vigorously hand working every day with saddle soap. Continue doing this until the skin is pliant.

After you have had some practice you may decide to attempt to free the skin of the skull also. This will take sharp sewing scissors and a lot of patience.

When you have taken the skin and any other part you need (claws, teeth, etc.) the carcass should be buried deeply. Place rocks over it and replace the dirt. An offering of feathers and tobacco is appropriate.

Should you feel it necessary to have the skull or skeleton of an animal there are two ways of cleaning the bones. If you have a really good ant's nest in your yard you can place the head or carcass in its vicinity. Cover the carcass with a bucket or bowl to keep dogs and cats away. Usually the ants will remove most of the flesh. Another method is to boil the carcass in water until all the flesh falls cleanly from the bones. Rinse the bones extremely well. Place them somewhere to dry completely. The flesh should be given respectful burial.

BEADING

Beadwork was developed to a very high level by the Indians. Everyone is familiar with the beautiful decorations made from seed beads on bags, moccasins, and other items. It is ironic that the first of these small beads suitable for decorative embroidery were brought by the unega. Prior to that time dyed porcupine quills and dyed animal hair were a primary means of decoration. Beads were hand made from shell and other hard materials. These were rarely small nor were they as colorful as the European beads. The shell, bone, and clay beads were used in necklaces and as decoration of clothes and other objects. Long tubular beads

LAZY STITCH BEADING

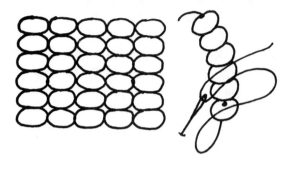

APPLIQUE STITCH

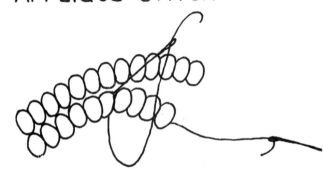

BACK STITCH

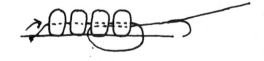

are still widely used for chokers and breastplates. Little cones of tin or other metal are used for decorating fringes as are bells, shells, teeth, and claws.

Bead looms may be bought at needlework and toy stores. They come with directions. Bead weaving is quite simple. It is the easiest and fastest method of beading.

There are three general methods of Indian bead embroidery; lazy (squaw) stitch, applique stitch, and backstitch. In lazy stitch six to twelve beads are threaded on waxed thread. The thread is sewn down at each end of the row of beads. This is done in even rows. All the stitches have the same number of beads. (See Illustration) This method is widely used by the plains Indians. It produces a characteristically striped look.

Applique beading uses two needles. On one, the beads are threaded with the colors in order. This thread is laid on top of the backing material, usually heavy fabric or leather. Sew down the beaded thread between every second or third bead with the other needle .

Back stitch beading sounds a little complicated but it isn't particularly difficult in practice. It is used primarily for rosettes. Thread one bead on the needle and sew it down in the center. Next take two beads on the needle. Sew down through the backing, come up, and go through the second bead again. After the second or third row, begin putting four beads on the needle. Come back up through the last two. At the end of each round run the thread through all the beads in that circle to even them up.

SHIELDS

Shields, as war weapons, were used primarily by the plains Indians. They made both ceremonial and war shields. Obviously, it wouldn't do to try to fight in the middle of the woods with a shield hanging up on every bush. The Indians of the eastern woodlands did not develop the medicine of the shield so extensively although they did sometimes make personal shields. The masks found in the east may be analogous. So perhaps are the elaborate circular pendants found in these areas.

Frequently the various clan, totem, and medi-

cine societies had individual shields to identify their members, much like Masonic Rings or fraternity pins.

In modern medicine path the use and meaning of the shield is taken from the ceremonial traditions of the plains Indians. The design is usually found in a vision. The shield functions as a coat of arms, a statement of personal or group identity. It is also a means of communication with the power from whom one's vision came. The symbolism of every shield is a statement of personal knowledge or illumination. It is a visible reminder of your commitment to medicine path.

Shields may be made of hide or canvas stretched on a hoop, of thin plywood or composition board, or even of cardboard. Grey Cat's is a circle of black mat board with designs in construction paper. Hawk's is painted on leather stretched on a wooden hoop. The material is a great deal less important than the design and what it means to you.

Shields are also protective. You may choose to make shields protecting you from specific dangers or people. You might make shields for the four directions to place yourself in the full protection of the spirit keepers.

LEATHER OR CANVAS SHIELD

To make a shield of leather, you must make or buy a hoop. A wooden embroidery hoop of sufficient size will work. You need to use both pieces of the hoop for strength. If the larger hoop has a screw tightener this screw must be removed completely. Glue the outer hoop to the smaller hoop.

Hoops may also be made of small saplings about 1/2 inch in diameter. Willow, cottonwood, ash, oak, or other hardwood sprouts are usable. The hoop must be bent while the wood is green. It must be tied and held in a circular shape while the wood dries. Wrap the sapling around a barrel, wastebasket or drum. Tie the ends together very tightly. It may take a month for the wood to dry fully so it will permanently hold its circular form.

Cut leather or canvas about 3 or 4 inches larger than your hoop. Soak it in cold water until it is thoroughly wet. Make holes about 2 inches apart all the way around it. A wet leather thong should be laced through these holes. Place the hoop on the back of the leather or canvas. Pull the lacing string up very, very tightly. This will bring the leather up over the hoop. There will be a couple inches inside it in the back. A couple of softer, wider strips of leather are threaded across the back to let you slip your arm into the shield for carrying.

Leather should be painted while it is still slightly damp. Canvas should be left to dry completely. Acrylic artists' paints are suitable for most materials and are easy to handle. The colors most frequently encountered in true Indian work are white, black, red, yellow, light and dark blue, green, and a rust or buff orange.

Shields made of plywood, thin composition board, or cardboard need only be cut into a circle and painted. Have some sort of handle on these so you can carry it over your arm.

Shields may be further decorated with feathers, red flannel, horsehair, and such. A special vision quest may be needed to give you the design for your shield.

STAFF

The staff is a symbol of ability, leadership, and authority. A staff is not made and carried lightly. It is a very powerful medicine tool if you are called to bear one.

A staff is usually within a foot or so, either way, of the standing height of its bearer although this isn't a hard and fast rule. Small staffs, 1 to 2 feet long, have certain advantages in packing and carrying around. Primarily the staff symbolizes medicine power which you HAVE AND USE. You are sticking your neck out if you carry one when you are not ready for it.

Making a staff is an activity of maximum intuition and minimum conventionality. To begin find a piece of wood. It may be taken from a living tree or found on the forest floor. Should it be dead wood, be sure that there isn't much decay and that it is strong enough to last.

Shape the two ends. Remove bark, small branches, rough spots, etc. This can be done with any sort of knife. Do the shaping and cleaning with the knife carefully and with precision. Many people do not use sandpaper in finishing their staff.

Once the staff has been cleaned up and

smoothed, a good quality paste wax, linseed oil, or tung oil should be applied. The more coats applied the better. You may want to attach precious and semi-precious stones to the staff. This may be done with glue, either Crazy Glue, a good transparent glue, or hot glue. Take a chip off with the knife exactly where you will be gluing. Otherwise the glue will not adhere to the waxed or oiled staff. Feathers, medicine bags, and other items may be tied on with leather thongs, colored yarn, or ribbon.

No one can tell you what to put on your staff. Each staff is different. Each one is the expression of an individual's vision. As with shields some of the secret societies had a special staff or lance decorated in a particular way. Coup sticks and ceremonial lances are in essence a form of staff.

PRAYER STICKS, FANS

The differences between a so-called prayer stick, a stick fan, a small staff, and, indeed, a magick wand are extremely difficult to identify. The dance rattle even slips over into the same general category.

This tool is between six inches and three feet long. It is carved and/or decorated with fur, feathers, stones, beads, etc. It is used in dance or in other ceremonies. The prayer stick is sometimes like an inside-out totem bag. It is used to communicate with the individual's totem spirit. It may be wrapped with fur or carved. It may have feathers attached stiffly to the end making it a fan. It may have feathers hung from it on loops. Bells and metal decorations may be hung on it so as to strike together. This blurs the distinction between a prayer stick and a rattle.

Feathers are usually an important part of a prayer stick. Birds in general are message carriers to the spirit world. Putting feathers on the stick helps your message on its way.

A feathered prayer stick is a good beginning. Make it with several feathers (5 or more) and use as a fan for smudging. It may be carried in ceremony and dance to demonstrate and make stronger your ties with a totem spirit.

Choose a piece of sound wood between six and twelve inches long. If you wish to use the wood of a living tree offer tobacco to the tree before cutting your stick. A stick picked up from the woods or even a bought dowel should also be received gratefully with an offering of tobacco.

Take off the bark and smooth the stick carefully with a knife. Carve symbols which will increase its connection to the totem spirit to whom you wish to dedicated it. Carve a flat space on one side or hollows for each individual feather if your skill will allow.

Using string or yarn attach the feathers to one end of the stick. Wrap an inch or so of that end with the string. It is nice to thread pony beads on your yarn and include them in this wrapping. Secure both ends of the wrapping carefully, gluing if necessary.

Your prayer stick may be further decorated with small medicine objects; shells, beads, claws, other feathers, bells, streamers, etc. You can even wrap an appropriate fur or skin around it.

HEADBANDS

Headbands are worn to keep your hair from flying into your eyes. They are also worn as jewelry and decoration. There are headbands for the societies, clans, and tribes. A headband can be made to call to a totem spirit. As it lies naturally right over the third eye it is a convenient meditation aid.

To make a headband take a piece of leather or fabric. Bind fabric edges to prevent ravelling. Cut it slightly smaller than your head. This band should be between one and two inches wide. Add ties of soft leather thongs, yarn, or string at each end.

Your headband may be decorated with beading, painting, or embroidery. Stone beads may be sewn on or cabochon cut stones glued to leather. Frequently a small crystal point is sewn to the center front with an "X" shaped stitch.

HEADDRESSES

Headdresses are used to call in the totem powers of the animal(s) represented. Hawk's is made of a crow and a fox skin. It calls in the totem powers of those two animal spirits help him in ceremonies and healings. The headdress is a type of mantle. It is a crown the shaman wears to show he dresses up like the animal and is ONE with him. It brings the shaman into oneness with the animal(s) by covering his human head with the covering of the animal(s).

An entire animal or bird may be incorporated into a headdress. Just the fur, horns, or skull from the head of a large animal, a buffalo or bear, is used.

It isn't possible to tell you how to make a headdress. Each and every one is different. When you are ready for one beginning with a close-fitting skull cap will make the job easier. Attach appropriate objects to the cap.

Headdresses must be earned by study, devotion, and just plain hard work. Like many other medicine objects they do not forgive misuse.

MASKS

Masks are made to represent various supernatural beings, totem spirits, and animals. They are used primarily in dance. There are mask societies which are quite secretive. They often posses ancient and powerful masks which are not shown to non-members. By wearing these masks the individual not only represents the supernatural being, in many ways he or she becomes it.

Other masks are part of less serious customs such as the booger masks of the Cherokee. These boogers are the unega. They are portrayed in the dance as gross, unmannerly, and ludicrous. Non-people who are eventually defeated by the brave Human Beings of the clan.

Masks may be made out of a wide variety of things; wood, clay, animal skins and bones, papier-mache, corn shucks, cloth, cardboard, grocery bags, etc. One of the most effective I've seen pictured was a booger mask made of a hollowed out hornet's nest. Making and wearing a mask of your animal totem is a very powerful way to get into the skin of your totem spirit and to communicate with it.

Your own skills and experience will determine what materials you choose for a mask. Try not to copy some mask seen in a book. Talk to your totem and listen. Make a mask which will help you submerge your humanity into the being of your totem animal.

BAGS AND CONTAINERS:

All of the ceremonial objects we have talked about; the pipe, the smudging bowl, the staff, prayer stick, etc., should have it's own special bag or medicine bundle. These originally would have been made of leather, pottery, or basketry. None of these items should be left just lying around. When not in use they should be wrapped up or put into a container to be kept clean, undamaged, and out of sight.

Leather or cloth bags may be made using the directions for the medicine bag in Chapter 4. Measure the object and cut the material twice as wide as the finished bag and an inch or two longer. A bag which is a little too big is better than one which is a tight fit. Wings and other feathered objects should be provided with a sleeve, open on both ends, which is slid on the easy way before putting the object away. Because it is open on both ends the sleeve can be taken off the easy way. The feathers then are not ruffled up by being drawn out backwards.

A medicine bundle is a collection of all the objects which are used together. They are rolled up in a large piece of leather or cloth and carefully tied so that nothing falls out. Of course, a tote bag of appropriate size is also acceptable.

Medicine objects are expected to last at least for one entire lifetime. Many medicine objects have been handed down for many generations. The care in making the object as well as the careful storing of it is a part of their medicine power.

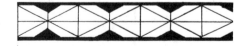

ON THE TRACK OF THE SEEN

The Seeking of the Totems

One day when the sun rose, the animals called a gathering of all the four-footeds to consider eradicating humankind from the face of Turtle Island. Every animal told of grievances against man. Yanu, the bear, told of the cutting of the woodlands. Dayi, the beaver, said that the rivers and streams were too dirty for raising her children. Awi, the deer, told of the plowing of the grasslands, Awahili, the eagle, cried her anger at the dirtying of the sky. Only Kiyaga, the chipmunk spoke in defense of man. Because she was so small, she was shown little or no animosity by this lumbering monster. Consequently, Kiyaga spoke up in defense of humans. At this the animals fell upon Kiyaga and tore her with their claws. To this day Chipmunk wears a stripe on her back as evidence of this attack and of the only charitable gesture made at the animal's council.

The idea of communicating with totem animals is a familiar aspect of American Indian custom. Animals commonly appear in Indian names; Crazy Crow, Grey Fox, Limping Buffalo. Indians wear and carry tokens of their totem spirits. They use their fur and feathers for drums, clothing, shields, prayer sticks, spirit bags, sacred pipes — in everything they do.

An Indian on his or her initial vision quest finds or is adopted by one or more totems. These frequently are animals although plant and mineral totems are plentiful. These totems set the pattern of the individuals life from that point forward. the totems brought back from a quest might indicate a future as a warrior, chief, medicine person, or other specialist of Indian life. Perhaps membership in a secret society goes along with the totem or other special distinction.

What is consistent is that the specific totem(s) are a major source of medicine throughout your life. The totem will protect, advise, and encourage you. It may bring the gift of a song useful for healing, a special dance, success in war, or in the hunt. You can depend upon your totem to take a supernatural interest in your life.

While the totems which come to you as a part of your vision quest may always remain your primary totem spirits, you are by no means limited to them. Each animal species (as with plants and minerals) has a different set of qualities. These are like skills which you may call upon. Do you need advice or assistance in the modern world of business and finance? The long seeing, quick hunting hawk may offer his expertise. Perhaps stubborn survival ability mixed with a talent for discovering hidden answers, qualities of the rat, is just what you need. For stalwart courage standing against adversity call upon the buffalo. For lightning quick decisions and skillful diversity the sparrow offers her expertise.

Through preparation and totem meditations you can avail yourself of the help of whatever totem(s) seem most likely to be of assistance in your particular situation. You may even discover that the totem you are calling upon has been attempting to communicate with you all along!

WHAT DO WE MEAN BY TOTEMS?

Totems, power animals, spirit guides — these are similar concepts. A follower of the medicine path will mention that the bear, the rabbit, or the hawk is their totem animal. A medicine person will contact the owl totem for help in obtaining direction for the future or the dragonfly totem to bring the power of fire into his or her medicine.

Don't assume that this is a symbolic communication. Indians did not work with what we call symbols. This is not to imply, however, that you will have a physical conversation with a specific, individual animal. Talking to your house cat, even when it answers, is not quite what is meant by speaking to the totems.

The first step to understanding what is meant by totems is to examine the way we speak of them. We contact THE bear totem, THE hawk totem, etc. Contact is made with THE spirit of all the individuals of each species. To contact the bear totem is to attempt speech with the essence, the spirit of all bearness. All bears are reflections of the essential bear-ness which is the bear totem.

This spirit of bearness is not a symbol. It is the essential reality of the bear spirit. Each individual bear is an expression of this spirit. Neither the bear itself, nor the totem spirit of bear is more or less real than the other.

Each totem possess knowledge and qualities of its own. These qualities are partially discovered through study of individual representatives of the totem. Observing the qualities, habits, and strengths of the bear will help lead you to a knowledge of the power of the bear totem. Tradition: the myths, legends and stories of the Indians also sheds light on the powers of the totems.

WHAT ARE THE DIFFERENT KINDS OF TOTEMS?

We have spoken of several different ways of referring to the totems. We may have found specific totem spirits which are ours. We may seek help of various totems for appropriate matters. We call the spirit keepers of the four quarters and the totem spirits of the moons in our medicine wheel

PERSONAL TOTEMS

Your personal totems will probably find you. You may seek a totem, but it is up to the individual totem spirit to let you know that he or she has adopted you. You may find your personal totem on a vision quest. Many medicine people take their name from the totem who comes to them on a vision quest. Subsequent vision quests undertaken for further learning, increase of medicine power, etc., may or may not produce additional personal totems. Personal totems are very important. They help you to discover the direction your medicine must take. They make themselves available to you to help you in following that direction.

SPIRIT KEEPERS, MOON TOTEMS, ETC.

Each direction of the compass is ruled by an animal totem called a spirit keeper. Each of the 12 moons has a totem animal, plant and mineral. The rabbit, spirit keeper of the south, may also be your personal totem spirit. The plantain, totem of the Thawing Moon of March, can be a personal totem. But as the spirit keeper of the south, tsistu also takes on the communications responsibilities of representing the powers and attributes of the south. Plantain, a totem spirit of perseverance, thrift, and survival in unfriendly environments, also represents (to the southern dwelling Cherokee) the early green of spring, health after privation, the turning of the season, and as a communication from the last moon of the winter.

You may contact awahili, the eagle, as the spirit keeper of the east, the power of light and thought. You may come to awahili in her role as patron of spirituality to ask help in increasing your awareness and abilities in spiritual matters. Awahili might appear to you on a vision quest and become one of your totem spirits. In all three of these guises awahili is still the eagle totem. Her powers and attributes retain their coherence. The totem does not change in these various roles. Our apprehension and interpretation may differ amongst them.

WHAT KINDS OF THINGS CAN BE TOTEMS?

Actually, just about anything can become a totem spirit. Animal totems are the most commonly spoken of and understood, but they are only one of the three kingdoms. Plants and minerals partake equally with animals of the spirit stuff. However, plants and minerals vibrate on a different frequency from animals. This frequency may be harder for some of us to receive or tune into.

In our modern world totem spirits can be found in the most unlikely of modern conveniences and irritations. Perhaps you have never thought about contacting the spirit of trains and railroads, of multi-story buildings, or telephones. Many computer users do feel a certain contact with the spirit of their thinking machines. Personally, when confronted by an insurmountable obstacle, I'm going to talk to the bulldozer totem!

WHEN SHOULD YOU SEEK CONTACT WITH THE TOTEMS?

You will contact many totem spirits in your work with the medicine wheel. You will establish communication through the sacred pipe. You will call upon them in smudging, give-away, sweat lodge, and in most any ritual or ceremony you do along your medicine path.

You need to keep in contact with your own personal totem spirits through meditation and ceremony. You should consult appropriate totems for guidance, strength, courage, and advice as you travel your medicine path. The totems offer their help and guidance to us and it would be foolish indeed to refuse their aid.

TOTEM COMMUNICATION

PREPARATION FOR TOTEM MEDITATIONS:

There are five steps in the preparation of a totem meditation.

1) Research the qualities of the specific animal in its mundane form. Read, and make notes, of its habits and life-style. What does it eat, where does it find it's food. Is it a vegetable eater, a hunter, a gatherer of insects? How does it hunt? Does it hide in the high grass, pounce suddenly, and break the neck of its prey. Does it scurry around the forest floor finding and hiding nuts? Does it pass unseen through the city streets banqueting upon the unreguarded leftovers of human kind? Where does it sleep? Is it awake during the day or at night? Does it have soft, fine fur; rough, bristly fur; or perhaps smooth lustrous feathers? Is it courageous, timid, wily, straightforward, fast, slow, streamlined, or awkward? You need to know a great deal about your animal in an ordinary sense before you are ready to become that animal in your quest for communication.

These behavioral and physical characteristics of the flesh-and-blood animal are essentially transferable to its totem spirit. Following is a very brief discussion of the life of a hawk as an example:

The hawk is primarily a diurnal bird of prey. Four hundred fifty species of this carnivorous raptor exist, with thirty-four species found in North America north of Mexico.

Hawks sit on high perches and fly in circles, searching for prey. When prey is located, she swoops down and seizes it in her talons. The kill will be torn apart and eaten or carried to the nest. Hawks prey on all categories of animal life: reptiles, amphibians, insects, birds, mammals and fish. Most hawks infinitely prefer fresh kills to gifts of (dead) food.

This description helps explain why the hawk is considered a totem of the modern-day business person — prospecting from a high vantage point and swooping down on profit. This identification is particularly apt as many anthropologists believe that the business realm has replaced the act of hunting in society.

2) The second step in preparing for your totem meditation is to find out the spiritual attributes of the totem animal. Think about the mole. What are some of its mundane activities and characteristics? It tunnels through the earth leaving raised burrows all over your yard; it has very weak eyesight; he evidently has compensatory senses. Other noticeable features of the mole include its extremely soft and lustrous black coat and its nearly human-seeming forefeet.

Without knowing any legends about the mole it seems safe to assume that he would be good at locating hidden things and bringing them to you. At the same time, you wouldn't go to the mole if you needed to find your object secretly. The mole doesn't attempt to hide his tracks.

Another way to discover the powers of a specific totem animal is to pay attention to your own intuition. If you feel that you should call upon a certain species of animal, don't fight it.

3) The third step in preparing for a totem meditation is to obtain a totem bag or some other physical means of tuning in on the totem spirit. The totem bag might contain a prayer feather, an offering bag of tobacco for the totem spirit, herbs and plants associated with the totem, and a stone associated with the totem. A crystal may afford the spirit a focus. For animal totems an object from the body of the animal is often included. This can be fur, feather, bone fragment, etc. A picture of the animal, a very small statue or figure (made or bought), or any other way of linking the totem bag to the animal should be included.

Plant and mineral totems have energies just as strong and vital as the animal totems although they vibrate somewhat more slowly to our human perception. It is usually easier to obtain a physical specimen from one of these kingdoms. One of the totems associated with your birth moon might be a good selection for your beginning meditations.

A bear totem bag might contain one of the following herbs which are considered bear herbs: violet, mullein, thistle, plantain, fennel and spruce. I would be tempted to add blueberry to this list as bears are notorious in their love of this fruit. One of the following semi-precious stones will also increase the bearness of a totem bag: amethyst, apache tear (a type of obsidian) and jasper. The bag should also contain some object more directly associated with bear - like a few strands of actual bear hair, a real or simulated bear claw, a small model of a bear, or even a picture of one.

You can assemble your own totem bag using the suggestions included in our short discussions of the individual totems, your own research, and your intuition. You can also buy one from some of the sources listed in this book.

4) Think out the psychosensory changes involved in becoming your chosen totem animal. Here is an example of a psychosensual imagery booster written for meditating on the wolf.

MICROCOSMIC:

Feel: from within: lightness and grace on feet, especially when running (as opposed to human) fluid movement of four legs, shock resistant walking on padded feet, heavy fur coat, coarse texture, faster heartbeat, slightly higher body temperature

from outside: thickness of fur while cleaning and preening, Movement of fur strands while scratching and searching for parasites,

Taste: of body while cleaning and preening, raspy sensation from rough texture of tongue,

Sight: of streamlined body of fur, greatly increased peripheral vision

Sound: of body moving, of heart beating, of your own growl

Smell: of coat and entire body

MACROCOSMIC

Feel: of prey hunted and stalked, of soft objects and surfaces which claws and teeth sink into, of objects which bump against a body covered with fur

Taste: of warm blood, of own pups fur, of living, raw meat

Sight: in near darkness, of the world from a low vantage point with a wide periphery, of prey, of other wolves

Sound: of noises humans cannot hear, acuity of sound, soft movements of prey being stalked

Smell: of prey, of food, of possible mates, of other animals, of familiar sounds

4) Your last preparation for a totem meditation is to decide upon the form of the meditation itself. If you are experienced at visualization and meditation you may not need to make any further preparations. Armed with knowledge of your chosen totem, its mundane and spiritual qualities, and aided by a totem bag, you may be able to communicate successfully using skills you have already learned.

For those inexperienced in meditation and visualization there are four steps of final preparation you may make.

1) Review the meditation methods explained in Chapter 3. If you have practiced you will have developed the basic skills needed for this meditation.

2) Review the mundane, psychosensory, and spiritual information you have gathered about the totem in 2), 3), and 4) above. Fix the information in your mind so you are not confused about what the totem is and does.

3) Choose a framework for your meditation. Begin with smudging. This cleanses you mentally, physically, and spiritually for the task you have set yourself.

A tobacco offering or tobacco ties may be given to the totem, to the four quarters, the sky, and earth. You may then wish to offer the sacred pipe especially to the particular totem with whom you wish to communicate. For some of the totems there are sets of related animals corresponding to the four directions, the sky, and the earth. We give examples of this in the discussions of the individual animals. You may wish to use these identifications instead of the usual spirit keepers.

4) Plan your meditation. You must enter the meditation, become the animal, and live it's life with it. At some point you must pause to speak to the totem and hear its communications to you. Before ending the meditation you must systematically return to your own human form. A totem meditation is shape changing magic. Attempting to return to ordinary life without properly changing back into human form may be the source of some werewolf stories!

DOING A TOTEM MEDITATION

Go to your place of meditation. A natural place where the animal, plant, or mineral of your totem would feel at home is ideal. Most important find a place where you are comfortable! Decide upon your position and get settled and comfortable. Wait a few moments until your mental, emotional, and physical beings are relaxed.

Once you are settled and relaxed take a pinch

of tobacco from your totem's bag and offer it to the six directions

Close the totem bag and place it over your third eye. A headband, bandanna or ribbon will help. Close your physical eyes. You should breath deeply and slowly and let your consciousness go deeply into the third eye and into the totem bag. You must become immersed in the essence of your totem. If your totem is the bear, imagine the fur and thick flesh which surrounds your body. Feel your immensity with respect to the smaller animals. If your totem is the eagle imagine feathers covering your body. Spread your wings, soar high over the earth. If your totem is the turtle picture the magnificent, protective covering surrounding you as you dive to the bottom of the lake; as you swim fluidly through the water.

Whatever your totem may be: goose, rat, buffalo, become that animal, plant, or mineral. Using your powers of imagery BECOME your totem. Wear the feathers, fur, bark, or hard covering of your totem. Make the noises and movements of your totem. Perceive the physical world through the eyes of your totem, with your totem's senses.

Do the things your totem does: sway in the wind, flap your wings, swim by the movement of your fins, watch millions of years go by as a stone whose very essence changes and coalesces with each movement of Grandmother Earth (Unchi).

Live where your totem lives: in the forest, in the sea, among the tall trees, in a cave, on a cliff or promontory. Experience life as your totem does: eat, sleep, hunt, kill, heal, breath, defecate, sense, as your totem senses.

Proceed in this imagery until you feel that you have achieved oneness with the totem. This may not happen in one session. Depending on your desire, the complexity of the totem, and your level of achievement of imagery it may take ten or more sessions. These sessions may last from a minute or so to many hours. The time necessary is individual.

It is important to end a meditation with a re-awakening process for both mind and body. Many of us recede so deeply into the essence of the totem that we must come out as slowly as we went in. Just as the diver paces herself when rising up from the ocean depths to avoid the bends, so must we reverse the process of becoming a totem archetype. You must unbecome the totem and (95) self?

return to your body in essence and form. This should be done in reverse of the process you used to begin. Move your consciousness away from the third eye and direct it to the crown of your head. Imagine the trappings of your outward totem form receding. The fur thins, the bark recedes leaving your human skin underneath. Paws or claws transform into arms and legs. Little by little become conscious of the rest of your body, of the sounds and sights around you. Reform slowly from the projected image of the totem back into human form. Put your hands and totem bag on the earth or floor to ground yourself. You may be surprised at how much better you can feel both physically and mentally after meditating.

RECORDING YOUR VISION

Your recording should begin with the date, time of day, and place of the meditation. Record the name of the totem with whom you were attempting to communicate. Describe the physical feelings you felt/assumed as you became the totem. Did you feel lighter or heavier, what was the movement of your limbs. Plants and minerals move as well as animals, rock has veins, promontories and outcroppings, plants have leaves, stems, which move in the wind. How did you perform movements? How was this different from your human movements? If you were a plant or stone did you move from your initial place, did the world move past you? What sounds did you make, How did the surface of your body look and feel? Smell, Taste?

What life-sustaining activities did you perform? Did you eat, kill, hunt, or photosynthesize? Did you sleep? Did the seasons change? Did you seek shelter? Did you breath? Did you bear or nurture young?

How has this meditation affected you in your ordinary self? Do you see yourself differently physically? Emotionally? Mentally? Spiritually? Do you see the world immediately around you differently? Do you see Grandmother Earth, the Great Spirit, the total universe, Miaheyyun, in a different way after your experience as a totem? How aware did you become of the totem on the cellular level? Describe this feeling. Have you brought some of this awareness to your ordinary self?

TALKING WITH THE FOUR-LEGGEDS

The Animal Kingdom Totems

When you begin totem meditations it can help to have specific guidelines. After following these guidelines for a little while you will be able to make your own way more easily.

CAT TOTEM MEDITATION

The following cat totem meditation focuses on a very familiar animal and gives you information about the Indian's imagery of the cat as fuel for your meditation. We have included some brief songs to aid you in your journey.

Take your chosen position for meditation and notice all around you. Touch the ground or floor to balance yourself and honor Grandmother Earth.

O Earth Mother, my heart, O brightest Queen,
Cast your blessings unto me.
I am your child, you are my mother,
So come be with me.
You are my provider, you give me strength,
Earth Mother inspire me.
O All Mother, O Earth Mother, O my mother
Come Close to me.

Acknowledge and/or invoke the nature spirits, the emissaries of the four directions, the sky, and the mother of four-Leggeds. Call on the powers of enlightenment and wisdom of your totem bag. Make an offering of incense or tobacco.

Invoke the cat totem. Call, Come:
(four times)
Come
come from the world beyond
Come and reach to me
Come and teach me. (four times)

Imagine yourself sitting upon a bare rock ledge in the wild. The sun is beating comfortably down

upon you. Feline energy envelopes your being.

Your feet begin to shrink smaller, smaller into paws with thick, tough pads. Your toenails grow outward into pointed claws. You sprout thick hair — spreading to cover your paws with fur. A tail begins to grow, longer and longer, with a twitchy tip. Your whole body is covered with fur; your hands grow pads and claws.

Your ears move to the top of your head and peak. Your nose and chin join to form a muzzle. Your teeth grow longer. Long, sensitive whiskers grow.

Night is falling as you look far out over the ledge. Your eyes can see more and further now. Your ears can hear many more sounds than you could before. You hear many beings, small and large.

Walk silently through the forest seeking your supper. Stalk patiently seeking one small sound you recognize as food.

POUNCE, trapping the tiny creature beneath your paw. Hold it in your long claws. Watch it a moment. Fling it up and pounce upon it again. Kill it neatly and bite into it.

Walk to a quiet place and curl yourself up into a warm, fuzzy ball. Open your inner eyes to see a shape in front of you. In this shape you will see negative thought-forms you produce. They stand between you and prosperity. Remember, understand, all these forms. Watch so long as the display continues. Look at your reflection.

Now it is time to return. Open the eyes of the cat and watch the lustrous fur slowly leave your body. See your hands and feet change from claws and pads back into human design. Feel your tail still and disappear. Your muzzle flattens out; your whiskers fade away.

To close your meditation thank the entities you called upon at the beginning. Touch your hands and your totem bag to the ground to release excess energy. Center your self within your human body. Find yourself in balance between all the forces. End your meditation with this song:

I walk with wisdom
from this hallowed place.
I walk with knowledge
from this hallowed place
I walk in balance,
not in haste

There are countless ways in which to contact

the totems. While we have given several suggestions this doesn't mean that they are the only ways YOU may use. They are intended only to give you a start.

THE ANIMAL KINGDOM TOTEMS

Following the research principles given in Chapter 13 we have compiled information on a number of totems in each of the three kingdoms. As you discover which totems are particularly yours add your own research to ours. This will make it much easier for you to contact the totem. It will also make the totem's communications to you much clearer. Like most other things as you practice totem communication it will become a second nature to you. It will no longer present the difficulties you may experience at first.

We have arranged information on the animal kingdom totems in a consistent form. You will note that we haven't been able to collect as much information on some of the totems as on others. Totem research is a new discipline in medicine path. Our understanding and accumulation of facts is constantly growing. Perhaps you will find yourself filling in some of these blanks as you concentrate on specific totems.

We have used a great number of sources in the compilation of the information in this chapter and the two following chapters. The books listed in the bibliography have been of great assistance in this work. However, virtually everything ever read by the authors has played a part. Nor have we hesitated to use information culled from personal observation and intuition. Our personal totem spirits have also added to our knowledge of their powers.

BEAR

Ursus species,
Cherokee - yanu: Chippewa - mudjekeewis: Piegan Blackfoot - kyaiyo [grizzly]; - paksikwoyi [honey bear]

PRIMARY POWERS: The bear is the great healer, particularly of the spirit

ZOOLOGICAL INFORMATION: The bear sleeps most of the winter. Bears do not hibernate in a strict sense. Their body temperature does not drop low enough. When he awakens in the spring yanu locates herbs and mud which are tonic. Bears are omnivorous like humans. They are very protective of their families. They have been observed placing their own hair in wounds to speed the healing process.

MYTHOLOGY: In many legends, the bear was the chief of the council of animals. She is credited with the ability to look within the spirit and discover weaknesses and impurities which require healing. The great strength of the bear comes from a healthy mind and spirit. She is the spirit keeper of the west. She is connected with the thunderers, the setting sun, water, and introspection. She is said to originally have been a person changed to a bear in the course of protecting the People. In Cherokee legend the bears know of an invisible lake in the mountains which can heal all injuries.

SPIRITUAL QUALITIES: The bear totem is useful particularly for healing information from and for the inner self; physical, spiritual, and psychic.

WEST - Black Bear: NORTH - Kodiak: EAST - Panda: SOUTH - Grizzly: SKY - Brown Bear: EARTH - Honey Bear

ASSOCIATED PLANTS: violet, mullein, thistle, plantain, fennel, spruce

ASSOCIATED MINERALS: amethyst, apache tear (a type of obsidian), jasper.

BEAVER

Castor canadensis
Cherokee - dayi: Shawnee - hamekw: Algonquian - poyawew: Chinook - enaqoa inene

PRIMARY POWERS: altering and building environments, water, balancing

ZOOLOGICAL INFORMATION: Beavers range almost the entire northern portions of the continent. They frequent streams in forested areas where there are trees and bushes for building materials and food. She feeds on the soft inner bark of aspen and poplar trees as well as twigs, leaves, grasses, shoots, and roots. The beaver is a rodent with few natural enemies other than man. Her fur is dense, soft, and silky. It is waterproofed by an oily secretion which allows her to spend long minutes under water. Her dam building activities are obsessive and characterized by ingenuity and neatness. HER dams provide shelter and storage.

MYTHOLOGY: The beaver's affinity to water places her in the west where the thunders live. However, the beaver's ability to make drastic alterations and her methods of deliberate, constant, and resourceful change corresponds to north energies. The Omaha tell a legend of Schinike, a hunter hero, who visits a beaver lodge. The beaver kills one of her children to provide supper for the hero. Afterwards she places the bones of the cub in its hide and puts the bundle under the water. From this bundle, a new beaver cub is born. The Cheyenne say that the earth rests on a large beam or post in the south. A green beaver, the father of all mankind, knaws on this post. Someday he will grow angry and gnaw through the support completely and the earth will fall.

SPIRITUAL QUALITIES: Beaver medicine encompasses all four directions. Its qualities include drastic alterations in the environment, building of new concepts, ideas, and structures. He represents water element powers; resurrection and rebirth: teething of children; and balance; and grounding. Use a beaver totem bag when beginning new projects. Urbanites will find the beaver gives stability and balance in the city's state of constant flux. It's water powers include healing, fluidity, and smoothness.

QUARTER IDENTITY: The Beaver's qualities encompass all four quarters as noted above.

ASSOCIATED PLANTS: blue camas, thistle

BLUE JAY

Cyanocitta cristata
Cherokee - tlayku

PRIMARY POWERS: Alertness in the morning, great courage

ZOOLOGICAL INFORMATION: The blue jay is a noisy, moderately territorial bird. He will not tolerate certain other birds, such as grackles and starlings, in his area. He will argue even with a trespassing hawk. He eats large insects, acorns, and, in breeding season, small birds and eggs. Occasionally he eats frogs or mice. He is a robber and can cause damage to crops. In general he stays in the same area year round.

MYTHOLOGY: The Cherokee give a child a tea of jay's feathers to make him an early riser.

SPIRITUAL QUALITIES: The jay offers great courage of the noisiest sort. He is up to the minute on everything going on. He is adaptable and always very proud of himself.

QUARTER IDENTITIES: WEST - Stellar Jay: NORTH - Canada Jay (Whiskey-jack): EAST - Blue Jay: SOUTH - Green Rio Grande Jay

ASSOCIATED PLANTS: pine tree

BUFFALO

Cherokee - yunsu: Hichitee - yanasi: Creek - yanasa: Choctaw - yanash: Ojibwa - waboose

PRIMARY POWERS: strength, truth, tenacity, power, provision

ZOOLOGICAL INFORMATION: Buffalo in the wild are not easily dissuaded from any given purpose. The mother bison refuses to leave the side of her young even when confronted by vicious predators. Actually few of whom can pose a threat to an adult. Buffalo was the food and clothing staple for the plains people and very important to many of the more eastern tribes.

MYTHOLOGY: According to the Ojibwa and the Cherokee the buffalo is the spirit keeper of the north. She provides a solid base for the coming of spring. The Sioux legend of Tsitsetse, the jumping mouse, tells how the buffalo shielded the mouse from predators as she travelled to the place of her vision. The White Buffalo Calf Woman brought the sacred pipe to the Lakota Sioux.

SPIRITUAL QUALITIES: Buffalo provides strength through purity of purpose. She embodies tenacity, veracity, and provision.

ASSOCIATED PLANTS: birch, aspen, plantain

CARDINAL

Richmondena cadrdinalis
Cherokee - tatsuhwa

PRIMARY POWERS: Hope in darkness, red-paint spirit

ZOOLOGICAL INFORMATION: The cardinal is a non-migratory songbird. "Their clear, whistle-like 'cheer, cheer, cheer' in late winter months is one of the most pleasing of all outdoor sounds." [Peterson Guide to Eastern Birds] They will come to your birdfeeder if you give them sunflower or melon seeds. The flash of the bright red male and the rich brown underlaid with crimson coloring of the female contrasted against snow lifts the gloom of winter.

MYTHOLOGY: When the daughter of the sun was killed, some say by the rattlesnake, her ghost took the shape of the cardinal. Later when the raccoon tricked the wolf and covered his eyes with dung; the cardinal cleaned him. The wolf in gratitude gave the red paint to the cardinal.

SPIRITUAL QUALITIES: The cardinal grants group cooperation and concern; living hope in the darkness of the soul; happiness; sprouting seed magic; birth and rebirth.

CAT

Felix spp.

Cherokee - wesa [cat in general]: tluntutsi [panther]: atsil tluntutse [fire panther, shooting stars]

PRIMARY POWERS: invulnerability, finding lost things, prosperity,

ZOOLOGICAL INFORMATION: All cats are basically primal and independent regardless of their home or degree of domesticity. Cats are flesh eaters. They are powerful, stealthy, carnivorous prowlers. The mountain lion (puma, cougar, panther) is considered one of the most elusive mammals on the continent.

MYTHOLOGY: Cherokee say that when a cat lies by the lodge fire purring he is saying "taladu-nungi, taladu-nungi", or sixteen-four, sixteen-four. The characteristics of the number four include tenacity and the four directions. Sixteen is, of course, four fours. Rabbit and wildcat once tricked the wily wild turkey. The Cherokee considered the panther invulnerable. They say that he could sustain many arrows to his head without harm. Creek legend says the mountain lion has a giant wheel which can find all lost objects. The cougar is the sacred totem of the Big Winds Moon to the Chippewa/Ojibwa. He had powers of hunting and healing. This is an example of the reciprocal/polarized nature of the totem powers. The lion is oom leeuw in South Africa, the Flying Hunter. The Cherokee call comets and meteors fire panthers. They tell stories of underground panthers who will invite you to visit. You go home after an evening of feasting and pleasure to find that many years have passed in your village.

SPIRITUAL QUALITIES: The cats grant aggressive protection and hunting success. They are used to find lost things, and to find and remove obstacles, particularly those in the way of prosperity. They offer great power in hunting, healing, seeing spirits, strength, and creative energy. The Strength card in the Native American Tarot deck

shows a cougar. Other powers are protective tenacity, love, and a talent for security.

QUARTER IDENTITIES: WEST - Everglades Panther NORTH - Snow Leopard EAST - African Lion SOUTH - Wildcat SKY - Mountain Lion EARTH - Cougar

ASSOCIATED PLANTS: catnip, rosemary, borage, fennel, mandrake, poppy

ASSOCIATED MINERALS: tigereye,

COYOTE

Canis latrans

Kiowa - saynday: Ojibwa - shawnodese

PRIMARY POWERS: growth, trust, maturity, wisdom

ZOOLOGICAL INFORMATION: The coyote is one of the few mammals to increase its range in the last two hundred years. He is almost entirely carnivorous although occasionally he feeds on fleshy fruit. Actually there is little that a coyote will not eat. He is a wily and generally successful hunter.

MYTHOLOGY: The coyote is the trickster of the plains and other western Indians. He is a great teacher and the hero/god of many stories. The Kiowa credit him with diverting a smallpox epidemic to their enemies, the Pawnee. The Ojibwa consider him the spirit keeper of the south.

SPIRITUAL QUALITIES: Coyote is the teacher of sacred truths, growth, trust, lessons, even if one is reluctant to learn. He specializes in reaching outward and testing wisdom. The holder of coyote medicine has the capacity for rapid growth on all levels, providing she centers herself first. The coyote's colors are green of plants growing and yellow of sun which feeds and nourishes her. Seek the coyote totem at mid-day especially during the summer.

QUARTER IDENTITIES: WEST - Dog NORTH - Wolf EAST - Fox SOUTH - Coyote

ASSOCIATED PLANTS: rose, raspberry, violet

CROW

Corvus brachyrhynchos

Cherokee - kagu

PRIMARY POWERS: seeing and interpreting signs and omens, curiosity.

ZOOLOGICAL INFORMATION: A large, black, loquacious bird, the crow is considered destructive by farmers. Frequently he does more good by eating insects than harm in stealing crops. Research has indicated that crows more often glean from harvested fields than raid standing crops. The crow steals and hides shiny objects, lacks fear, is intelligent, curious, and very clean. She is a good mimic and can reproduce many sounds. She is omnivorous and non-migratory.

MYTHOLOGY: One who has crow medicine possesses the gift of seeing and interpreting signs. In the modern world the crow may interpret sociological, political, and financial trends. The Cherokee tell frightening stories of the raven mockers, witch spirits who rob the dying of life. They look like old, withered humans but fly in a fiery shape. They will steal the soul of any who see them.

SPIRITUAL QUALITIES: Crow is concerned with giving and interpreting omens. Omens are delivered without fear of the message, whether they portend danger or security, prosperity or poverty. It cannot be polluted by the mundane world. There are two trails on the path of omens: the trail of the wolf: a nomad who might guide a war party and the trail of the crow: a non-migratory animal who interprets the signs near and about home. Crow medicine is paradoxical and dualistic.

QUARTER IDENTITIES: WEST - Storm Crow NORTH - Northern Raven EAST - Grackle SOUTH - Jackdaw SKY - Gunskaliski [killer of Raven-Mockers] EARTH - Kalanu ahyeliski [Raven-Mocker]

ASSOCIATED PLANTS: corn, hyacinth, bay laurel, fennel

ASSOCIATED MINERALS: gold, silver, diamond

DEER

Odocoilius virginianus

Cherokee - awi [doe]: galagina [buck]

PRIMARY POWERS: speed, quick thinking.

ZOOLOGICAL INFORMATION: The white-tailed or Virginia Deer is the most wide spread species. A forest dweller who often feeds in glades, she has adapted well to civilization. A vegetarian (although said to occasionally eat fish) she eats the twigs of shrubs and trees, herbaceous plants, acorns, and small fruit. Pine, spruce, and aldar are eaten in winter. She is shy and a fast runner.

MYTHOLOGY: The chief of the deer tribe is

called Little Deer, Awi Usdi. He checks to be sure that the proper prayers have been said when one of his tribe is killed for food. He is pure white and very small. His antlers provide one of the Cherokee's most valued talismans. The Cherokee say that the deer visited rheumatism on man in revenge for being killed. The deer won his horns in a race with the rabbit. Cherokee invoked deer medicine to prevent frostbite. Awi, the doe spirit, brought corn to the People.

SPIRITUAL QUALITIES: Speed, quick thinking, acute hearing.

QUARTER IDENTITIES: WEST - Reindeer NORTH - Elk [Wapiti] EAST - Spotted Deer SOUTH - Swamp Deer SKY - Buck [Galagina] EARTH - Doe [Awi]

ASSOCIATED PLANTS: yarrow, spruce, hazel, mugwort, rue, willow

DRAGONFLY

Order Odonata, various genuses and species

PRIMARY POWERS: Emotional, physical and spiritual fire.

ZOOLOGICAL INFORMATION: Dragonflys frequent moist areas around ponds and swampy places in meadows. They range from four inches to one inch from wing-tip to wing-tip.

MYTHOLOGY: Assisted the water spider in obtaining the gift of fire.

SPIRITUAL QUALITIES: Again we observe the reciprocal, dualistic nature of medicine power. The firefly, a water insect, brings fire to us. There is a heyoka quality to dragonfly medicine power. It is the fire which stimulates to action, breaking inertial cycles. It lights the way to new concepts or new ways of seeing situations. It is the physical fire which helps well or maimed bodies participate in life. It is a form of the kundalini energy, dragon power. It is a powerful helper in times of major change.

QUARTER IDENTITIES: WEST - Dragonfly NORTH - Spider EAST - Fly SOUTH - Dragonfly SKY - Butterfly EARTH - Grubworm

ASSOCIATED PLANTS: fireweed, water plants

ASSOCIATED MINERALS: aquamarine, obsidian

EAGLE

Aquila chrysaetos canadensis [golden]: Halieotus leucocephalus [bald]

Cherokee - awahili: Hopi - kwahu, kwatoko: Sioux - wabun: Algonquian - apatenew

PRIMARY POWERS: Communication to and from Galunlati, the great sacred medicine

ZOOLOGICAL INFORMATION: The eagle makes no direct use of plants in his diet but lives by killing small mammals. He soars effortlessly for many miles while searching for food. He has strong talons and bill. Many times eagles have controlled sudden population outbursts of small rodents which would be extremely uncomfortable to man. The bald eagle's diet consists primarily of fish while the golden eagle prefers mammals. They build large, untidy looking nests and are devoted to their young.

MYTHOLOGY: Every tribe has legends about the eagle. The eagle dance is an important ceremony throughout Turtle Island. Eagle feathers constitute the highest possible award for bravery or other notable service to the tribe (a President's Medal so to say). Catching an eagle, whether to preserve alive or to kill, is surrounded with an enormous amount of ceremony. Frequently, as with the Cherokee, only a certain few individuals are trained to kill an eagle or know the ceremonies of propitiation to the eagle spirit. Many tribes share a special method of killing an eagle. In it the hunter is cleansed. He hides in a pit. A stuffed coyote or wolf skin is arranged very close to the pit to simulate a scavenger feeding on a kill. When an eagle flies down to share in the feast, the hunter grabs the eagle's feet. Obviously, the hunter chances maiming blows from the eagle's wings, talons, and beak.

An eagle bone whistle is used by the road man who presides over the Peyote Ceremony. Eagle bone whistles are also important in the Sun Dance. A dream of eagles is the occasion of an eagle dance among the Cherokee lest someone in the dreamer's family should die. Eagle feathers were of such value and importance that among the Blackfoot the tail feathers were the standard of exchange. Such feathers are used to decorate virtually every ceremonial tool, vessel, or item of clothing. Wabun, to the Chippewa, is the spirit keeper of the east and is associated with wisdom.

SPIRITUAL QUALITIES: The power of the eagle is the sacred medicine of the Great Spirit. The true holder of eagle medicine must separate him/herself from the mundane before beginning to under-

stand the intricacies involved in its mystery. To others the eagle is the direct connection to Galunlati. Dreaming of an eagle portends a message from Grandfather Sky.

QUARTER IDENTITIES: WEST - California Condor NORTH - Snowy Owl EAST - Golden Eagle SOUTH - Turkey Buzzard SKY - Bald Eagle EARTH - Screech Owl, Burrowing Owl

ASSOCIATED PLANTS: sage, pennyroyal, anise, spearmint, cypress

FISH

Cherokee - atsadi: Algonquian - namess: Alabama - lalo: Choctaw - nani: Mobilian - slasu

PRIMARY POWERS: transformation

ZOOLOGICAL INFORMATION: Fish live in and breath water. Fish drown when exposed to air. They are cold-blooded vertebrates. The diet of fish ranges from predatory carnivores to eaters of microscopic algae. One fish is even legally [the mullet] a chicken as it has a crop. Each fish species has a separate totem spirit with specific powers.

MYTHOLOGY: It seems that every tribe has a story about someone getting swallowed by a large fish. The Creek tell of Dakwa, a great fish living in the Tennessee River. Dakwa swallowed whole canoes full of people. One day he swallowed a warrior who cut his way out with a mussel shell. Manabozho, the superman of Ojibwa legend was also swallowed by a fish. He beat on the fish's ribs with his war club causing the river-dweller to head for deep water. The hero then turned his canoe sideways in the fish's throat. This caused the great fish to beach and the hero escaped. The Cheyenne tell of two young men who found a couple of very large eggs on the bank of the Mississippi. One hunter ate his egg. The other, fearing the repercussions of eating such a curious and magically-appearing object, kept his. The hunter who ate the egg was transformed into a great fish. The Seminole and Cherokee believe that fish cause dream diseases, or fish ghosts [indigestion], out of vengeance for being caught. The totems of larger fish or fish-eating birds are invoked for a cure of this disease. The Chippewa consider the sturgeon the totem spirit of the Ripe Berries Moon with powers of clairvoyance, sensitivity, and perception.

SPIRITUAL QUALITIES: The fish stories all share the qualities of transformation. The general fish totem, as well as many of the separate specie totems, are invoked in times of complete change.

QUARTER IDENTITIES: WEST - Sturgeon NORTH - Pike EAST - Ugunsteli [a fish which transforms itself into a lizard according to the Creeks] SOUTH - Rainbow trout

ASSOCIATED PLANTS: water plants, algae

FOX

Vulpes fulva [Eastern Red], Urocyon cinereoargenteus [Grey]

Cherokee - tsula [red fox], inali [black fox]

PRIMARY POWERS: balance, cunning, shrewdness

ZOOLOGICAL INFORMATION: Black and silver foxes are normal color variations of the red fox. Foxes have a talent for escaping danger of all types, in ancient as well as modern environments. Mastery of a small range area where he memorizes every detail of terrain provides him with an almost supernatural power to avoid all enemies. The fox is generally a carnivore feeding on small rodents and other small animals. The fox and grapes story in Aesop, however, needs a new moral as foxes do eat fruit.

MYTHOLOGY: The Cherokee invoke the fox as protection against frostbite.

SPIRITUAL QUALITIES: Fox brings balance, cunning, and shrewdness. He represents adaptation and family ties, especially those of fatherhood. Fox medicine affords the qualities of balance of the spiritual and practical worlds; the cunning and shrewdness needed to discern the finer points of psychic phenomena; and adaptation to new spiritual concepts.

ASSOCIATED PLANTS: cinquefoil, cloves, mastic

FROG

Cherokee - walasi

PRIMARY POWERS: transformation, rebirth

ZOOLOGICAL INFORMATION: Frogs and toads go through a remarkable transformation from water dweller (tadpoles) to land dweller (adults). Both frogs and toads require reasonably damp environments. Toads, however, have far greater range away from the water, some living in what we call desert. Both return to the water to lay eggs. Both primarily eat insects.

MYTHOLOGY: The Cherokee agree with European legend that warts are caught from toads. The frog was the marshal and leader in the Council of

(102)

the Animals. She eats the sun or moon to cause eclipses. At this time the people must make a great deal of noise to scare her away from her lunch. She also brings disease to mankind as a result of the council held to punish mankinds' evil deeds.

SPIRITUAL QUALITIES: Frog and toad totem spirits are important resources in times of transformational change.

ASSOCIATED PLANTS: poppy, camas, frankincense, camphor

GOOSE

Chen species, and others

Cherokee - dagulku, sasa: Algonquian - apkirahk, kahakak

PRIMARY POWERS: protection, organization, leadership

ZOOLOGICAL INFORMATION: Geese are migratory birds who fly great distances from their summer grounds in the far north to winter quarters in the United States and further south. In winter they feed primarily on plants, particularly those found in the vicinity of bodies of relatively still water.

MYTHOLOGY: Cherokee legend says the goose stole the first tobacco from the people. She is, therefore, the master of the sacred tobacco [tsalu wakan]. To the Cheyenne, she played a part in the creation of the world. The Chippewa/Ojibwa consider her the totem of the Earth Renewal Moon.

SPIRITUAL QUALITIES: The goose is symbolic of protection and organization; leadership qualities. Goose medicine will empower you with qualities allowing you to grace those contacted and give them the blessings of organization and guidance. Carrying a goose totem bag will give you self-confidence and security.

QUARTER IDENTITIES: WEST - Barnacle Goose NORTH - Snow Goose EAST - Red-Breasted Goose SOUTH - Pied (Magpie) Goose SKY - Hawaiian Goose EARTH - Graylag Goose

ASSOCIATED PLANTS: camphor, frankencense

HAWK

Accipiter species, Buteo species

Cherokee - tlanuwa, tlanuwa usdi [little hawk]

PRIMARY POWERS: aggressive conquering medicine

ZOOLOGICAL INFORMATION: The hawk is a

diurnal bird of prey with a few exceptions (night-hawk for one). He sits on a high perch or flies in circles searching for prey. When prey is located, he swoops down, seizing it in his talons. He tears it apart and eats it there or carries it to his nest. Hawks prey on all categories of animal life: reptiles, amphibians, insects, birds, mammals and fish.

MYTHOLOGY: The Cherokee tell of a great hawk who nested in a cliff and carried off dogs and children. A shaman threw the hatchings to an uktena (great serpent, dragon). In retaliation the parent hawks tore the uktena to pieces and then departed for the sky country. tlanuwa usdi, the little hawk is the leader of the hawks.

SPIRITUAL QUALITIES: The hawk is a good totem for the modern business person as she swoops down on profit and prospect from a high vantage point. She is a hunting totem and modern anthropologists believe that the business realm has replaced hunting in societal pursuit. It serves in all conquering and coup situations.

QUARTER IDENTITIES: WEST - Marsh Hawk [Harrier] NORTH - Gyrfalcon EAST - Red-Tailed Hawk SOUTH - Magpie SKY - Sparrowhawk [kestrel] EARTH - Goshawk

ASSOCIATED PLANTS: dandelion, mullein

HORSE

Equiis spp.

Cherokee - sagwali [means a pack or burden]

PRIMARY POWERS: strength in speed, wide vision, adjustment and adaptability, visions

ZOOLOGICAL INFORMATION: Horses' eyes are located on the sides of their heads making it difficult to sneak up upon them. They escape danger at a very high speed. They can adapt to nearly every terrestrial environment and are able to change from wild to domesticated state and back to the wild.

MYTHOLOGY: Cherokee believed that eating of horse meat (and that of other quick animals) would contribute to the development of speed in the individual. Horses have excellent psychic abilities. While the Spaniards are generally credited with the introduction the horse to Turtle Island there are some reasons to believe that this is not entirely true.

Nearly every tribe has a legend about the coming of the horses. Moctezuma, the gambler of Hopi, Navajo and other Athabascan tribal legend, lost everything he had to Jicarilla who then shot him with an arrow. The arrow carried Moctezuma up to the Great Spirit who showed him the horse of the southern Mexican plains. The gambler brought the horse back to his people. The Kiowa and Cheyenne say that the milky way is the dusty track along which the buffalo and the horse ran a race (The Cherokee say that this is corn meal spilled by the dog.) There are horse dances, particularly one of the Lakota described by Black Elk. Horse hair was used in belts, ropes, anklets, bridles, and many other objects.

SPIRITUAL QUALITIES: The holder of horse medicine is ever wary of the negative psychic forces which lurk and stalk about the darkness. Upon the first sign of these forces the horse totem will break away with blinding speed. Horse medicine displays a flowing elasticity in practical and spiritual situations. It brings the power to see visions.

ASSOCIATED PLANTS: elecampagne, olive, lovage, ash

OWL

Order Strigiformes and Tytonidae

Cherokee - uguku [barred or hoot owl, *Syrnium nebulosum*]: wahuhu [screech owl, *Megascops asio*]: tskiki or atskili [dusky horned owl, *Bubo virginianus saturatus*]

PRIMARY POWERS: sight in darkness, watch-fulness, clairvoyance and prophecy

ZOOLOGICAL INFORMATION: Owls feed on small rodents and large insects. The larger owls prey on rabbits, rats, squirrels, gamebirds, crayfish, and frogs. Owls range in size from the elf owl which is smaller than a robin to quite large barred and horned owls. Owls will regurgitate pellets of the fur, feathers, and bones of their prey. Owls have uncanny abilities of silent flight as well as terrifying banshee cries.

MYTHOLOGY: Many legends say that night birds are ghosts or witches. Their cry is taken as an evil omen. It may be that when their trained medicine priests were somehow lost the Cherokee also lost all those who could interpret the owl's omens. A Kiowa medicine man of great power once kept the body of an owl wrapped in red cloth suspended from a pole outside his tipi. At night when he heard the owl's call he would follow it into the forest. There he would be given a new prophecy or revelation. Only a very wise one was capable of understanding the language of the owl from whom come prophetic tidings. The Cherokee believe a tea of owl tail or wing feathers could provide extended wakefulness.

SPIRITUAL QUALITIES: The medicine powers of the owl are escape; sight in darkness (both literally and spiritually); watchfulness over home and loved ones at night; clairvoyance and prophecy; transmutation; and hunting.

ASSOCIATED PLANTS: olive, apple
ASSOCIATED MINERALS: crystal

RABBIT

Lepus species
Cherokee - tsistu: Algonquian - wabos
PRIMARY POWERS: messenger, protector, trickster

ZOOLOGICAL INFORMATION: Rabbits are capable of great speed. Some jack rabbits can make leaps of ten feet or more. They also can change direction, apparently in mid-air. They have large, mule-like ears. Rabbits are vegetarians, eating herbaceous plants in summer and twigs and bark in winter. They dig comfortable burrows and produce lots of little rabbits. Grey Cat says they particularly like to tease cars at night. They run across the road in front of you, the game being just how many crossings may be made. She also notes that the rabbit count of road kills is infinitely small.

MYTHOLOGY: The rabbit was the hero-god, wonder-worker of all the tribes east of the Mississippi from Hudson Bay to the Gulf. The Algonquian people connected him with the dawn. They saw him as the bringer of light and life, driving away the darkness which held the world in chains. This places him in the east where according to the Chippewa/Ojibwa he is spirit keeper. The rabbit totem also is unexpectedly associated with saynday, the coyote trickster. This explains why he is spirit keeper of the south for the woodlands Indians.

In Cherokee legend the rabbit stole the otter's coat and the opossum's beautiful tail. He tried to trick the wildcat out of turkeys caught by guile. He failed to beat the terrapin in a race and to win the antlers of the buck. But he is always willing to attempt anything which takes chutzpah. The Luo and Wayano tribes of Africa say that the hare tricked the elephant out of his meat and killed the hyena by rope magic (illusory binding ritual).

SPIRITUAL QUALITIES: Rabbit medicine has a dual nature: trickster and mischief maker while at the same time a giver of life. To call upon the dawn rabbit, face east. To consult the trickster, face south.

QUARTER IDENTITIES: WEST - Welsh Giant NORTH - Snowshoe Rabbit EAST - Jackrabbit SOUTH - Trickster Hare SKY - Belgian Hare EARTH - Angora

RAT

Cricetidae Family
Cherokee - tsisdetsi
PRIMARY POWERS: survival, warfare, urban medicine

ZOOLOGICAL INFORMATION: There are several species of rat native to Turtle Island including the cotton rat, *Sigmodon hispidus* and the eastern wood rat, *Neotoma floridana*. The most common rat however, is the house rat or norway rat, *Rattus norvegicus*. He now far outnumbers his aboriginal brothers (sound familiar?). Rats simply eat everything and live anywhere. They can survive being flushed down a toilet or can enter a building through that same route. They can fall six stories and scurry away unharmed. They can gnaw through lead pipe and cinder blocks (their teeth can exert 24,000 lbs. psi); swim 1/2 mile; and tread water for three days. They can wriggle through a hole no larger than a quarter and grow to the size of a rather large puppy. Rats have efficiently taken over man's own created environment. They steal from him, destroy his home and goods, and carry on the longest and most successful guerrilla operation in history. The rat is king of all in urbania inspiring more fear than the lion ever thought about.

MYTHOLOGY: If there are any legends about rats they are doubtless too frightening to pass on.

SPIRITUAL QUALITIES: Rat medicine powers include survival and prosperity in the face of incredible resistance; stubborn tenacity; adaptation; and fertility in a material sense as well as physical. He can infiltrate psychic strongholds with astounding accuracy. The holder of rat medicine need not fear for survival and protection in hostile environments. One of the most awesome totem powers, Rat medicine is survival. It is learning the answers to things hidden and discovering that which is camouflaged. The rat can get into many places we cannot. He knows all the nooks and crannies of urbania which elude our attention. When something perplexes you - when something is hidden from you — it is time for rat medicine.

RATTLESNAKE

Crotalus spp.

Cherokee - utsanati [he has a bell]

PRIMARY POWERS: Attracting rain, hunting medicine

ZOOLOGICAL INFORMATION: All snakes are carnivorous or insectivorous and the prey, which under natural conditions must be captured alive, is swallowed whole. A snake can swallow masses of considerably greater diameter than itself. Rattlesnakes have a curious extra sense organ on the face between the eye and nostril. Each shedding of skin adds a "button" to the collection of rattles the snake carries on its tail. Rattlesnakes are very rarely aggressive towards humans even when shedding their skins or during mating season. The courteous rattle generally gives you sufficient warning to avoid trespassing upon his territory.

MYTHOLOGY: To the Cherokee the rattlesnake was the thunder's necklace. The rattlesnake bit and killed the sun's evil daughter. Having once been a man, the rattlesnake is kindly towards mankind. While the rattler's rattles and skin are powerful talismans, only a specially trained individual can safely kill one. It is believed that they would not bite unless disturbed. The rattler has given the people a special prayer song which will combat the effect of its poison. The Hopi release rattlesnakes after a rainmaking ceremony to carry messages to the thunderers (sistsekom).

There are other interesting items about snakes in Cherokee mythology: The black racer, uksuhi, was scorched in the attempt to obtain the first fire, as was gulegi, the blacksnake. The blacksnake may be hung on a tree to obtain rain within three or four days, or bite the body of one as a cure for toothache.

The copperhead, wadige-askali [brown head] was bronzed through getting too near the sun. It is hated more than revered. It is a descendant of the great mystic serpent and has eyes of fire. A great invisible serpent is conjured by a shaman around the home of a sick person to keep witches (the raven mockers) out.

There are a number of supernatural snakes. The ustutli, foot snake, moved on four feet, rather like an inch worm. It could only move up or down the mountains. He would fall should he attempt to move sideways. Uwtsunta, bouncer, was another inch-worm type dragon. Uktena, a dragon-like snake with a brilliant talisman stone in her forehead, will be discussed in the entry on Crystal.

SPIRITUAL QUALITIES: The strongest medicine of the rattlesnake is to attract rain and bring an end to drought. The rattles are hunting talismans.

ASSOCIATED PLANTS: bistort, bryony, henbane. Rattlesnakes are afraid of campion and it shouldn't be allowed near when making rattlesnake medicine. Snakes, deer, and ginseng act as allies according to the Cherokee. Injury to any one of them is avenged by all.

SPARROW

Fringillidae family

Cherokee - tsiskwaya [the real or principal bird

PRIMARY POWERS: wide coverage of a problem, variety of approach

ZOOLOGICAL INFORMATION: Sparrows have evolved to fit all the available niches. While all looking pretty much alike they have adapted countless sub-species which eat all sorts of foods. Cheeky and happy tempered, they are ubiquitous. Generally unvalued by the bird watcher their subtle variety and truly superb song should bring them more respect.

MYTHOLOGY: The Cherokee considered the sparrow the original of all the birds, the prototype.

SPIRITUAL QUALITIES: The sparrow has the ability to make small, expertly judged changes. As a species they are able to approach a problem from every conceivable direction. They also bring brilliant, beautiful song to the dusty, dull, and dirty city creating the beauty of nature out of their hearts.

ASSOCIATED PLANTS: Dry weeds of midwinter, anemone, burdock, tonka-bean

ASSOCIATED MINERALS: ordinary pebbles

SPIDER, WATER

Cherokee - kananeski amaiyehi: dilstayati [scissors]: Seminole - tequa

PRIMARY POWERS: powers of fire, thread magic, time

MYTHOLOGY: The water spider succeeded in bringing back the first fire to the People. The fire was on an island and none of the animals found a way to carry it. The spider succeeded by weaving a pocket of her thread in which she hauled coals of fire on her back. The Cherokee also believed that evil conjurors invoked her and used her thread to entangle souls. After the coming of the unega, the Cherokee applied the spider's name to watches and clocks. The Seminole say that tequa had countless children and that she was going to take over all of the great swamp for her own use. When the animals resisted she spun her web round and round so swiftly that it created a great, driving storm - the first hurricane. All the animals were overcome by the storm and driven from their homes except the mud dauber wasp. The wasp hid in her house of mud until the eye of the storm came over it. Then she came out of her safe little house, captured the spider, and fed her to her children.

SPIRITUAL QUALITIES: Kananeski amaiyehi brings the powers of binding and, under the reciprocal tendency of totems, of cutting through bonds. Because of the similarity of her web to the faces of the unega clocks she can also traverse time. Although a water creature, she is associated with the sacred fire.

SQUIRREL

Tree dwelling squirrels: *Tamiasciurus, Sciurus,* and *Glaucomys* families; Ground squirrels: Sciuridae family; Chipmunks: *Tamias* species

Cherokee - salali, tewa, kiyaga [chipmunk]: Algonquian - messanik: Alabaman - iplo: Mobilian - fani

PRIMARY POWERS: provision, husbandry, concern for mankind

ZOOLOGICAL INFORMATION: Most squirrels are diurnal although the flying squirrel is nocturnal. Squirrels eat primarily vegetarian food: leaves, twigs, nuts, and berries. They industriously store food away in secret hiding places - which they frequently forget all about. These hiding places include hollows in trees, miniature caves, and holes in the ground. Quick and nearly invisible, fun loving and noisy at play, the squirrel lives happily beside man (except for the Red Squirrel and the Fox Squirrel which have nearly been exterminated by over-hunting.)

MYTHOLOGY: In Cherokee legend when the Council of Animals met to discuss the eradication of mankind, every animal expressed a grievance against Homo sapiens except the chipmunk. Being so small, man had failed to demonstrate animosity against her. The other animals were outraged by her defense of man. They sprang upon her and tore her with their claws. To this day kiyaga wears on her back the stripes left by their claws.

When the flyers and the four-leggeds met to play a game of ball the flying squirrel (along with the bat) took the side of the birds. In order for her to be able to play as a flyer, squirrel's skin was stretched. With squirrel's help, the wingeds won. The Cherokee attach the skin of the squirrel to their ball equipment to assure victory. Because the squirrel has a hunched posture the Cherokee would not feed its meat to sufferers of rheumatism.

The Ila of Africa call the squirrel the rabbits brother-in-law. They say that squirrel borrowed rabbit's beautiful tail and refused to return it. The squirrel must live in a tree to escape the rabbit. Rabbit was so embarrassed after the loss of his lovely tail he refused to return to live with the other animals.

SPIRITUAL QUALITIES: Powers of the squirrel are provision and husbandry. Provision, in that she stores food away for times of need. In this act of provision, the squirrel becomes the instrument of hokshichankiya, spiritual seed. The nuts and cones buried and forgotten by squirrel have been planted encouraging the regeneration of nature.

ASSOCIATED PLANTS: acorns, other nuts, pine cones

TURTLE

Cherokee - tuksi [land tortoise]: tulanawa [soft shell]: saligugi [water]

PRIMARY POWERS: symbolic of the world; slow, sure power; protection

ZOOLOGICAL INFORMATION: Most turtles

are primarily vegetarian although few species are entirely so. Snapping turtles catch, kill, and eat waterfowl.

MYTHOLOGY: In Cheyenne and other legend the turtle carries the world upon her back. The turtle appears in the World card of the Native American Tarot deck. She beat the rabbit in a foot race by a trick according to the Cherokee. She uses the wolf's ears for a spoon. In retaliation for this the wolf threw the turtle onto a rock in the water and broke her shell. You can still see where it was mended. The turtle was once the thunderer's messenger. When the thunderer's wolf was injured he sent turtle to fetch the healer.

SPIRITUAL QUALITIES: Turtle is used as a focus for the transfer of earth energy to the individual. She offers slow, absolutely sure power and the strong protection of her shell as well as the fluid element of water. A turtle totem bag may be hung over the doorway of a house for protection.

QUARTER IDENTITIES: WEST - Logger-head Turtle NORTH - Box Turtle (Land Tortoise) EAST - Spotted Turtle SOUTH - Painted Turtle SKY/SUN - Snapping Turtle EARTH - Soft-Shell Turtle

ASSOCIATED PLANTS: caraway, pimpernel, dill

WASP, MUD DAUBER

Psammocharidae family

Seminole - tequah quin [spider bane]

PRIMARY POWERS: counteracting spider medicine, general strength

MYTHOLOGY: When tequa, the water spider, decided to take over the swamp for her own children, she spun her web so fast she created the first hurricane. This overwhelmed all the animals except for the mud dauber wasp. She crouched in her hard, strong house of rock-like mud and waited patiently until the center of tequa's web, now known as the calm or eye of the hurricane, spun over her home. At that time she sprang out and stung tequa paralyzing her with poison. The mud dauber then imprisoned the spider in a quartz crystal and placed her in the nest as food for her young. To this day, a quartz crystal with a black phantom mark inside is called by the mud dauber's name: tequa-quin, spider bane.

SPIRITUAL QUALITIES: Counteraction of iktomi [negative spider] medicine; quick-striking power

to paralyze enemies; security of home; provision; general strength. If oppressed by negative spider or iktomi medicine, carry a tequa quin crystal or stone - or a mud dauber's nest.

ASSOCIATED MINERALS: Quartz crystal with a black inclusion

WOLF

Canis lupus, C. niger

Cherokee - waya

PRIMARY POWERS: omens applying to travel and war

ZOOLOGICAL INFORMATION: The unega have pushed the wolf into a tiny, tiny portion of his original range. He is almost entirely carnivorous. He is a pack animal and rarely lives alone.

SPIRITUAL QUALITIES: Wolf medicine produces the reciprocal omen to crow medicine. It provides omens applicable to moving about, traveling, and going to war.

ASSOCIATED PLANTS: wolf-bane (aconite), marigold, hops, ash

THE WORLD OF GREEN
The Vegetable Kingdom Totems

There are two methods of meditating with the totems of the vegetable kingdom. The first is much like the cat meditation in the last chapter. To do this sort of meditation visualize your body assuming the form and being of the plant. Grow bark, leaves, flowers, and fruit. The second method of communicating with one of the plant totems is to place yourself quite close to a member of the species you wish to contact. Allow the plant to become the focus of your mind. Either way your concentration will allow the plant to speak to you.

PINE TREE MEDITATION

Select your location. Walk around the area mentally pushing away from that place all confusion, negativity - all the ordinary world. Take your chosen position for meditation and notice all around you. Touch the ground, or floor, to balance yourself and honor Grandmother Earth.

> O Earth Mother, my heart, O brightest Queen,
> Cast your blessings unto me.
> I am your child, you are my mother,
> So come be with me.
>
> You are my provider, you give me strength,
> Earth Mother inspire me.
> O All Mother, O Earth Mother, O my mother
> Come Close to me.

Acknowledge and/or invoke the nature spirits, the emissaries of the four directions, the sky, and the earth Call on the powers of enlightenment and wisdom of your totem bag. Make an offering of incense or tobacco.

> Come
> Come from the world beyond
> Come and reach to me
> Come and teach me. (four times)

Feel your toes reaching into the earth and forming long, strong fibrous roots. Let your roots reach deep, deep into the Earth Mother. Your body is slowly being covered with strong plates of bark. Your skin is dry, hard, and rough. Your arms are becoming limbs and are reaching way up into the sky. They too are covered with bark but it is much smoother than the bark on your body. Your fingers turn into millions of soft green needles.

Feel the wind pass through the needles. They flutter in the breeze. A blue jay perches on one of your high branches and calls. Squirrels run up and down your bark.

Rain falls around you and turns to snow. All the other trees have lost their lovely green leaves. Your needles are the only color in the snow. All the forest is asleep except you. You hold your head high above all the other trees and watch as you have been told.

The sun comes up in the east and casts your shadow against the clouds of the west. Watch the shadow and see what it has to tell you. Watch for danger or evil in your life. Ask the pine how to guard yourself against it.

Spring has come and you begin to wake up. Your needles turn back into fingers and you get very, very short. The bark falls off your body and it is human again. Your roots draw up into your legs and are again feet. You can move, breathe, and speak.

In closing your meditation thank the entities you called upon at the beginning. Touch your hands and your totem bag to the ground to release excess energy. Center your self within your human body.

Find yourself in balance between all the forces. End your meditation with this song:

> I walk with wisdom
> from this hallowed place.
>
> I walk with knowledge
> from this hallowed place
>
> I walk in balance,
> not in haste

THE VEGETABLE KINGDOM TOTEMS

AMARANTH

Amaranthus hypochondriacus, A. spp.

OTHER COMMON NAMES: Love-lies-Bleeding, Red Cockscomb, Velvet Flower, Strawberry Blite

Aztec: huauhtli (Flower of Immortality)

PRIMARY POWERS: healing heartache, calling forth dead ancestors, burial rites, protection from bullets

MYTHOLOGY: It is an herb of awahili, the eagle. The Blackfoot placed it in medicine bundles worn over the breast to protect from bullets. Central American Indians used it to call forth dead ancestors. In European mythology it conferred invisibility, called forth the dead, and promoted harmony. It was sacred to the Goddess Artemis and to the Horned God.

MEDICINAL EFFECTS: Astringent, diaphoretic, diuretic, emmenagogue, stimulant, bitter tonic, vesicant.

USED IN THE FOLLOWING ILLNESSES: dysentery, diarrhea, excessive menses, ulcers, intestinal bleeding, skin problems, sore throat

SPIRITUAL QUALITIES: Used to place one in touch with the ancestors. It is an herb of Saturn and relates to fire and receptive energies. It is used in love divination.

RITUAL OR CEREMONIAL USES: Wear or place in medicine bundle for protection and/or harmony. Use in rituals honoring the ancestors or when attempting to contact the ancestors. Use at handfastings (weddings) and in protective amulets for an individual or dwelling.

CAUTIONS: the seeds of some species are mildly poisonous as they contain saponin.

CEDAR

Thuja spp.

OTHER COMMON NAMES: Tree of Life, Arbor Vitae, White Cedar, Red Cedar, Western Cedar

Cherokee: atsina

PRIMARY POWERS: Purification, banishing evil spirits and negative atmosphere

MYTHOLOGY: The most sacred tree of the Cherokee. Ghosts are thought to be unable to endure the smell. Cedar was never used as fuel. Trophies were hung upon it. The red of the wood is said to be the blood of an evil magician who died when he touched the tree. In European tradition it is an herb of the Sun with active energy and affinity to fire.

MEDICINAL EFFECTS: aromatic, astringent, diuretic, abortifacient (dangerous as it causes extreme irritation), heart stimulant, emmenagogue

USED IN THE FOLLOWING ILLNESSES: intermittent fevers, rheumatism, dropsy, coughs, scurvy, warts

SPIRITUAL QUALITIES: Cedar is an extremely powerful protective herb. Use as an incense, in smudging mixtures, or hang in the home to guard against lightning and to protect against evil. It is also used to draw money. In incense it increases psychic powers. It is an herb of the plant Pluto and of the Sun; its season is winter.

RITUAL OR CEREMONIAL USES: Practically always an ingredient of smudging mixtures. The needles or branches are frequently used in sweat lodges.

ASSOCIATED MINERALS: Sapphire

CAUTIONS: Oil of cedar is quite dangerous and should not be used on the skin or in anything to be ingested.

CONE FLOWER

Echinacea augustifolia, E. spp.

OTHER COMMON NAMES: Black Sampson

Cherokee: ahawi akata (deer eye)

PRIMARY POWERS: offering to the nunahe

MYTHOLOGY: strengthens magickal workings.

MEDICINAL EFFECTS: analgesic, antibiotic, antiphlogistic, antiseptic, depurative, exanthematous, sudorific, bitter tonic, stimulates the immune system.

USED IN THE FOLLOWING ILLNESSES: poisonous bites, toothaches, enlarged glands, headache, blood purifier, infections, old and new wounds, boils, stimulates immune system (cancer, aids). The Cherokee used it for flux (diarrhea), venereal disease, snake bite, eye infections and as a wash for swellings

SPIRITUAL QUALITIES: Use as an offering to the surrounding spirits and ancestors encouraging them to increase the power and effectiveness of your medicine work.

RITUAL OR CEREMONIAL USES: include in

medicine bag or offer through fire or water.

CORN

Zea maise

OTHER COMMON NAMES: Maize, Indian Corn, Corn Mother, Corn Grandmother, The Old Woman

Cherokee: selu (commonly) agawela, old woman (ceremonial usage)

PRIMARY POWERS: banish negativity, aid in divination, bring luck, plenty, protection, attract money or rain. Used in birthing magick. MYTHOLOGY: Most tribes of Indians in North and South America depended upon corn as their major food. Every tribe had many myths about the gift of the first corn. Each had one or more especially sacred ceremonies celebrating the planting and harvesting of the corn (see Chapter 4). The Cherokee Green Corn Dance was the most sacred ceremony of the year. They planted 7 grains of corn to each hill and did not thin it.

MEDICINAL EFFECTS: diuretic, mild stimulant, emollient

USED IN THE FOLLOWING ILLNESSES: ulcers, swellings, rheumatic pains, nausea. Excellent diet for convalescents.

SPIRITUAL QUALITIES: Corn grants luck and plenty. It is used for protection and in some divination spells. It is an herb of Venus and is sympathetic with the element of earth. Its energy is receptive. RITUAL OR CEREMONIAL USES: Corn meal may be scattered as an offering. It protects you from negative forces. Red corncobs are burned to aid a difficult birth.

DOGWOOD

Cornus amomum

OTHER COMMON NAMES: Red American Osier, Swamp Dogwood, Red Willow, Silky Cornel, Female Dogwood, Blueberry, Kinnikinnik, Rose Willow, Boxwood, Budwood, Dogtree, Blueberry Cornell, Red brush, Squaw Bush

Cherokee: kanunsita

PRIMARY POWERS: granting wishes, protection, banishing negative energies

MEDICINAL EFFECTS: Antiperiodic, appetizer, diaphoretic, vulnerary

USED IN THE FOLLOWING ILLNESSES: typhoid, elevated temperature, tooth powder to whiten teeth and make gums more healthy. The Cherokee used it with other herbs to treat a disease called; "something is causing something to eat him".

SPIRITUAL QUALITIES: Cornel is another of the kinnikinnik herbs and as such would posses the qualities of attracting good energies and repelling negative energies.

RITUAL OR CEREMONIAL USES: The dry bark is added to smudging and/or smoking mixtures

CAUTIONS: Should be used dry only. The fresh green bark may upset the stomach

GINSENG

Panax quinquefolius

OTHER COMMON NAMES: Five Fingers, Tartar Root, Red Berry, Man's Health, Cure All,

Cherokee - atali kuli (commonly) [the mountain climber] - yunwi usdi (ceremonial) [little man] - yunwi usdiga adawehiyu [most powerful magician]

PRIMARY POWERS: Love, health, sexual potency, banishing and exorcism, beauty, breaking spells, protection, granting wishes, image magick

MYTHOLOGY: The Cherokee considered the ginseng plant a sentient being. They would pass up the first three plants found, give an offering to the fourth and take it as needed.

MEDICINAL EFFECTS: stimulant, tonic

USED IN THE FOLLOWING ILLNESSES: Take daily to counteract stress. It may help prevent colds and is of some utility in maintaining good health. The Cherokee used it for headache, cramps and female troubles.

SPIRITUAL QUALITIES: For protection and is an aid to powerful medicine. It is an herb of the Sun with active energy and affinity to fire.

RITUAL OR CEREMONIAL USES: Carry as a protective amulet or offer to spirits to increase medicine power.

CAUTIONS: Ginseng is rare and shouldn't be gathered from the wild

JIMSON WEED

Datura spp.

OTHER COMMON NAMES: Datura, Devil's Apple, Ghost Flower, Love-Will, Mad Apple, Madherb, Manicon, Stinkweed, Sorcerer's Herb, Thornapple, Toloache, Witches' Thimble, Yerba del Diablo, Devil's Trumpet, Apple of Peru

Southwestern Indian: momoy

PRIMARY POWERS: visionary, one of the shaman's herbs

MYTHOLOGY: The datura is the old woman who lived before the flood. She gives of her great knowledge to those who drink part of her bath water or eat of her bones.

MEDICINAL EFFECTS: analgesic, antispasmodic, narcotic, vulnerary

USED IN THE FOLLOWING ILLNESSES: asthma, boils, epilepsy, neuralgia

SPIRITUAL QUALITIES: This herb is of receptive energy, and is sympathetic to the element water, it is an herb of Saturn. It is used in European tradition in hex-breaking, sleep, and protection.

RITUAL OR CEREMONIAL USES: Datura is one of the herbs which are used by that minority of Indians who employ mind altering drugs in their visionary practice. It is extremely dangerous. A great deal of preparation must be undertaken before its use. Never use it unless under the direction of an extremely qualified person.

CAUTIONS: Extremely poisonous

MULLEIN

Verbascum thapsus

OTHER COMMON NAMES: Torches, Our Lady's Flannel, Velvet Dock, Blanket Herb, Velvet Plant, Woolen, Rag Paper, Candlewick Plant, Wild Ice Leaf, Clown's Lungwort, Bullock's Lungwort, Aaron's Rod, Jupiter's Staff, Golden Rod, Adam's Flannel, Beggar's Blanket, Clot, Cuddy's Lungs, Duffle, Feltwort, Fluffweed, Hare's Beard, Old Man's Flannel, Hag's Taper, Graveyard Dust, Hedge Taper, Lady's Foxglove, Peter's Staff, Velvetback

Cherokee: tsaliyusti (means like tobacco)

PRIMARY POWERS: exorcism, courage, healing, love divination, protection

MYTHOLOGY: The witches of Europe are said to have used this plant for candle wicks. It has the power of driving away evil spirits. It is the plant which Ulysses used to protect himself against Circe.

MEDICINAL EFFECTS: antiphlogistic, demulcent, expectorant, pulmonary

USED IN THE FOLLOWING ILLNESSES: chest colds, bronchitis, asthma, inflammations, ear problems

SPIRITUAL QUALITIES: Mullein is an herb of Jupiter with receptive energies. It is sympathetic to the element of fire. It is used to bring sleep, to protect travelers, for courage, fertility, general protection, and as a substitute for graveyard dust.

RITUAL OR CEREMONIAL USES: Carry in a medicine bag for protection and courage particularly in the wilds (good to take on a vision quest). Place around house for protection. Can be added to smudge for protection. Can also be added to smoking mixtures.

ASSOCIATED MINERALS: Jasper

ASSOCIATED ANIMALS: Bear, duck, eagle, raven, red hawk, sheep, mudjekeewis, the Ducks Fly Moon

CAUTIONS: The seeds contain a small amount of a narcotic substance and should not be ingested, made into an oil to be rubbed on the skin, burned, or smoked.

OAK

Quercus spp.

OTHER COMMON NAMES: Tanner's Bark, Duir, Jove's Nuts

Cherokee: ataya, aya - principal wood

PRIMARY POWERS: protection, luck, healing, longevity

MYTHOLOGY: The acorn, gule, was a principal food of the eastern tribes. A fire of post oak and summer grape will bring a spell of warm weather even in the cold of winter according to the Cherokee. In European mythology it is strongly connected with the Druids of England, Wales, and Ireland. It is said to be the wood from which the round table was constructed. The Greeks and Romans also held the oak sacred.

MEDICINAL EFFECTS: astringent, homeostatic, vulnerary, nutrient, tonic

USED IN THE FOLLOWING ILLNESSES: to stop bleeding, as a substitute for quinine, diarrhea, dysentery, bleeding gums, and hemorrhoids.

SPIRITUAL QUALITIES: The oak represents impressive spiritual qualities in itself for its strength, resiliency (a combination of qualities found in no other wood), and ability to grow to great age. It is used to bring luck, fertility and healing, to achieve immortality (or at least longevity), to increase sexual potency and maintain good health, to gain wealth, and to recover youth. It is an important protective herb. It is an herb of the Sun, of active energies and is in sympathy with the element of fire. It is connected with a number of European Deities including, Dagda, Dianus, Jupiter, Thor, Zeus, Herne, Janus, Rhea, Cybele, Hecate, Pan, Erato, Odin and Blodeuwedd, Apollo, Hercules, Cerridwen, and Cernnunnos.

RITUAL OR CEREMONIAL USES: The following directional identifications help in communing or requesting the help of the oak totem: West, Water Oak; North, Overcup Oak; East, Scarlet Oak; South, Red Oak; Sun, Blackjack Oak; Earth, Post Oak

CAUTIONS: Almost all acorns contain too much tannin to be edible without special leaching procedures.

PINE

Pinus spp.
Cherokee: natsi
PRIMARY POWERS: unsleeping guardianship, problem solving

MYTHOLOGY: The Cherokee say that once Galunlati told all the trees to watch over the world. Most of the trees finally dozed off. The pine and a few other trees stayed awake and maintained their watch. As a punishment, all other trees must drop their beautiful leaves and sleep for part of the year while natsi keeps watch.

MEDICINAL EFFECTS: rubefacient, diuretic, irritant

USED IN THE FOLLOWING ILLNESSES: bladder, kidney and rheumatic afflictions, diseases of the mucous membrane, respiratory complaints

SPIRITUAL QUALITIES: Cleansing, exorcism, fertility, happiness, healing, longevity, protection, wealth, spell reversing, visions, answers

RITUAL OR CEREMONIAL USES: Burn as incense or smudge (either the needles, bark, or resin) to banish evil emanations. Drink of the pine sap to aid visions (since the pine is tall and can see all). Lean against the trunk when perplexed. The pine will whisper the answer. The pine is sacred to Poseidon, Cybele, Pan, Enus, Attis, Dionysus, Astarte, Sylvanus. It is an herb of Mars with active energy, sympathetic with the element of air. A pine cone, gathered on midsummer eve, with the seeds inside, is a very powerful magickal item. A pine outside your door, or a pine branch over the door, will watch out for evil spirits while you sleep.

ASSOCIATED MINERALS: amber
ASSOCIATED ANIMALS: woodpecker

SAGEBRUSH

Artemisia spp.
OTHER COMMON NAMES: Red Sage
PRIMARY POWERS: purification, healing, cleansing

MYTHOLOGY: This sage is not the same as the sage of European tradition. Western sage is the preferred cleansing herb of the plains Indians. Garden sage is an acceptable substitute.

MEDICINAL EFFECTS: analgesic, antiemetic, astringent, carminative, vulnerary, stomachic

USED IN THE FOLLOWING ILLNESSES: colds, headache, diarrhea, sore throat, eye problems

SPIRITUAL QUALITIES: Primarily used as a purifying ingredient in rituals. Artemisias are useful as meditation aids.

RITUAL OR CEREMONIAL USES: Use in the sweat lodge, perhaps spread all over the floor, and in smudging or pipe mixtures.

ASSOCIATED ANIMALS: toads

CAUTIONS: It isn't wise to use a great deal of any Artemisia as its effects become unpredictable and frequently unpleasant if a lot is inhaled or ingested

SASSAFRAS

Sassafras albidum
OTHER COMMON NAMES: Ague tree, Saxifrax, Cinnamon Wood, Salop
Cherokee: kunstutsi [green wood]
PRIMARY POWERS: healing, increasing medicine power, love, wealth

MYTHOLOGY: The Cherokee never burned sassafras. Strangely enough, the root bark of sassafras was the first major cash crop for the Europeans in Turtle Island and thus had a great deal to do with the success of many of the early settlements.

MEDICINAL EFFECTS: antiperiodic, antiphlogistic, antiseptic, carminative, diuretic, febrifuge, aromatic, flavoring, stimulant, diaphoretic, alterative

USED IN THE FOLLOWING ILLNESSES: pain caused by menstrual obstructions and following parturition, rheumatism, syphilis, gonorrhea, and skin diseases.

SPIRITUAL QUALITIES: Sassafras is an herb of Jupiter with active energies sympathetic to the element of fire.

RITUAL OR CEREMONIAL USES: The root bark makes a wonderful tea. The finely powdered root bark is an excellent addition to sachets. It may be added to smudging and smoking mixtures in small amounts.

CAUTIONS: The FDA, having tested a chemical compound extracted from sassafras bark (one which cannot be produced by home methods) found that in great quantities it can cause cancer, has forbidden all sale of the bark for human consumption.

TOBACCO

Nicotiana tabacum, N. rustica
OTHER COMMON NAMES: Tabacca
Cherokee - tsalu: The wild plant, N. rustica is called tsalagayunli [old tobacco]: Tuscarora - charhu [fire to hold in the mouth]

PRIMARY POWERS: banishing negativity, communicating with the unseen

MYTHOLOGY: Most tribes, including the Cherokee, have a story about the time that tobacco was stolen by one of the four-leggeds or wingeds. It was finally rescued and returned to the people although in the process a number of animals tried and fail. All the myths emphasize the value of the herb to the people.

MEDICINAL EFFECTS: local irritant, sialagogue, expectorant, antiseptic, sedative, diuretic, discutient, emetic

USED IN THE FOLLOWING ILLNESSES: Tobacco is very rarely used as a medicinal at this time. Because its poisonous qualities are difficult to judge, its use is dangerous.

SPIRITUAL QUALITIES: The use of tobacco as a medium of communication with the unseen worlds and beings cannot be overemphasized. Its sacredness to the Indians is impossible to overestimate. In modern times you can observe a traditional Indian quietly gesturing to the four directions with a cigarette before settling down to smoke it. Tobacco is used in smudging mixtures as well as in the pipe. It is also frequently offered unburned either in small pinches or bundled neatly and colorfully as tobacco ties. Tobacco is an herb of Mars with active energies and sympathy with the element of fire. It is sacred to the Great Mystery, Galunlati, in all forms.

RITUAL OR CEREMONIAL USES: Endless: add to smudging mixtures, smoking mixtures; as offerings in pinches or in tobacco ties. A small bundle is often tied to a present such as a bow. Throw into a river to communicate with or thank river spirits. It not only puts you in touch with the sacred, it purifies the area and you.

ASSOCIATED MINERALS: catlinite, pipestone
ASSOCIATED ANIMALS: goose
CAUTIONS: Nicotine is a poison, particularly in a tea or decoction. Never make or use an oil of tobacco as it can quickly go through the skin. As a drug nicotine has some very good effects but the side effects are all too well known. It is at its least dangerous when burned.

WILLOW

Salix alba, S. spp.
OTHER COMMON NAMES: Osier, Pussy Willow, Saille, Salicyn Willow, Saugh Tree, Tree of Enchantment, White Willow, Witches' Asprin, Withe, Withy.

Chippewa — ozisigobimic
PRIMARY POWERS: Banishing negativity, healing, love attraction, communicating with spirits

MYTHOLOGY: In England burial sites were frequently planted with willow. It is a wood frequently used for magick wands. Willow bark is burned to aid in communicating with spirits.

MEDICINAL EFFECTS: Antiseptic, astringent, disinfectant, febrifuge, anodyne

USED IN THE FOLLOWING ILLNESSES: The bark of the willow contains a chemical called salicin - a form of salicylic acid or aspirin. It is used as a decoction in all the ways aspirin generally is used: to relieve pain, for insomnia, colds, rheumatism, dysentery, dyspepsia, etc. Many people find it easier on their stomachs than commercial aspirin although note that many also find it more irritating. There is little argument that it tastes really terrible.

SPIRITUAL QUALITIES: Willow is an herb of the Moon of receptive energies and sympathetic with the element of water. In European traditions it is linked with the following Deity figures; Artemis, Ceres, Hecate, Persephone, Hera, Mercury, Belili, Belinus, Orpheus, Hermes.

RITUAL OR CEREMONIAL USES: It is used as an incense at funerals and as an aid in communication with spirits or nunahe. It may be used in a smudging mixture or in very small quantities in a smoking mixture.

CAUTIONS: Precautions suitable for commercial aspirin should be observed.

YARROW

Achillea millefolium

OTHER COMMON NAMES: Achillea, Arrowroot, Bad Man's Plaything, Carpenter's Weed, Death Flower, Devil's Nettle, Eerie, Field Hops, Gearwe, Hundred Leaved Grass, Knight's Milfoil, Knyghten, Lady's Mantle, Milfoil, Militaris, Military Herb, Millefolium, Noble Yarrow, Nosebleed, Old Man's Mustard, Old Man's Pepper, Sanguinary, Seven Year's Love, Snake's Grass, Soldier's Woundwort, Stanch Grass, Stanch Weed, Tansy, Thousand Seal, Woundwort, Yarroway, Yerwe, Nose Bleed, Bloodwort, Staunchweed, Devil's Plaything,

Ojibwa - wabeno-wusk; plant of the eastern dawn

PRIMARY POWERS: strengthening psychic powers, courage, friendship

MYTHOLOGY: Said to be the plant with which Achilles stanched the wounds of his soldiers. It has a long history as a wound herb. It is frequently used in divination. I Ching sticks are made of yarrow stalks.

MEDICINAL EFFECTS: antidontalgic, referigerant, antiphlogistic, astringent, homeostatic, febrifuge, bitter tonic, vulnerary

USED IN THE FOLLOWING ILLNESSES: urinary problems, head colds, wounds, toothache, blood purification

SPIRITUAL QUALITIES: Yarrow is an herb of Venus and has receptive energies sympathetic to the element of water. It's qualities include courage, love attraction, increase of psychic powers, divination, and exorcism.

RITUAL OR CEREMONIAL USES: Add to smudge to help diminish a negative atmosphere or to bring in a more loving one. Also use when divination is to be done. Carry in medicine bag for courage and/or to banish negativity.

ASSOCIATED MINERALS: agate

ASSOCIATED ANIMALS: awahili, the eagle; Cornplanting Moon; deer

THE SHINING STONES, THE CHANGELESS ROCKS

The Mineral Kingdom Totems

You may find the totems of the mineral kingdom more difficult to reach in meditation than animal and plant totems. The following meditation should help you in your first attempt at this communication.

THE STANDING STONE

It once stood as a sentinel at the edge of the Cumberland Plateau of Tennessee. An old standing stone called the Wolf by the Cherokee and Shawnee who hunted the land. The stone itself is gone, but you may see with its eyes.

Select your location. Walk around the area mentally pushing away from that place all confusion, negativity - all the ordinary world. Take your chosen position for meditation and notice all around you. Touch the ground or floor to balance yourself and honor Grandmother Earth.

> O Earth Mother, my heart, O brightest Queen,
> Cast your blessings unto me.
> I am your child, you are my mother,
> So come be with me.
> You are my provider, you give me strength,
> Earth Mother inspire me.
> O All Mother, O Earth Mother, O my mother
> Come Close to me.

Acknowledge and/or invoke the nature spirits, the emissaries of the four cardinal directions, the sky and the mother of four-leggeds. Call on the powers of enlightenment and wisdom contained in your totem bag. Make an offering of incense or tobacco.

> Come
> come from the world beyond
> Come and reach to me
> Come and teach me. (four times)

Let yourself grow extremely still. Your outside is hard. The sun strikes on the grainy surface but cannot warm you. At your center is peaceful coolness. You stand tall on the edge of a cliff. A highway below you disappears. Trees grow in its place leaving only a faint trail. Untidy wagons go by and disappear; men on horses ride by and are gone. Soon only red bodies of the People may be seen slipping silently through the trees.

You see the seasons pass. The sun, the wind, the rain, and the snow hardly affect you. The land begins to sink; the waters of the seas rise over the land. The time of beginnings is approaching. You feel yourself getting younger and younger. Soon you are far, far under the water. The sand of which you were made begins to separate into separate grains. Soon you are floating in a billion separate grains through the primeval sea.

Reflected on the water you can see a message to the life of the earth. Read the message and reflect on it as long as you wish. You have all time.

Slowly let your grains come back together. Beneath the unimaginable pressure of the waters you become hard and whole. The waters run off you; you are thrust again high on the cliff. Let your body soften and warm. Let movement again make itself felt within you. Feel your breath moving; feel your heart beating. Find your arms and legs within your solid form.

In closing your meditation thank the entities you called upon at the beginning. Touch your hands and your totem bag to the ground to release excess energy. Center your self within your human body. Find yourself in balance between all the forces. End your meditation with this song:

> I walk with wisdom
> from this hallowed place.
> I walk with knowledge
> from this hallowed place
> I walk in balance,
> not in haste

THE MINERAL KINGDOM TOTEMS
AGATE

COMPOSITION: A variety of quartz so minutely developed that it does not mature crystals. The general group is called chalcedony. It includes onyx, carnelian, sard, chrysoprase, bloodstone, jasper, and flint.

COLOR, DESCRIPTION: Banded, spotted or filled with fernlike designs. It is variegated in color with curved, multi-colored stripes. It also comes in solid white, brown, and red. The agatized patterns are caused by gas bubbles in the liquid magma which leave spaces for colored fluid silicon compounds to fill. This process creates whorls, ridges, eyes, circles, and crosses which mirror the symbolic archetypes of a particular stone's inherent power.

PRIMARY POWERS: works with fire and air; aid to meditation and seeing; deepens powers of concentration; is an aid to achievement of spiritual balance.

MYTHOLOGY: Associated with Shiva the destroyer and Vulcan the Smith God. Worn to placate the gods; illuminate the mind; bestow eloquence; give courage; assist in the discovery of treasures; and attract inheritances. It can calm storms and avert tempests. It can keep its wearer from licentiousness, making him serious and well-balanced. In Mexico dog heads were carved from agate and buried with the dead to keep them strong and wakeful. It is recommended for guarding against lightning, scorpion stings, and rain. It promotes childbirth and makes a person loveable. It grants an even temperament and acceptance of circumstances.

HEALING POWERS: Poison antidote; aids the circulatory system; is good for the excretory system and related organs; gum disease; and helps the body to utilize calcium.

RITUAL OR CEREMONIAL USES: Use on headband to aid in meditation. Wear as an amulet to guard against afflictions, particularly against snake bite; paralysis; mental illness; epilepsy; and the plague. Use in ritual to prevent storms.

ASSOCIATED ANIMALS: dog, lion, snake

ASSOCIATED PLANTS: ferns, moss (in moss agate)

QUARTER IDENTITY: west or according to color.

ASTROLOGICAL AFFINITY: Mars, Sun, Mercury, Saturn and Pluto depending upon color, etc.

AMETHYST

COMPOSITION: A form of quartz crystal.

COLOR, DESCRIPTION: The color is provided by manganese oxide, iron, titanium, and other metals. Colors range from lilac to purple. They are transparent.

PRIMARY POWERS: peace of mind, sobriety, control of passions, spiritual attunement.

MYTHOLOGY: The word, amethyst, comes from a Greek derivative which means "not intoxicating". The stone was set in goblets for this purpose. It promotes wittiness; wisdom; humility; philanthropy; friendship; a good memory; love and worship of the Great Spirit; meditation and creative thinking; clarity in prophecy; and interpretation of dreams. If worn to bed it promotes sleep and brings good dreams. Protects against hatred, rage, fear, grief, and homesickness It promotes good judgement, justice, courage, and spiritual attunement.

HEALING POWERS: Prevention of intoxication, poisoning, sterility, and absent-mindedness. Protection against blood and venereal diseases, neuralgia, hysteria, and fits. It disinfects adverse conditions of the central nervous system. It combats insomnia and skin impurities.

RITUAL OR CEREMONIAL USES: Use it for soul-cleansing and spiritual ennoblement. Wear on headband for meditation. Carry when fishing to improve catch. Encourages the growth of plant roots.

QUARTER IDENTITY: north.

ASTROLOGICAL AFFINITY: Neptune, Jupiter, Mercury, and Pisces.

APATITE

COMPOSITION: Calcium phosphate with some fluorine. It occurs in veins with quartz, feldspar, and iron ores.

COLOR, DESCRIPTION: Apatite gets its name from a Greek derivative meaning "to deceive" due to its resemblance to many other minerals. It comes in green, brown, greenish yellow, purple, and blue.

PRIMARY POWERS: clearing mental confusion; stability.

RITUAL OR CEREMONIAL USES: Place on third eye (or on a headband) as an aid to clearing confusion from mental stratas. It will allow you to think more clearly and make more intelligent decisions in a variety of situations. It promotes stability in many different environments.

QUARTER IDENTITY: east
ASTROLOGICAL AFFINITY: Mercury

BLOODSTONE, HELIOTROPE

COMPOSITION: One of the cryptocrystalline forms of quartz generally called chalcedony.

COLOR, DESCRIPTION: Bloodstone is green with red spots which resemble drops of blood.

PRIMARY POWERS: mental balance, peace, concentration, aid in childbirth.

MYTHOLOGY: One of the sacred stones of Atlantis. It has a reverse force-field and can emit directly into a physical vehicle. It gives peace in the emotional and physical realms. It has the ability to vitalize brain tissue and to keep oxygen circulating as it pours iron into the etheric body or web. It purifies body, mind, and spirit. It is useful in grounding earth energies. Under a pillow it induces visionary dreams. It strengthens the will to do good and to offer oneself as an instrument of the divine spirit. In ancient times it was polished as a mirror in which to watch eclipses of the sun. It resonates to earth energies.

HEALING POWERS: Stops bleeding, helps heal wounds. Use during pregnancy and childbirth. When worn on the left arm it is believed to prevent miscarriage. Worn on the right arm it promotes ease in delivery.

RITUAL OR CEREMONIAL USES: Wear as an amulet to bring fame; long life; and to promote wisdom. Place under pillow for prophetic dreams.

QUARTER IDENTITY: north
ASTROLOGICAL AFFINITY: Pluto and Mars

CHRYSOPHRASE

COMPOSITION: A cryptocrystaline form of quartz in the chalcedony family.

COLOR, DESCRIPTION: Green

PRIMARY POWERS: Invoking fire, clarifying problems, encouraging hope, strengthening insight.

MYTHOLOGY: Used to invoke the Goddess Vesta and to give the user control and understanding of fire. It contains healing lore. It protects the

wearer from ill health. During the middle ages it was used as a cure for restlessness, making the wearer quick witted and adaptable. It gives protection during sea voyages.

HEALING POWERS: General healing, especially of the digestive tract. Specifically it can prevent ulcers and cancer due to karma. It prevents emotional congestion.

RITUAL OR CEREMONIAL USES: Use in working with fire; to promote calm; and for general good health.

QUARTER IDENTITY: south
ASTROLOGICAL AFFINITY: Uranus, Moon, Venus, and Saturn

CRYSTAL

COMPOSITION: Oxide of silicon, the parent of many stones: smoky quartz, cairngorm, rose quartz, tiger's eye, and amethyst.

COLOR, DESCRIPTION: Quartz crystals or rock crystals are clear in color. Some have inclusions of various colors.

PRIMARY POWERS: strengthens intuitive powers. The ulunsuti or igaguti crystal of the Cherokee is a clear crystal with a blood-red streak running from top to bottom. It is a very great talisman and source of medicine power.

MYTHOLOGY: To the Cherokee this crystal was the horn or third eye of the uktena, the sometimes winged snake or dragon. Perfectly clear crystals, called ulunsu, were the scales of this beast. The ulunsuti, which contains a blood-red streak, is kept in a secret place preferably a cave. It is wrapped in deerskin and placed inside a sealed jar. It must be fed with blood every seven days unless put to sleep. It will cause sudden death if any but the owner comes close. According to legend these stones were buried with the owner at death. (Don't ask us how you found them or were able to approach them. Perhaps the death of the owner broke the protection.) These stones are used for prophecy — as quartz crystals have been used by many cultures throughout many ages. Quartz has the ability to convert physical energy into electrical energy and visa versa. These physical abilities are transferred into the psychic realm. Quartz crystal is in harmony with all the elements: earth, air, fire, water, and spirit; with all 7 directions;

and all the powers.

HEALING POWERS: Crystal is used as an amplifier of healing energies regardless of the disease.

RITUAL OR CEREMONIAL USES: Both the ulunsuti and the ulunsu are valuable psychic energy amplifiers and are used for an absolute multitude of purposes. The ulunsuti is particularly helpful in any sort of divination.

ASSOCIATED ANIMALS: uktena, dragon

QUARTER IDENTITY: north, sky

ASTROLOGICAL AFFINITY: Just about everything: Moon, Mercury, Cancer, Uranus, Sun

FLUORITE

COMPOSITION: Calcium Fluoride

COLOR, DESCRIPTION: Fluorite comes in nearly every color: blue, sea-green, brown, purple, clear, plum, and rose. It consists of crystals in an angular configuration.

PRIMARY POWERS: energy grounding, strengthening, warding off negativity.

MYTHOLOGY: The Cherokee believe that crystals with brownish blemishes have the power of the thunders and call it uk'denok. They carry the crystal in a bag of antelope hide. Fluorites ground excessive energies and help you operate at optimum efficiency. Purple strengthens influences while other colors phase them out. When used with copper or silver fluorite becomes a transmuting agent.

RITUAL OR CEREMONIAL USES: Carry purple stone to use as a strengthener in all situations where courage, enthusiasm, or motivation are needed. Use in meditations to rid yourself of adverse influences. Place with a coin for strong transmutational powers. Carry colors other than purple to ward off negativity.

QUARTER IDENTITY: west

ASTROLOGICAL AFFINITY: thunders

JADE

COMPOSITION: One of two minerals, jadeite or nephrite. Jadite is a pyroxene, a mineral formed at very high temperature. It is a silicate with many other constituents. Nephrite, called true jade, is a type of amphibole and is a complex silicate.

COLOR, DESCRIPTION: While jade is thought of as green, it comes in black, blue, brown, lavender, red, white, and yellow.

PRIMARY POWERS: Mercy, courage, justice, wisdom, and modesty. It is the patron stone of gardeners.

MYTHOLOGY: Jade is a link between the arcane and mundane. It is said to aid in longevity due to its yang or vital masculine principle. It is the special stone of the herbalist. Disks of white jade, pierced in the center, were used by the emperors of China to communicate with heaven. The Chinese had six ritual uses of jade each utilizing a different color. Jade can be used to help hasten sending negativity back to its origins. It has been used to make weapons in Central Europe, Alaska, Mexico, and Ireland as well as in the Orient. The Mayans carved jadite for burial offerings.

HEALING POWERS: It soothes the nervous system through the liver making it very healing to the emotions. It prolongs life; helps in childbirth; protects from accidents; promotes a large family; is said to cure kidney disease; aids in the passing of kidney-stones; and keeps ones eyesight in good shape.

RITUAL OR CEREMONIAL USES: Use to dispel negativity and promote clearing vibrations. Use as a consciousness raiser in groups. It will establish links among all mental layers increasing intelligence.

QUARTER IDENTITY: north

ASTROLOGICAL AFFINITY: Scorpio, Venus, Moon, Neptune, water signs, 5th house, Venus or Mars in Libra, Taurus

MOONSTONE

COMPOSITION: calcium sulfate, a transparent form of gypsum. Called adularia and selenite.

COLOR, DESCRIPTION: A pearly-blue, semi-transparent, opalescent stone

PRIMARY POWERS: Happiness, health, good fortune, companionship, energy channeling, inner growth.

MYTHOLOGY: Moonstone is said to be connected to the heart and emotional bodies in the astral realms. It is associated with the changing of the moon. It is the symbol of the third eye.

HEALING POWERS: It stimulates the pineal gland lessening a tendency to over-react to emotional and personal situations. It will deal with mild endocrine imbalances in women. Protects against dropsy.

RITUAL OR CEREMONIAL USES: Wear to help in channeling healing energy. Use to dispel internal fear, particularly fears of the night and the darkness of the unknown. Wear to strengthen psychic abilities. Take care of it for it scratches easily. When held in the mouth things which should be done are more clearly impressed upon the conscious mind. During the waxing moon it favors consumptives and sweethearts. During the waning moon it helps one to look into the future. Hang in the branches of a blossoming fruit tree when the moon is waxing to insure a plentiful crop. It ennobles emotional life, unmasks enemies, and gives inspiration and success in love. Moonstone is particularly favorable to women.

QUARTER IDENTITY: north
ASTROLOGICAL AFFINITY: Moon, Venus, Neptune. Has an affinity with water.

OPAL

COMPOSITION: Hydrous silicon dioxide (quartz with water in it). Does not have a definite atomic structure and never occurs in crystal form.

COLOR, DESCRIPTION: Opal has no color of its own except as a background. White is the usual background but black opal, with dark-blue or grey coloration, and fire opal, which is redish orange, also occur. The water held within the stone allows it to show rainbow colors when the light hits it.

PRIMARY POWERS: carries the spirit of truth, promotes clairvoyance.

MYTHOLOGY: Opal protects the wearer from drunkenness, blindness, death by fire, and bad health. It turns pale to warn of danger and shines brightly when near beneficial energies. Black opal is said to be particularly lucky. In much of Europe a fire opal is said to bring bad luck.

HEALING POWERS: Beneficial to the pituitary, the lungs, and all spinal centers. It is also said to cure eye diseases, protect from contagion, and dispel melancholy.

RITUAL OR CEREMONIAL USES: Wear in a headband to benefit spinal centers. Carry a charged stone to build self esteem and to bring enjoyable dreams.

QUARTER IDENTITY: south and west
ASTROLOGICAL AFFINITY: has an affinity to fire: Moon, Venus in Libra, Sun, Mars, Pluto, Neptune, and Uranus.

PYRITE

COMPOSITION: Iron sulfide.
COLOR, DESCRIPTION: Also called fool's gold. It has pale brass colored crystals in a dark tan matrix.

PRIMARY POWERS: transmitter.
MYTHOLOGY: Pyrite is found in ancient Incan graves.

HEALING POWERS: Homeopathic remedy for inflammation of the respiratory passages, tonic for circulatory system, and brain stimulator.

RITUAL OR CEREMONIAL USES: Use in rituals where power is to be sent or relayed.

QUARTER IDENTITY: east
ASTROLOGICAL AFFINITY: Sun

RUBY

COMPOSITION: Aluminum oxide, a form of corundum (as are sapphires)

COLOR, DESCRIPTION: Yellowish-red to bluish-red. The blue tinged ones are known as pigeon blood ruby and are found in Burma. The color is provided by chromium oxide.

PRIMARY POWERS: Symbol of spiritual love and devotion, emotional stimulant.

MYTHOLOGY: Known as the lord of all stones in India. The Romany say it repels enemies, disease, and the evil eye. They also believe the stone brings energy, courage, passion, and victory. Alchemists believe the ruby works through the element of fire to purify the circulatory system. It is also believed that divine love is translated into divine will by it. It represents freedom, charity, dignity, divine power, health, and strength. Wearing a ruby is said to keep sadness away from your life. Pliny thought that some rubies were male and others female. He recommended using the male stones against plague and to banish all evil.

HEALING POWERS: Renews vital life-forces; increases vigor; cleanses the blood; and works on the circulatory system.

RITUAL OR CEREMONIAL USES: Use in a staff or prayer stick to symbolize the balance of divine and earthly powers. Rubies darken under threat. A ruby amulet may be worn to insure success.

QUARTER IDENTITY: east
ASTROLOGICAL AFFINITY: Mars, Pluto

SAPPHIRE

COMPOSITION: Aluminum oxide, corundum. The sapphire of antiquity was the lapis lazuli, a form of sodalite.

COLOR, DESCRIPTION: Sapphires are thought of as blue but come in many colors including green, orange, pink, purple, yellow, and black. The star is the result of needlelike impurities or inclusions.

PRIMARY POWERS: Heightened awareness, protection, wisdom, truthfulness.

MYTHOLOGY: One of the stones of the Apocalypse. It promotes spiritual development and heightens awareness of the macrocosm. Sapphire gives devotion, fellow-feeling, chastity, veracity, imagination, faith, noble conduct, prophetic gifts, and peace of mind. It attracts good people; brings help in times of need, particularly when trapped by fire or lost, makes thoughts pure and genial in preparation for meditation; protects against false friends; and defends against black magick. It's color will change when one is about to come into contact with calamity, treachery, or poison. It is a binder in life and love. The plains tribes found small sapphires in ant's nests. These were used in the yuwipi ceremony as an aid to communication with the nunahe, particularly those of trees.

HEALING POWERS: It protects the eyes and heart; corrects respiratory disorders; cools fevers and swellings; augments strength; and prevent ulcers. It also dispels fears; brings inner peace; and cures mental and nervous disorders.

RITUAL OR CEREMONIAL USES: Place on the solar plexus in healing meditation. Use as a focus before beginning meditation. Carry for protection from a variety of dangers. Use in all bridge building medicine.

ASSOCIATED ANIMALS: ants
ASSOCIATED PLANTS: trees
ASTROLOGICAL AFFINITY: Taurus, Mercury, Jupiter, Neptune, Saturn (star sapphires), Venus (in engagement ring)

SUNSTONE

COMPOSITION: There are at least two different stones called sunstones. Oregon sunstone is a form of translucent quartz with an orangy color. The sunstone of Europe is a form of feldspar. It resembles an orange opal with a multicolored flash.

COLOR, DESCRIPTION: Clear, fiery; a pale orange.

PRIMARY POWERS: purging impurities, energy, health, sexual energy

MYTHOLOGY: Sunstone is sacred to Taiowa, Hopi god of the Sun. The Blackfoot drew ikuto-wapi (supernatural power) from the sun with this gem. Connected directly to the Great Spirit, sunstone is a bird stone. Feathers were often used in combination with sunstones.

The sunstone is a bean aflame with a holy and formless fire according to the southern swamp-dwelling tribes. It is used to bake away impurities. It is likened to the practice of spreading moldy objects out to dry in the sun. Remember that this practice can be overdone. That which is too long exposed to the sun will dry and crack.

HEALING POWERS: Used to effect cures for cancer and related cellular disorders. Shamen felt that only sun power could hope to affect such powerful degeneration within the physical being.

RITUAL OR CEREMONIAL USES: Use in the sun to purge impurities directly or indirectly, either physically or astrally. European magicians set it in gold to bring the influences of the sun to the magician. Carried close to other magickal ingredients it will increase the energy of your work. It is of active energy and associated with the element of fire.

ASSOCIATED ANIMALS: wingeds
ASSOCIATED PLANTS: Sun

TOPAZ

COMPOSITION: Hydrous aluminum silicate with fluorine.

COLOR, DESCRIPTION: Although usually thought of as yellow, it comes more frequently in many other colors, blue, clear, pink, gray, and green. Some topaz may fade when exposed to sunlight; others can be altered in hue by applying heat.

PRIMARY POWERS: power of thought, wisdom, and knowledge.

MYTHOLOGY: It holds some aspects of the sun; carry it at all times. As a talisman it controls lust and greed; cures insanity; calms anger or prevents its arousal; and prevents insomnia. It increases happiness and joy and decreases depression and low spirits. It transforms physical energy into thought power and higher consciousness. It wards off false friends and the evil eye. It gives chastity, happiness, and faithful friends. It intensifies the creative energy flow of artists, writers, and scientists and makes it easier to grasp abstractions and innovative projects. It polarizes force fields.

HEALING POWERS: Increases physical strength, particularly for women. It relieves the pain of headache. It integrates the solar plexus force center of the spine; aids the liver; improves circulation; and heightens the sense of taste. It aids the heart, stops bleeding, and corrects poor vision.

RITUAL OR CEREMONIAL USES: Wear or carry in spirit bag for good temper, lightened spirits, and joy.

ASTROLOGICAL AFFINITY: Mercury, Sagitarius, Moon, Saturn, Uranus, Sun, Venus, Gemini

TURQUOISE

COMPOSITION: Hydrous aluminum silicate with copper, aluminum phosphates, water, silica, and iron

COLOR, DESCRIPTION: blue or greenish blue with streaks of brown. Turquoise is a soft stone: a gel which has been converted into a crystalline structure. There is more life in it than in harder stones. It is delicate and must be protected from soap, sunlight, caustic liquids, perspiration, grease, perfume, dirt, and heat.

PRIMARY POWERS: protection, contact with plant spirits

MYTHOLOGY: Some of the tribes say that turquoise is stone in the process of being transformed into a plant. They think of the stone as being more alive than other stones. It is used as a bridge to plant spirits. It is the primary protective stone of the Moslems who use it against the evil eye; to reduce quarrels in marriage; and to guard against poison, snakebite, black magick, blindness, and wild beasts. It is a useful meditative stone and will absorb harmful vibrations. In Russia it is given to a bride to give peace of mind. Given to a husband it grants strength for labor, prosperity, popularity, and health. It enters into the spontaneous upsurge of romantic love and leads to remarkable encounters with people from past lives. It protects virtue, true love, and innocence. It will change color with the aura of the wearer.

HEALING POWERS: Used to treat melancholy, malaria; diseases of the lungs; and respiratory system. It protects from ill health.

RITUAL OR CEREMONIAL USES: Wear or carry for communication with Grandmother Earth or with plant spirits. Use in meditation.

ASSOCIATED PLANTS: all plants

ASTROLOGICAL AFFINITY: Venus, Moon, Sun, Jupiter, Neptune, Pluto, Saturn,

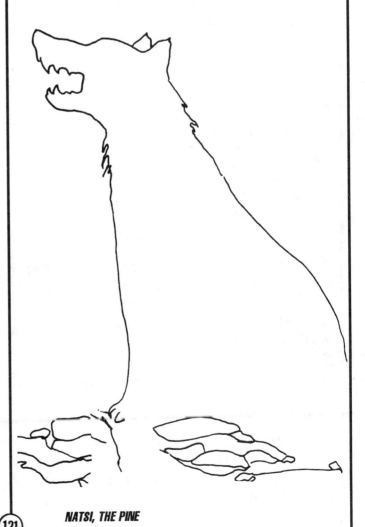

NATSI, THE PINE

CHAPTER 17

CONCRETE CANYONS WITH MANY-COLORED LEAVES
Urban Medicine

I was born, Ghost Drum in my hand
Staked and tied, I made my final stand
A hundred years pass 'ere I'm reborn
Steering wheel replaces saddle horn
Buffalo, now made of chrome and steel
White man on a tree, in place of Medicine   Wheel
Painted boats leap between the stars
Fences rise, just like prison bars
Concrete hills loom before my eye
Talking ropes beneath where steel birds fly
Fires flame inside globes of glass
Asphalt fields replace plains of grass
Lodges rise to the clouds, I've seen
Counting coup is now a war machine.
And the people cried for stone medicine
And I can't deny them, no....
Stone medicine, on the day I died.
                                        -Medicine Hawk

As I look out over the skyline of a sprawling Atlanta, I see a concrete mountain range. Long ago, man lumbered into the piedmont plain, pillaging the earth to raise these peaks of glass and metal. Most animal and plant totems ran away to the last vestiges of nature. Some remained. These mutated survivors created a massive core of medicine power still vibrant and living within the urban confines.

Dandelions push up through solid asphalt reaching for the sky. Pigeons perch high on the ledges of steel canyons looking down on the earthbound residents. Indeed, the rat remained, defiant and glorious, feeding and thriving off the designs of man; driving him away as drums along the ghetto sounded over his retreating shoulder. These are truly strong totems; the survivors, the adapters, those who charged headlong into the violence of the sun and returned alive to tell the tales of power.

Medicine path teachings are traditionally geographic in character. As they evolved the center of concern was the wilderness in which most tribes dwelt. This focus helped build relationships to the earth as it appeared at the time; natural, unpolluted, and basically unchanged for hundreds - thousands - of years.

The face of Agisegua, the Earth Mother has changed since then. The earth is now covered with the structures and designs of only one of its multitude of species - humans. Whether or not these structures and designs are beneficial to the well-being of the earth is immaterial. They exist.

After our many years of striving for the elimination of pollution and destruction the effects of these ills continue to increase. We must, therefore, take another avenue towards the improvement of the earth. We must change the attitudes which have produced such sterile results. No longer can we afford to escape to the last vestiges of nature to pursue the medicine path. These band-aids upon the posterior of the planet will not achieve rehabilitation of the spirit.

We must seek solutions where we are, where we live, and where we exist. The urban areas need medicine power, blessing, and spirit much more than the wild areas. On some level we chose to live where we are. To run away to the wilderness for short intervals is to deny the divine providence which placed us where we are. If we continually desire escape, our flesh incarnation (this time around) has become essentially valueless.

We must begin to work on Mother Earth at the sore spots — the wounds. Petting her on the healthy, fleshy spots does not heal the inner being of our earth mother. Furthermore, we already live within the wounds. We must begin healing here.

In the course of the development of civilization the mutated forms of man's creation sprang into being ("mutate" means "changed", not "perverted", as some science-fictions writers would have us believe). These creations gained form and life through the designs of man. Their spirits rumbled into being just as did the plant and animal species which Darwin's theory suggests happened millions of years ago in the coal swamps. They took on bodies of metal, wire, rubber, plastic, circuitry, and stone. Different bodies from their predecessors, the plants, animals, and minerals. The technological breath of life spawned three more parallel kingdoms: the architectural kingdom; the transporational kingdom; and the communications kingdom.

The transportational kingdom moves, corresponding to the animal kingdom. The architectural kingdom remains stationary, corresponding to the mineral kingdom. (Although stones move when they expand and contract with the effects of heat and cold.) The communications kingdom fell between these parameters corresponding to the plant kingdom. The plants have branches and root systems which spread out in all directions much like the wires and connections of communications devices and systems.

The members of these three worlds breathe with the same spirit as their predecessors. They yearn to be free as all beings do. But we have shackled and imprisoned them in our prejudice and bigotry. We malign their existence with the dubious justification of hatred for the pollution and change wrought in their making.

This is our legacy - our heritage - our inheritance. We can turn out backs refusing to believe that spirit inhabits these "inanimate" objects or we can seek to free all things.

The members of these kingdoms are very simple. We already know them all in a superficial manner. Now we must communicate with their spirits. Each member of each kingdom has a spirit. We can become the totem spirit in much the same manner as we did the animal, plant, and mineral totems.

TRANSPORTATIONAL TOTEM SPIRITS

It is best to closely observe your chosen transporational totem in movement. Watch actual planes, cars, trains, or boats in movement as they go from place to place. Do not take it for granted that you already understand all this. We absentmindedly watch these beings in the course of a day without actually noticing them. Truly examine the movements of your totem. If possible, handle, feel, and listen to the subject (preferably up close). Feel the vibration of the motor, its lifeforce. Hear it as it starts, runs, shuts off. Feel its energy at rest. Observe its media (roads, tracks, airways, waterways). Take a short time to read up on its history if you are not familiar with its invention and development. If possible get your hands down into the bowels of the subject. Get the grease, oil, fluids upon your hands. No mundane mechanic would discount the power of a car's lifeblood: the fluids.

Obtain or prepare a medicine bag for the totem spirit you have chosen. For a train put in some rock from beside the tracks, a piece of iron or steel. Perhaps you can find a spike or an old tie nail. A piece of coal can symbolize the fuel even of the modern diesel locomotive. Add a piece or oak or pine to symbolize the great forests cut for the ties. Make the bag black for the locomotive; red or yellow for the caboose.

This new step into the urban environment involves a new skill: meditation and individual personification while you are exposed to various levels of noise. In animal, plant, and mineral meditations, we had the dubious luxury of quiet during the process. Urban medicine is louder, more cacophonous, than traditional medicine. The raucous nature of this delivery system is its power. If you are a quiet person, at first it may be best to isolate all but the sound of your totem subject. At the very least shut out as much noise that is extraneous to your subject as possible. Get INTO the noise of your subject. THAT is its form of vocal expression. Its power is the work which it performs. This noise is good. It is the call of your transportational totem spirit.

Depending upon your subject pick an area conducive to this contact. If you wish to contact plane get in or near an airport - or at least in the flight path. If you wish to contact train get near a railroad track. You may BEGIN the meditation on the tracks. For obvious reasons it is best to move before really getting into the meditation. The best place to contact boat is near water or in a boat. Automobiles are easiest. You would be hard-pressed to find a place on earth where you cannot get into a car. This is the ideal spot for an automobile meditation. Have a friend drive you through traffic to feel movement under pressure. Meditate in a parking lot or garage. The same principles work for buses, monorails, etc. If close proximity is not possible use pictures, movies, videos, or audio tapes.

THE TRANSPORTATIONAL SPIRIT MEDITATION

You should now have a feel for your totem subject. Choosing your spot, stand or sit comfortably and maintain your position throughout the meditation. Slowly, steadily, picture your subject. See every contour, every attachment, nut, bolt, glass — everything — until it forms into an identifiable whole. At the same rate "start" the motor. Feel it begin from the spark and roar into life pulsating in a steady cycle. Let it drone on, beating a cyclic rhythm through your being. Materialize yourself at the spark - the starting place of the motor (or other place as appropriate). Travel throughout the being. To the combustion chamber, the pistons, the drive shaft, all through its engine. See it as it explodes gloriously, spreading force out across the entire structure. Be one with its power, engine, body. Now being to move. Accelerate along your medium (highway, railroad track, waterway, runway). As you accelerate the world around you begins to change. The face of reality wrinkles more and more the faster you go. The bends in the fabric of the world become more and more pronounced until .... BANG! The same spark which started the engine cycles through again catapulting you into another plane. All is smooth, rhythmic movement. All is clear for you to seek the new vistas which speed has brought you. Glide for as long as necessary observing and experiencing all that touches you in this dimension. Feel, smell, taste all of this realm — all that it has to offer. Reach out with your sixth sense into the void. Glide smoothly along so long as you like.

Soon, you will hear a signal; automobile horn, train whistle, fog horn, jet engine. It is time to return. Accelerate your motor as its spark flies. Faster, faster until you have crossed over once again. Slow down gradually and come to a stop. Cut the motor off. Rest for a time with the noise of your surroundings. For a further time rest in a place without noise. Record your experiences as always.

COMMUNICATIONS KINGDOM TOTEMS

It is not difficult to find an area surrounded by the machinations of communications technology. Almost every mansion, home, office, school, hotel, and shack in the U.S. has a phone and/or television. Many have computers, sophisticated recording equipment, and even devices to enable communications with other planetary bodies. The point is that you have access to an environment conducive to communion with totem spirits of the communications kingdom. For that matter high-frequency waves are transmitted throughout all the atmosphere of earth.

Once again, do not take this activity for granted. Although you use the physical devices of communications constantly you may not have reached for the true soul of these devices. You must listen to the hum of the MECHANISM — the completed circuit — the actual WAVES and PARTICLES which flow through the air or wire. Do not limit yourself to sound in this experience but rather the entire sensory sphere. Feel the movement; taste, smell, see the essence of technological communication. Examine the contours — the wired circuits if possible — the connections which spread out like branches and roots of a plant. Feel the movement of power along these paths.

Obtain or make a medicine bag for your totem spirit. For the telephone: a piece of directory, a snip of phone wire, a connector, a transmitter, or receiver. For others: transistors, ticker tape, telegrams, TV Guide, tubes, and antenna wire are possible inclusions. Floppy disks, digital code, print-outs, or manuals will go into a computation medicine bag.

Again, we are dealing with a noise factor which exceeds that of the three "natural" kingdoms. Unlike a transportational meditation we do not need to communicate with roaring engines or motors. A difference in volume of sound exists but a diverse quantity of sounds replaces the raucous clamor. Choose an area in close proximity to a physical example, a device, of your totem spirit. Make sure it is working but do not look at the screen or listen at the receiver. In other words if you are working with the totem spirit of a TV or computer, do not face the screen. Sit behind it where you can feel the vibrations but not become involved with the images. If it is phone, do not lift the receiver. The idea is to feel the life of the physical example but to stay separate from its product. We have already had years of that.

COMMUNICATIONS TOTEM MEDITATION

Place your hands upon the physical example if convenient. Be sure you are clear of the high-voltage connectors. This touch gives you a feel for the life of the totem spirit. Place the totem bag on this physical example for the maximum effect.

Much as you did with the motor of the transportational examples begin to feel the movement of current as it runs through circuits and transistors, channeling along the myriad routes throughout the device. Let it move up your arms, through the heart, and into your brain. Let your awareness spread out in a nexus of connectors. Let your nerve cells vibrate with the essence of communicative power. Reduce your self in vision to a WAVE of electrons.

Let the wave shake itself out to full length and snap into place. Allow yourself, as this wave, to travel out further, further, until you have left the atmosphere traveling at the speed of light.

Suddenly you transfer over into another world, another dimension, another place. In this place all the surroundings are different: all is light; all is enlightenment. Standing just ahead of you is a light being — the spirit keeper. He or she has much to tell you. Approach this spirit keeper with love and light. Rest within its glow. Listen to the messages, the learning, the enlightenment. Listen to all that it has to tell you. Give your spirit keeper all the time needed.

When your spirit keeper gives you a signal it will be time to go. Generate movement of your wave again. Return along the path by which you came. You break through into your own dimension again. Traveling at the speed of light return through the atmosphere to your body. Reenter as the wave of light. Feel your body and spirit return to their original forms. Remember all that you experienced. Rest for a time still feeling the current. Release the current into the physical example. As always record your experiences.

ARCHITECTURAL TOTEMS

Closely observe your physical totem example. This is not difficult in the architectural kingdom. The best environment for this meditation is INSIDE your physical totem example. Watch the building/structure from many different vantage points. Look at it far away, close up, inside. Look out the windows and doors. Look in the rooms. Walk around inside of it getting to know what goes on there. Touch the walls, fixtures, panels, etc. Smell it - every building and home has its own distinctive smell. If a water receptacle is there, taste the water. Listen to the noises of the people who use the building. Then listen to the noises of the building itself: doors opening and closing, elevators moving, windows opening and closing, actual movements of the structure settling, floors creaking, carpet sounds as people walk, etc. Check into the history of the building, look at photographs of its construction.

Remember that the architectural kingdom corresponds to the mineral kingdom. Many of the metals used in the structures of large buildings are much more refined and pure than the natural forms. The actual power of that type of metal or mineral may manifest with more force of purpose once activated by spirit.

Obtain or make a totem bag for your chosen structure. Make it of fabric similar to the drapes or upholstery - or of Naugahyde. Put in it glass, wood, steel, concrete, wallpaper, paint chips, wallboard, floor tile, carpet lint. Nails, screws, bolts, and plastics are other possible inclusions.

Once again it is possible that you will have to use a noisy space for this meditation. Sometimes an architectural kingdom totem spirit example will provide a quiet environment for the meditation. If not you should be able to flow with the noise and company of fellow humans not particularly sympathetic to what you are doing.

If you can, get actually inside your physical totem example. Seek out the HEART of the structure. If this is not possible due to people controls or shielding walls, find a place as close to the heart as possible.

ARCHITECTURAL TOTEM MEDITATION

Stand or sit with your back in contact with a wall. Hold the totem bag to your solar plexus. Feel the pulsations of the energy carried by the metal, stone, or wood which run on energy lines through the structure. When the stimulus of this energy has established contact with your body allow it to run through the connectors of your own system.

We know that a building exists on many levels of reality. You sit or stand in only one of these dimensions. Radiate the energy now coursing through you out, away from your body. The atmosphere now begins to wrinkle, beginning the change. Movement of the fabric of reality steps up until you are shifted into the next dimension of this building. You are there following this energy.

Observe the details of this place. Mark them well. There are two doors in front of you. Rise, in your spirit body, and open one of them. As you step into the next room all is light. You glow as well when you walk into this new place. In front of you is a large screen upon which images have begun to appear. Watch them closely and remember all the symbols you see. Continue to watch, enjoying the panorama.

When the images stop close your spirit eyes and remember well all that you have seen and felt. Open your eyes again. Turn and go back through the door. Close it. Slowly settle back down into your body. Let the energy of the building leave your body and settle back down into the structure. Rest a while and then leave the place. Record your experiences.

CREATING SACRED SPACE - THE PORTABLE MEDICINE WHEEL

The medicine wheel exists once it has been created in the mind's eye (chante ishta, the one, true eye of the heart). You need not build with stones each time you wish to utilize its power. It becomes three-dimensional at first by virtue of your imagery. Then it becomes multi-dimensional, crossing and pulsating simultaneously in and out of all the levels of reality affecting our existence. It sanctifies the area in which we are that we may perform any task there in a galunky'ti'yu manner. This wheel will follow us, surrounding us, in all our movements if we desire it to do so.

Review your work with the medicine wheel in Chapter 6. Learn the configurations of the stones. The names are less important than the arrangement and meaning.

Now begin to build the medicine wheel in your mind's eye. Begin with it flat, two-dimensional on the floor, or on a table, or desk in front of you. Practice this in a quiet meditation place at first until you can build up the image easily.

Now in your mind let the circle of the wheel separate into two hoops. Let one stay flat on the surface and let the other float upwards, leaving an invisible connection to the lower hoop until they form a tube. There is a medicine wheel at each end of this tube with the Great Spirit stone at the center of each hoop.

Place yourself at the center of this tube where the Great Spirit is. Now you are inside the medicine wheel. Practice this in quiet without outside interference until you are proficient at the imagery. Keep practicing forming this wheel with all 36 stones in the hoops at each end of the tube. You should be able to see the shapes and colors of each of the stones.

Now you are ready to attempt this visualization where you will actually need it, under noisy conditions with people all around you. You will probably do best to begin in a moderately quiet place - in your own office or the break room or some such. Practice until you can build the medicine wheel under an assortment of conditions.

Once you have conquered building the tube wheel add to it a vertical wheel. Image the wheel facing you as if on a TV screen. Expand this wheel into a tube or let it roll in a circle round and round you. Then overlap this wheel with the one built flat on the floor. This will center you in a multi-dimensional medicine wheel.

When you have the power and ability to create multi-dimensional sacred space surrounding you and you can maintain this under adverse conditions, the wheel can assist and protect you. It will increase creativity and help you achieve harmony and union. You can expand this multi-dimensional wheel to include larger areas as your house and yard, your workplace, your neighborhood, or the entire city, state, country, even the planet. The strength of this medicine wheel can be increased and/or maintained by doing smudging and pipe ceremonies directed towards it sacred energy.

You will probably have to repeat the building of this multi-dimensional medicine wheel at intervals as much of what we imperfect beings create does not last forever. Remember that the valuations for the moon stones given for the medicine wheel are not the only possible ones. As you work with the wheel you may develop totemic systems of your own. As you begin to become proficient with the wheel you may wish to make connections between the moons opposite on the wheel, thus providing spokes for it.

THE URBAN PIPE CEREMONY

It is possible to bring the kanunnawu into the environs of urbania. The sore places of the earth, highly populated and modernized areas, need it more than the wild areas anyway. Those mundanes who inhabit urbania would be alarmed to see an elaborate sacred pipe. Our mission in the city is not to alarm or to make an ostentatious show. We use non-threatening offspring of the pipe ceremony in this area: cigarettes, tobacco alone, regular pipes.

To prepare for an urban pipe ceremony you must provide yourself with tools which are not out of place in the city. Do not perform this in a non-smoking area. Non-smokers have become literally rabid about this — don't antagonize them. Choose the place, object, or the area you wish to bless and in or near which you wish to offer the pipe.

With your non-threatening pipe surrogate face the directions or gesture towards them. Say the callings out loud or project yourself into these directions silently so as not to call attention to yourself.

Two friends who are both medicine path people can easily look as if they are conversing and gesturing while actually doing an urban pipe ceremony. In any case the idea is to perform a pipe ceremony anywhere, under any circumstances. The smallest pinch of tobacco is still sacred whether or not it is in your decorated and dedicated pipe.

You can use this ceremony to bless your workplace from the board room, to the office, to McDonalds. Negative vibrations find easy access to these areas and a pipe ceremony can do much

to disperse them. Any portion of your home can be so blessed no matter who lives there. Public buildings can profit from such a blessing — or bless the room of a friend in the hospital, in jail, or attending court. Bless your daily transportation, even your bus stop. And don't forget the communications devices with which you come into contact daily.

Every puff of smoke, every grain of tobacco, goes out from you to bring life, freedom and harmony, to that which surrounds your life. Make sacred all that you touch and do, that life itself may be lived in a galunky'ti'yu manner.

THE UNDERGROUND RAILROAD OF SPIRIT

In the early 1800's Medicine Hawk's ancestor, Keegan Brammar, ran a link in the underground railroad. He carried hundreds of slaves between Jellico, Tennessee and Ironton, Ohio to assure their freedom. In twenty-six years he never lost a passenger. Not sharing the Quakers' believe in non-violence, he was undoubtedly responsible for the disappearance of many a slave-catcher.

We are confronted today by a new form of slavery. It poses the same questions of bigotry and prejudice as those blanketing Turtle Island before our Civil War. Not too long ago we civilized beings began a losing war against pollution. In resisting the effects of pollution and crowd mentality we have created a mass hatred of all things urban. At present one would be hard-pressed to locate a New Age son or daughter who would admit to LIKING urban life. Adding fuel to this fire is the widely accepted theory that all the machinations and creations of man are mutated beyond the stages of life. A belief that they are inanimate, sociopathic, abortions of the earth. Needless to say this attitude is not conducive to an understanding of living, breathing medicine power in an urban environment. If we can overcome our basic prejudice in the face of new concepts perhaps we can begin to understand the being and life of urbania. At that time we will begin to be ready to grapple with the problems therein.

You have now done some communication with the totem spirits of the modern world. Your understanding of these beings should be such that your attitude is free of extreme prejudice regarding urban environments. Pick three physical totem examples from each of the kingdoms of the city. Make or obtain totem bags for each of these totems and supply yourself with a sacred pipe (or city sneaker substitute) and hokshichankiya materials.

In the city it may not be expedient to pull out a sacred pipe and perform a pipe ceremony. With practice you will become adept in the art of becoming invisible. For this ceremony it IS important to **LIGHT** the tobacco. It is the **SMOKE** which frees the spirit. Remember there is no need to inhale.

Get as close as is practical to the object or area; whatever you wish to free. Offer the pipe or cigarette in the regular way. Be sure you have checked up on the directions before you begin. After offering a puff of smoke to the seven directions put out the pipe or cigarette. Dig a little unburned tobacco out of the pipe or break off part of the cigarette. Leave this tobacco actually touching the physical example you are blessing. Do make absolutely sure the tobacco is no longer burning. Just one or two grains are sufficient so don't feel you need to be a litter-bug.

Release the spirit of your physical example by saying, "I release the spirit(s) of this ....[building, bus, etc.] to its/their highest potential".

Plant from your hokshichankiya packet if there is any earth available. Otherwise scatter a little tobacco dust around the area to symbolize such a planting. Don't fail, however, to plant seeds in an appropriate place later.

This is a very simply ceremony but earth shaking in its intent. Imagine a world of spirit, without any slavery, no thralldom whatsoever.

Do this blessing with a member of each of the three kingdoms. Do it often. Do it on the way to work or school. Free the roads on which you drive, the buildings in which you work or study, the machines you work on. Free the natural; trees, animals, and stones, as well as the city totem spirits. Run your link in the underground railroad and keep it functioning. Free ALL things. Liberate ALL spirit.

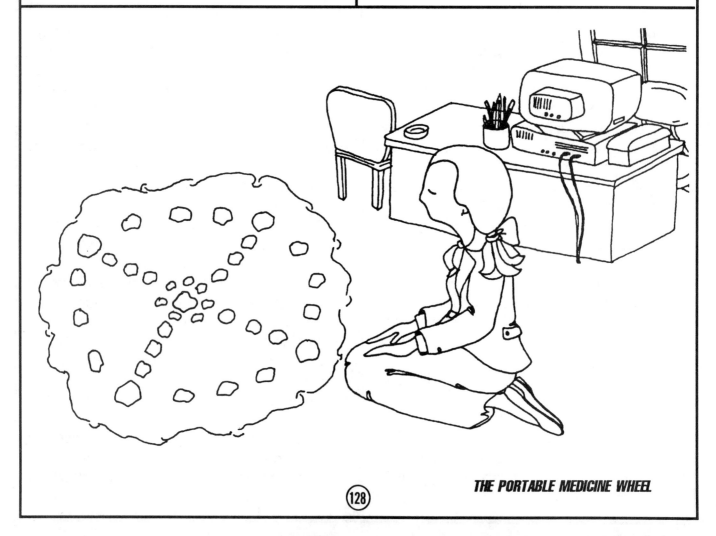

THE PORTABLE MEDICINE WHEEL

CHRONICLES OF SAND, ROCK, AND SKIN

Magick in Letters and Symbols

We have discussed many forms which medicine power may take. We have seen power in the scent of the smudge and in the form of the medicine wheel. We have watched the power of the sacred smoke ascending to the Great Mysterious and have experienced the cleansing steam. We have talked about power in drum beats, in dance and in song. We have made medicine power with our hands by constructing tools. We have reached out to touch medicine power in the spirits of the totems of the four-leggeds, the green world, and the slow world of stone. We have even opened for ourselves the medicine power of the man-made world of the city.

The unega who first came to live on Turtle Island considered the native peoples illiterate because they did not write down the words of their languages. [Do note that there may have been some exceptions to this belief.] It is perhaps understandable that a people, totally dependent upon written language, should consider peoples who did not do so to be ignorant savages. Certainly this is not the first time such a conclusion has been reached. The Roman conquerors of Britain considered the Celts ignorant, not because they did not possess a written language, but because they declined to use it for their most important records.

The Native Americans, like the Celts, the Germanic Tribes, and hundreds of tribes in Africa, remembered their history and their important philosophies in the form of living, oral traditions. To a society enamored of the myth that written history is somehow much more accurate. This oral history was despised and discounted. While much evidence exists showing that oral history is at least as accurate as written history; we, as a society committed to the written word, remain doubtful of all non-written traditions.

While there were a great many languages and dialects spoken by the Native Americans, they had also developed a number of trade languages facilitating the extensive exchanges of goods which were maintained. In addition to trade languages an extremely sophisticated sign language was developed. This seems to have been quite widespread and understood by a majority of the tribes.

It isn't exactly true that the Native Americans kept no written histories. A number of the tribes maintained pictographic histories which can still be read by anyone familiar with the symbols.

Years were counted by some great happening and events of interest were noted in their proper order. These histories can frequently be cross-referenced with the histories kept in writing by the unega.

In addition to making records of events and maintaining chronologies the pictographs were used as decoration.

This decoration touched, as did most things the AmerInds did, upon the sacred. Pictographic symbols of courage, invulnerability, and speed might be placed upon one's war gear in order to enlist those totems for protection and success in battle. An eagle feather might be attached to a pipe to underline the hope that prayers would be carried to Galunlati. In the same manner the pictograph of an eagle engraved on the stem of the pipe would invoke that messenger.

There was agreement about the forms and meanings of these pictographs among tribes. Individuals of one tribe could often understand messages written by a member of another. You have seen many of these pictographs on drawings, photographs, or actual examples of bead work, painted shields, teepee decorations, pots, etc.

The following pictograph chart a very small sampling of the many which were used. You will note that you can understand many of them with-

EARTH MOTHER

SKY FATHER

NORTH

SOUTH

EAST

ANCESTORS

BEAR

RABBIT

PLENTY FOOD

FAMINE

WOLF

HAWK

COUNCIL

SPIRITUAL SEED

THUNDERBIRD

SACRED LODGE

HUNGRY

FEAR

EAT

DEER TRACKS

WEST

SACRED PIPE

CAMP FIRE

DRUM

TIPI

SPIRIT

STARS

SWALLOW

TURTLE

DEER, MOOSE

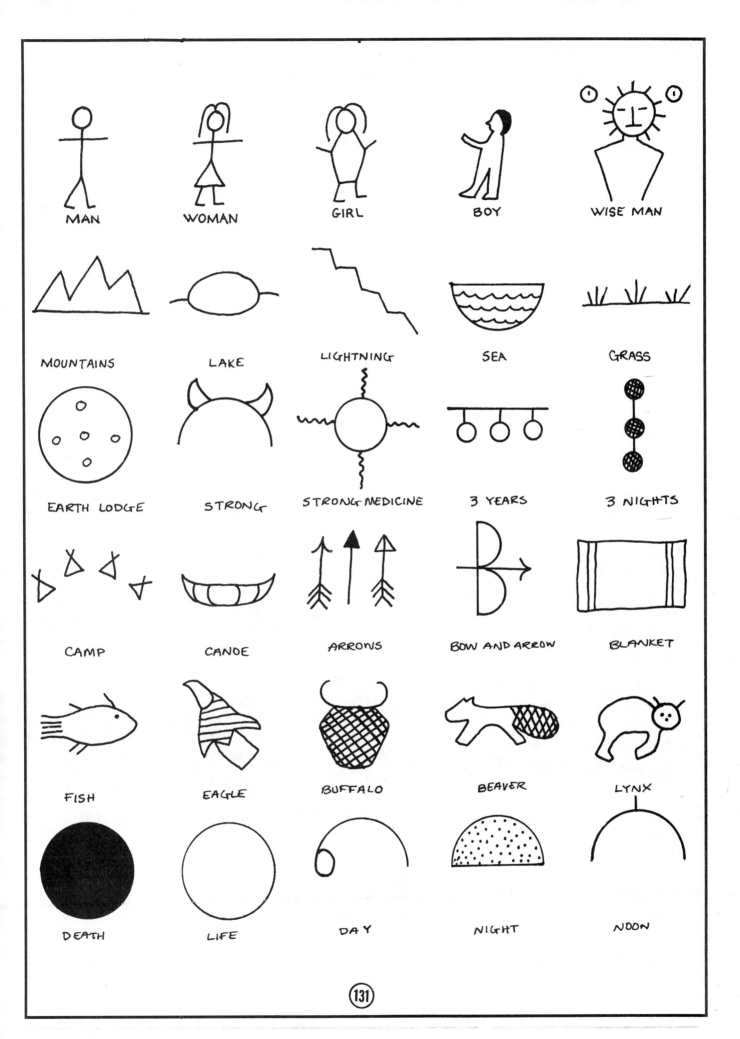

MAN   WOMAN   GIRL   BOY   WISE MAN

MOUNTAINS   LAKE   LIGHTNING   SEA   GRASS

EARTH LODGE   STRONG   STRONG MEDICINE   3 YEARS   3 NIGHTS

CAMP   CANOE   ARROWS   BOW AND ARROW   BLANKET

FISH   EAGLE   BUFFALO   BEAVER   LYNX

DEATH   LIFE   DAY   NIGHT   NOON

out the written translation. Feel free to invent more to fulfill your own needs.

Most of the pictographs stand for concrete objects: crow, camp, buffalo, or hunt. Others express abstract concepts: death, bad, famine, or ancestors. Obviously it is far more difficult to agree upon a pictograph to symbolize spirit than one to symbolize snake. Probably not all tribes agreed about these abstract pictographs.

Use pictographs to mark your tools and costumes. Use them in spirit Bags to call to particular powers and spirits. They offer just one more way of bringing your modern mind into communication with the spirits who exist here. Invent pictographs which evoke the spirits of the urban totems as well. You may even find that this is a good way to express what you have learned during your work on the medicine path.

MEDICINE PATH RUNES

An interesting way of using the pictographs is to create a set of runes or divination stones. A great variety of runes are used world wide as divination devices. Most runes consist of tiles or stones marked with the letters of a written language. However, pictographs of totem animals, other spirits, and concepts may be painted or engraved on stones. These provide a very powerful and a very interesting set of runes.

To make a set of American Indian runes first choose a set of symbols which will speak to human life and possibilities. Below is a SUGGESTED selection of symbols for a rune set. To use these runes think of a specific question. Draw three or more of the rune stones from a bag. Consider deeply the symbols on the rune stones you drew. With careful interpretation an answer to the question can be deduced from these symbols.

1. West - Introspection, death, need to seek knowledge
2. North - cleansing, wisdom, stability
3. East - Knowledge, enlightenment, beginning new things
4. South - misunderstanding, humor, things aren't what they seem
5. Sky Father - seek guidance from the spirits
6. Earth Mother - look deeply within your question, depend upon your intuition
7. Ancestors - examine the past, the root of the problem, the answer may be there

8. Eagle - a message, the power to succeed
9. Bear - seek healing, or offer it
10. Buffalo - be steadfast, perhaps someone is blocking you
11. Rabbit or Coyote - examine everything carefully, someone or something may be distracting you or lying to you
12. Wise man - seek help from a man, or the problem may be solved by aggressive action
13. Wise Woman - seek or expect help from a woman, or the problem may be solved by avoiding it or waiting it out
14. Plenty food - things will be good, favorable outcome
15. Famine - expect trouble or misfortune
16. Spirit - be concerned with non-material things
17. Wolf - cooperation is needed
18. Wild Cat - independence, you're on your own
19. Hawk - stand up for yourself, don't let others push you around
20. Treaty - a disagreement resolved
21. Council - it's time to talk
22. Spiritual Seed - expect growth, or expect to be called upon to teach
23. Thunder bird - Change, undesired messages
24. Sacred Pipe - Reach out to others, talk to the spirits
25. Sacred Lodge - go into yourself, examine your own feelings
26. Crow - Listen for secret information, expect news

These very short interpretations should not be memorized or used exactly as they are stated here. As you learn to use your runes you will add the information received during your vision quest and totem meditations to your understanding of the messages of the stones. Runestones are interpreted in light of all which you drew from the bag. For instance if you draw the eagle first, then plenty food, and last the lightning, the interpretation might run: A message will bring great good but will cause a lot of change in your life.

Runes,, like other methods of divination depend upon your own psychic, intuitional connection with the runestones. The more you work with the stones, the totems, and the concepts they represent the more useful your work with the stones will be.

SAND PAINTING

I imagine that most people reading this book have seen the complex sand paintings of the Navajo. These paintings are not merely pictures. Each one is part of a ritual cycle intended to invoke the powers of the spirits to do a particular healing. Each ritual cycle, which may include a great many songs and chants as well as one or several sand paintings, can take an apprentice several years to learn.

We would be utterly foolish even to attempt to teach sand painting this book. We can, however, teach a method of divination which draws its inspiration from the Navajo sand painting. To practice this form of divination you need several colors of powdered incense. You may prefer to use colored sand available from hobby stores. Preferred colors are those traditional to AmerInd decorative work: black, white, blue, red, yellow, green, and brown. Begin with only four colors: black, yellow or blue, white or brown, and red.

Provide yourself with a large sheet of white paper or a carefully swept area of the ground. A smooth rock is also good. If you are working outside the wind currents may play a part in your reading. Some painters prefer to let the wind participate, blowing new patterns in the grains. Others prefer to work inside where only their own hand plays a part.

Place your colored incense or sand in small bowls. Place them in easy reach. If you use incense light a charcoal block in a censor or non-flammable container. Make yourself comfortable and meditate for a time on the question you wish to ask. Soon you should let yourself reach toward one of the colors. Take up some of the color and sprinkle it on the paper or ground. Continue with the same or other colors until you feel that the painting is completed.

Below we have listed a number of possible interpretations of the forms the sand makes. These are by no means the last word nor is the list complete. Use your own intuition and interpretations freely.

After your interpretation of this painting is complete meditate again for a few minutes on your question. Sprinkle incense from your painting on the charcoal block. Again note the patterns of the incense and the smoke. Interpret the patterns again.

DIVINATORY ARCHETYPES:

I. Colors
1. Black - west: hard lessons, learn to learn more easily
2. Yellow or blue - east: enlightenment through the assimilation of hard lessons
3. White or brown - north: pure, undifferentiated energy, the place where power is built.
4. Red - south: place where power is put into use.
II. Shapes
1. Circle - life force
2. Square - imbalanced life force
3. Equilateral triangle - roadways, paths, decisions, edge of reality
4. Mountains - places you need to go in your life.
5. Jagged lines - hard lessons, rough going.
6. Curvy, zig-zag lines - water, adaptability, versatility, learning, flow with the spirit instead of flowing against it.
7. Points, dots - something specific in life that you have to go through (color is particularly important here).
8. Animal tracks - interpret these in light of the power of the totem for you.
   a. coyote/dog - wiliness
   b. bear - strength
   c. bird - farsightedness
   e. deer - earth power
   f. cat - hunting
   g. horse - perseverance
   h. small mammal - intelligence
   i. rodent - survival
9. Spirals - building energy or power
10. Zig-zag lines - thunders, hard lessons, death, destruction, that which brings about new life.
11. Cars, planes, trains, etc - travel
12. straight lines - only a partial reality - you don't have all the facts
13. Angles - The width of the angle is important
   a. Narrow - narrow viewpoint of life
   b. Wide - open viewpoint of life
   c. 45 degree - only observing one particular side of a problem
   d. 90 degree - balanced outlook on the problem at hand
14. Oval - incorrectly used life force.
15. Egg shape - birthing, life force about to give way to something creative.
16. Rectangle - hole or an empty place in life
17. Infinity sign (8 on its side) - joining of two separate life forces, the true creative force
19. Loops - exhausted life force
20. Island - ("0" with line through it) - taking a small part of reality and stressing it.

Once again, this is not a complete listing of archetypes. The diviner should seek to interpret as the spirit leads. Add archetypes to this list and connect the many symbols and colors in both sand and smoke divination.

CHEROKEE ALPHABET

Once, before the unega had taken all the eastern lands, a young man of the Cherokee nation was told that the black-bird tracks on thin white leaves could speak. The young man did not know the language of the unega nor did the black-bird tracks say anything to him.

The idea of the talking tracks stayed with this young man. He dreamed of making his own language speak through the black-bird tracks on the white leaves. Then the wisdom and traditions of the People could live forever. This young man sat down all by himself to invent talking signs for the Cherokee. After trying several paths which led nowhere, he found 85 symbols with which all the words of the Cherokee could be written down.

Modern linguists say that this is the second best system for writing a language that has ever been invented. They consider the 26 letters with which this book was written to be better. However, all of us spent two to three years learning to read and write English. A Cherokee speaker can study the alphabet invented by Siquoya for two or three WEEKS and then read and write any word in the language! I'm sure that systems for writing English just as logical and as quick to learn have been invented—but you know what happened to the "change over into the metric system".

The Cherokee alphabet is not suited for writing English, words. There are sounds in English which don't occur in Cherokee and sounds in Cherokee which aren't in English. We show the names of the seven directions written in Cherokee and you may enjoy using them. (Illustration 2) The Cherokee alphabet is such an amazing accomplishment that we felt you would wish to share in it.

WIGWAGS:

We're not at all sure that wigwags were an instrument of AmerInd spiritual practice. What are "wigwags" you ask? They are the tiny pictures you build while sitting on the ground listening to someone. Your hands don't have anything much to do so you scrape a little bit of the earth clear of loose stuff. Then you place leaves, stones, twigs, cones, and a bit of tinfoil from a chewing gum wrapper in a pattern.

"Those are just meaningless doodles," you say. Well, doodles themselves are not meaningless. These wigwags are your interaction with a tiny little bit of nature. It is a way you can communicate with the totem spirits. It is a way in which you express your own ideas of order and beauty in cooperation with the order and beauty of the nature spirits themselves.

A wigwag is very much like the altar you build in the earth in the asi. While there are conventions indicating of the altar in the asi is built; wigwags are entirely free from all rules. The only person who will ever know if it is done right is you.

Next time you are doing a totem meditation outdoors, begin by building a small wigwag. Find a small stick or rock which is just right for scraping away the loose litter. Usually a wigwag is no larger than your reach as you sit in front of it.

Look for things to put in your wigwag. These, too, are usually within your reach. Place sticks, stones, cones, your totem spirit bag, whatever seems right, in the wigwag. Maybe it will have a little row of sticks or stones around the edge; perhaps it won't really have an edge. It may just join with the surroundings. It may be a circle, a square, or a totally irregular shape. There are no rules. You will know what should go where; and you will know when it is finished.

Somehow this idle wigwag has become an altar through which you may contact the totem you have chosen. It was made to speak to the dog, the bear, the eagle, or the fish and it does.

A CHEROKEE FINDING DIVINATION

The Cherokee have a special method for locating things which are lost. Look in a stream or creek for a small brown, quartz-like pebble. This brown rock is called nunya watigei. Tie the rock to a string or thin, flexible leather thong and hold the end of the thong so that the nunya watigei swings freely. Speak to the nunya watigei as follows:

"Sge! (listen) Ha, Now you have drawn near to hearken, O nunya watigei. You never lie about anything. Ha. Now I am about to look for it. I have lost a ....[fill in what you are looking for]. Now tell me

D a	R e	T i	Ꭷ o	Oʻ u	I v
f ga	Ʌv ge	y gi	A go	J gu	E gv
ꭺ ka					
Ꮴ ha	Ᏽ he	A hi	Ᏺ ho	Ꭲ hu	Ꮹ hv
W la	Ᏻ le	Ꮈ li	Ᏻ lo	M lu	Ꮿ lv
ᎠᎧ ma	Ꮋ me	H mi	Ꮙ mo	y mu	Ꮹ nu
θ na	Ꭼ ne	ꞁ ni	Z no		Oʻ nv
ꮠ hna	Ᏻ nah				
I qwa	ω qwe	ꝑ qwi	Ꮴ qwo	ω qwu	Ɛ qwv
Ꮵ sa	4 se	Ᏺ si	Ꮅ so	Ᏻ su	R sv
Ꮥ s					
Ꮣ da	Ꮪ de	J di	Ꮴ do	S du	Ꮙ dv
W ta	Ꮦ te	Ꭲ ti			
Ꮪ dla					
Ꮭ tla	L tle	C tli	Ꮱ tlo	Ᏻ tlu	P tlv
Ꮐ tsa	Ꮴ tse	Ꮶ tsi	K tso	J tsu	Ꮳ tsv
Ꮐ wa	Ꮺ we	Ꮾ wi	Ꮼ wo	Ꮽ wu	Ꮞ wv
Ꮽ ya	Ᏼ ye	Ꮵ yi	Ꮹ yo	Ꮽ yu	B yv

about where I shall find it. For is it not Mine? My Name is ....

The rock should swing towards one direction. Follow in that direction a short distance; perhaps to a place where you feel that further instruction is needed. At this point repeat the verse and watch the pebble. Should the pebble go around in circles rather than indicating a direction you can figure that there is some other problem to solve. The object may not just be lost.

SOME SPECIAL SIGNIFICANCES

As in most spiritual systems, the AmerInd found colors, numbers, and symbols of particular importance. It is a sign of our limitations that we find it remarkable that these significances tend to match up from culture to culture.

Obviously if your first grade teacher always hit you with a blue ruler, you are going to have personal attitudes towards the color blue which are at odds to the general attributes assigned to that color. It shouldn't come as a surprise that there are differences in these associations amongst peoples and cultures. We present below some common associations found among the AmerInd peoples. These are only to be used as guidance for your own development.

NUMBERS

Seven is one of the most sacred numbers to the Cherokee. It is viewed as a special number by most AmerInd peoples as well as by a majority of the cultures of the entire world. To the Cherokee it represents the seven sacred streams: matter, life, energy, time, motion, dimension, and spirit. There are seven major festivals in the Cherokee year and seven clans; the bird, deer, wolf, wild potato, paint, blue, and long hair. Their council house is seven-sided in which burns a fire of the seven sacred woods.

The Seneca tell of the seven sacred stones: blood stone, fertility stone, sun stone, blossoming stone, water stone, charity stone, and healing stone. The Sioux speak of seven arrows which are the seven directions: west, north, east, south, sky, earth, and all around (or center).

COLORS

It is a little more difficult to set down the color symbolism of the AmerInds as there isn't entire agreement. At Shadowlight we tend to use the following associations without assuming that they are the only ones:

Black - west, the thunders
White - north, the great white giant
Red - east, the beginning
Green - South, energy, action
Blue - the earth, water, the plant kingdom
Yellow - the sun, the sky, the wingeds

It isn't necessary to decide once and for all exactly what each color stands for. One can stand for one thing today and another tomorrow. Of course, consistency will probably help those who work with you.

THE SEARCH FOR THE LODGE OF YOUR GRANDSIRES

Continuing Along the Path

We have tried to present a very practical set of instructions to help you begin an understanding, perhaps even a personal journey, on the medicine path. We had to leave a great deal out. Even if we had had the time and space to attempt to get everything you should know into this book, we are ourselves students of the medicine path. Certainly we don't pretend to know everything - not even everything that WE should know.

It isn't possible to learn all you need to know about any spiritual path from just one book. Even if someone could write such a book, it could convey no more than a single understanding. It is the nature of a spiritual path that it is impractical to study it from only one book. Spiritual paths are too complicated for that; they touch too much of your life to allow one source to provide your only information. We have given you what no other book we know of has done; we have explained the practical methods of medicine path.

We have also introduced you to the spiritual essence which these practical matters are designed to promote. We had to make a decision that we would try to do just one thing well. We chose to teach the practical, hands-on aspects of medicine path.

If your interest in medicine path has been aroused by this book, we highly recommend that you now set forth to find other teachers to help guide your journey. There are a number of ways by which you may do this. The very best is to find a personal teacher, close to where you live, who can give you his/her personal help, advice, and guidance.

Sadly, medicine path people have only recently begun to reach out to others in the regular society with teaching and leadership. There is resistance to this trend. There are people who genuinely feel that these teachings should be given only to other Indians. We have given you our vision in this matter. There are also plastic medicine men; individuals who advertise classes and ceremonies but who actually know less of true medicine path than you now do. The worst is that most of these fakes charge - and get - large amounts of money.

Perhaps your ideal is to find a genuine, full-blood Indian shaman to guide you. It IS possible and we wish you luck. We will warn you that traditionally this lore is taught through allegorical stories. You may need to learn this allegorical language in order to profit from such an association.

You are faced with two problems in your search for a medicine path teacher. One is to find a teacher. The other is to know if it is the right teacher! To find a teacher you might begin with a local new age newspaper. Look for notices of a tribal society, classes, or public ceremonies to give you a start. Check with the Chamber of Commerce or Community Action group to see if there is a tribal association listed. Ask at the public library or anywhere else you can think of. Once you have found a name, whether of an individual or group, write a very short letter asking if they can give you any help in finding a teacher or a group. Enclose a stamped, self-addressed envelope with each enquiry. Few of these groups or individuals can afford to pay postage on a lot of inquiry letters.

We list a few names and addresses of groups and tribal societies with whom we have been in contact. We have not, however, made an effort to hunt out great numbers of these. Be warned that some of these groups will not be able to help you. They may even feel hostility towards anyone not blood Indian. All we can suggest is to keep trying until you do find a group or individual who wishes to communicate with you.

IS THIS TEACHER FOR YOU?

Once you have made contact with a teacher you must decide if he or she will be a good teacher for you. It is nearly impossible to set forth guidelines for this! A very wise woman once set forth some guidelines for selecting a teacher. We don't believe that they can be improved upon:

1. How did you feel when you first came into contact with this teacher? Did he or she convey a sense of clarity, serenity, joy, love, groundedness, and self-confidence?

2. Does the information this teacher provides match with things you already know to be true? Sometimes there is a stylistic or vocabulary barrier here which you must surmount before you really know what they are teaching.

3. Is this teacher in touch with other teachers of the medicine path? Does he or she join with other teachers in rituals and/or in information exchanges?

4. Does this teacher's behavior seem ethical? Does he or she try to manipulate or coerce people?

5. Does this teacher share with all members of the group? Are others allowed to offer the pipe or do the smudging; or does the teacher hog the spotlight?

6. Does this teacher teach a variety of rituals and approaches? Does he or she depend totally on just one expression of the path?

7. Do this teacher's other students seem capable and intelligent?

8. Does this teacher teach without large monetary demands? It isn't reasonable for a teacher to ask for no recompense for time and materials. However large fees for short workshops don't generally indicate a dedicated, serious teacher. You must be realistic about what IS a large fee. Compare costs to what eating out and a movie might cost — or a course at a local college.

9. Is this teacher well regarded by people you know who follow the medicine path?

OTHER LEARNING OPTIONS

There are some correspondence courses for medicine path students. Shadowlight has taught one for a number of years. We are listing a few which we know of. Outside of Shadowlight we don't really know much about the other courses. We can only suggest you write them and think about what they tell you about themselves.

Pan American Indian Association
Post Office Box 244
Nocatee, FL 33864
(813) 494-6930
Heritage revival, genealogy, resources, public and private meetings of shamanism, earth magic, crafts, special speakers, personal instruction in beadwork. Send for free sample copy of 16-page tabloid newspaper. Postcards preferred.

The Good Medicine Society
HCR 62 Box 15
Old Joe, AR 72659
The Good Medicine Society exists to make the teachings of Eli Gatoga, Cherokee, available to the people. Before his death in 1983, Eli organized his teachings into a progressive series of lessons which begin by introducing the basic concepts of our relationships with all nature's life, here and hereafter. Further teachings provide on-going guidance and practical application toward the student's goal of motal, mental, and spiritual health, for the most progress in this life.

Four Winds Circle
Annie Lane
Mill Valley, CA 94941
A non-profit educational center that bridges cultures and supports ancient traditions for survival in our world. "We live and travel together, sing and pray on a journey that takes us inward to our ancient grandmothers/grandfathers. We will live in sacred awareness."

Xat Medicine Society
1404 Gale Lane
Nashville, TN 37212
(615) 298-9932
Organization promoting American Indian spirituality with branches in several cities.

Susan Redwing, Archivist
Lenape Cultural Council and Native Scholars Network
c/o 252 East Summit
Souderton, PA 18964
Publisher of Volumes 1 and 2 in the Wik-Wum life series on traditional ways of living and the new earth by WM. Sauts Netamuxwe Bock.

Caney Indian Spiritual Circle
P. O. Box 6874
Pittsburgh, PA 15212
A non-profit religious organization doing spiritual work and conducting monthly ceremonies based closely upon the traditions of the Native Peoples of Central and South America. Publish Moon Breath magazine quarterly at $6.00 per year.

The Shadowlight Institute
1965 Prince Albert
Riverside, California 92507
The educational division of the Shadowlight Medicine Clan. It fulfills the metaphysical education

needs of the 30+ Shadowlight Medicine Clans, friends and associates. Includes departments in Medicine Path, Metaphysical Healing, Martial Arts and Metaphysical Science.

There are a lot of magazines published by and for followers of the Medicine Path and/or American Indians. A few of these follow:

Shadowlight publishes the following newsletters:
Pipe Dreams, news of the Shadowlight Clans

The Healing Network Newsletter, a network of individuals from all religious paths gathered to seek healing for all who ask.

Shaman's Drum
A Journal of Experiential Shamanism
P. O. 2636
Berkeley, CA 94702
A beautiful, slick magazine attempting to offer firsthand experiences, in-depth coverage, and a variety of viewpoints on shamanism. $15 per year, quarterly.

Daybreak
P. O. Box 98
Highland, MD 20777-0098
An American Indian magazine dedicated to the Seventh Generation. - keeping an lookout for and reflecting dangers and opportunities in the horizons of Fourth World, indigenous, American Indian peoples and all our relations. Offers a serious focus toward an abundant, life-enhancing future.

The Northeast Indian Quarterly
American Indian Program, Cornell University
400 Caldwell Hall
Cornell University
Ithaca, NY 14853
Topics: The Great Law of Peace, language and culture, curriculum development, environmental ethics, Cultural Encounter: Looking toward 1992. $12 yearly. Quarterly

Native Self-Sufficiency Magazine
P. O. Box 10A
6450 1st Street
Forestville, CA 95436
Political and Social issues, native values to preserve culture and environment, re-vitalizing communities, how-to, childrens' features. $8 per year, Quarterly.

Turtle Quarterly
25 Rainbow Mall
Niagara Falls, NY 14303
Native American art and culture; arts, crafts, history, culture, dance, health, athletics, philosophy, conservation, beliefs, cosmology. $10 yearly.

Indian Affairs
95 Madison Avenue
New York, NY 10016
Newsletter of the Association on American Indian Affairs, Inc. Voting membership $25.

Native American Rights Fund
Legal Review

1506 Broadway
Boulder, CO 80302
Nonprofit organization specializing in the protection of Indian Rights. Staffed by Indians. They respond to requests for legal assistance. Contributions always welcome.

Wildfire
The Bear Tribe
P. O. Box 9167
Spokane, WA 99209
Publication of Sun Bear's group. Features articles on Indian culture, crafts, self-sufficiency, spirituality.

A number of medicine people travel around the country doing workshops and weekend sessions on the medicine path. Medicine Hawk and Grey Cat are among this group. Sun Bear of the Bear Tribe usually has an extensive schedule; Wallace Black Elk makes a lecture tour most years; as does Mary Thunder. Quite a number of the teachers of medicine path do this. These lectures, workshops, and weekends can be extremely valuable to you. You may get a chance to ask an author what he or she meant by something in their book. You might learn to understand a point which wasn't clear to you. You will meet and work with a group of people who share some of your aims, beliefs, and goals. Again, the costs of these sessions should seem reasonable to you. If one seems a little expensive, contact the sponsors of the event. It may be that the money is going for some particular project which you do wish to support.

BOOKS ON THE MEDICINE PATH

Since you are reading a book now we assume that you will be interested in reading other books to increase your understanding and knowledge of the medicine path. In this chapter we are listing a short selection of books which we consider particularly helpful to those new to medicine path. There is a bibliography later which lists as many as possible of the books which we feel contributed to this book. However, some books in the bibliography aren't recommended to one just beginning. There are some listed which we didn't fully understand.

SOURCES OF MEDICINE PATH ITEMS

Where do you get eagle feathers, sacred pipes, leather, leather bags, beads, and wildcat claws? Quite a number of good mail-order sources of Amerind medicine objects and materials to construct them exist.

We are listing just a few. This listing does not constitute a recommendation of these businesses. We have not had the opportunity to do business with all of them. All we can say is that they answered our letters of inquiry and that their catalogs didn't turn us off.

Crazy Crow Trading Post
P. O. Box 314
Denison, TX 75020
Excellent variety of beads, beading supplies, leather and furs, leather working supplies, leather goods, feathers, jewelry, incense and smudge, warbonnets, hats, clothing, blackpower accessories, pipes, tobaccos, ironware, knives, knife making accessories, kits, cassettes, books, bead work, blankets. Color Catalog: $3.00

Pipestone Indian Shrine Association
Pipestone National Monument
P. O. Box 727
Pipestone, MN 56164
Genuine Indian reproductions of pipes and artifacts. Operated by the National Park Service. Request catalog.

Prarie Edge
P. O. Box 8303
Rapid City, SD 57709
Source of unique, individually handcrafted northern plains Indian art, artifacts, and jewelry. Original techniques and materials used. Authentic to smallest details. Expensive. Write for catalog.

Winona Trading Post
P. O. Box 324
Santa Fe, NM 87504
Wide variety of beads, handmade and machine-made, some in unusual colors and styles, antique and semi-precioius beads and stones, jewelry, beading supplies and books, feathers, cassettes of AmerInd music and prayer songs. Reasonable prices.

Wakeda Trading Post
P. O. Box 19146
Sacramento, CA 95819
Highly descriptive catalog, wide variety of beads in a wide variety of colors, some unusual beads, beading supplies, jewelry and supplies, bells, hides, furs, leathers and tails, feathers, shells, bone, tobacco and herbal blends, knives, pipes, tomahawks, blankets, drums, kits, patterns, recordings, books. Neat stuff!

Turtle Island Books
P. O. Box 9167
Spokane, WA 99209
Wide variety of books, videos, cassettes, herbs, rugs, crafted items, t-shirts, posters, drums.

Santa Fe Natural Tobacco
P. O. Box 1840
Santa Fe, NM 87504
Tobacco - American Spirit Tobacco and special blends. Very pleasant to deal with.

Phil & Susan Miller
P. O. Box 8178
Incline Village, NV 89450
Fine rawhide drums, handcrafted by Phil Miller. High energy, high quality drums, handcrafted especially for use in dance, ceremony, and a tools for spiritual growth. All have cottonwood hoops, each is signed. Specializing in large drums. Write or phone (702) 831-5320.

One World Products
Box L
Taos, NM 87571
Excellent smudge sticks, sachets, potpourri, incense, perfume, and gift items. Wholesale/retail. Made by Indians in Taos who are paid well over minimum wage.

Grey Owl Indian Craft Co.
113-15 Springfield Blvd.
Queens Village, NY 11429
Just about everything you could possibly want. Catalog of nearly 200 pages of crafts, supplies, and books.

Garden of Beadin
P. O. Box 1535
Redway, CA 95560
Wide variety of beads: bugle, glass, crystals, rhinestones, hand-painted, ethnic, metal, semi-precious, natural material, wood and more. Beading supplies, books, and findings. Sample assortments available. If you are into beading, their catalog is a must.

The Freed Company
415 Central
Albuquerque, NM 87103
Offer quartz crystal balls, points, many gem stones and beads. Leathers, furs, wigs, sequined motifs for costumes and many related Indian items. A main item is seashells used for jewelry making and ceremonies.

All Tribes Spiritual Center
2075 Shore Drive
Bosque Farms, NM 87608
Variety of incenses, smudge, feathers, furs, horns and skulls, leather items, rattles, drums, crafted items, medicine shields, semi-precious stones.

Thunder Studio
P. O. Box 1552
Cedar Ridge, CA 95924
"At Thunder Studio we appreciate that from the give-away of animals and trees we have the opportunity to create our beautiful drums. With these gifts of the Mother Earth, we may hold the power of Thunder, the music of the drum.

The Trading Post
Kit-Han-Ne
R. D. #8, Box 6
West Kittanning, PA 16201
Direct Reservation traders. Original works, some antique. Shopping by phone (with card) possible but catalog sketchy due to the fact that most of their merchandise is one of a kind.

Earth Nation
P. O. Box 929
Nashville, IN 47448

A not-for-profit organization which assists people in living harmoniously with the Earth and all her beings. Books, tapes, a tarot deck, postcards, newsletter calendar.

Otowi Designs
P. O. Box 9123
Santa Fe, NM 87504
Lovely silver jewelry featuring Mimbres and San Ildefonso designs. Free catalog, jewelry at medium prices.

Bovis Bead Company
P.O. Box 111
Bisbee, AZ 85603
Enormous catalog of beads - including rare collector and trade beads - from American Indian cultures as well as world-wide. You won't believe there are this many kinds of beads.

The Bear Tribe Catalog
P. O. Box 9167
Spokane, WA 99209
Many books, crafts, supplies from Sun Bear.

Wear It Well
1070 Mt. Philo
No. Ferrisburg, VT 05473
Jewelry from the Earth, made of natural elements too bring attunement and balance to the wearer. Reasonably priced beaded necklaces, pendants and earrings.

Shadowlight Products
P. O. Box 33568
Decatur, GA 30033
A division of the Shadowlight Medicine Clan, it offers many items needed for following Medicine Path including totem bags, smudging and smoking mixtures, minerals, herbs, crystals, etc. from Medicine Hawk.

BIBLIOGRAPHY

Bear, Sun and Wabun. The Medicine Wheel, Earth Astrology. Englewood Cliffs; Prentice-Hall. 1980.

Beyerl, Paul. The Master Book of Herbalism. Custer; Phoeni~. 1984.

Bolton, Brett L. The Secret Powers of Plants. New York; Berkeley. 1974.

Brown, Joseph Epes. The Sacred Pipe; Black Eld's Account Of The Seven Rites Of The Oglala. Norman; University of Oklahoma Press. 1953

Furst, Peter T. and Furst, Jill L. North American Indian Art. New York; Rissoli. 1982.

Harner, Michael. The Way Of The Shaman, A Guide To Power And Healing. New York; Harper & Row. 1980.

Hawken, Paul. The Magic Of Findhorn. New York; Bantam. 11g75.

Headstrom, Richard. Suburban Wildlife, An Introduction To The Common Animals Of Your Back Yark And Local Park. Englewood Cliffs; Prentice Hall. 1~84.

Hunt, W.Ben. The Gomplete Book Of Indian Grafts And Lore. New°York; Golden. 1954.

Kloss, Jethro. Back To Eden. Santa Barbara; Woodbridge. 1939.

Mooney, James. Myths Of The Cherokee And Sacred Forrmulas Of The Cherokees. Nashville; Elder. 1975.

Mooney, James. Myths Of The Cherokee. St. Clair Shores; Scholarly. 1970.

Neilhardt, John G. Black Elk Speaks; Being The Life Story Of A Holy Man Of The Oglala. New York; Pocket Books. 1932.

Parker, Arthur C. The Indian How Book. New York; Dover. 1927.

Steiger, Brad. Indian Medicine Power. Gloucester; Para Research. 1984.

Tomkins, William. Indian Sign Language. New York; Dover. 1969.

Uyldert, Mellie. The Magic Of Precious Stones. Wellingborough; Turnstone. 1984.

Woodward, Grace Steele. The Cherokees. Norman, University of Oklahoma. 1963.

Speck, Frank G. and Leonard Broom, [a collaboration with Will West Long]; Cherokee Dance and Drama; Univ. of California Press; Berkeley; 1951.

Steiger, Brad; Indian Medicine Power; Para Research; Gloucester, MA; 1984.

Storm, Heyemeyhosts; Seven Arrows

Terrell, John and Donna Terrell; Indian Women of the Western
Morning

Wolf, B. Hungry; The Ways of My Grandmothers

Woodward, Grace Steele; The Cherokees; University of Oklahoma Press; Norman; 1963.

GLOSSARY OF INDIAN WORDS

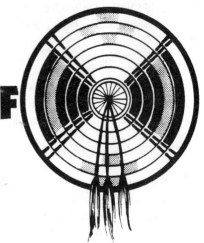

Words are in Cherokee unless otherwise indicated:

adanvdo, adanudo; Great Spirit
adawehiyu; Very great magician - part of name for ginseng
agawela; Literally old woman, the spirit of corn
agayunli; ancestral spirits
agisegwa; Earth Mother; Mother of Four-Legged
ahawi; form of awi, female deer
amaiyenehi; dwellers in the water
asi; sweat lodge, house
atagahi; the secret lake which cures illness
atali; mountain, part of ginseng's names
atali kuli; mountain climber, ginseng
ataya; oak, the principal or real wood; adayahi
atsadi; fish
atsila; fire
atsina; cedar tree
atskili; witch, horned owl
awahili; eagle
awi; deer (doe)
catlinite; red pipe stone found in Minnesota (
chante ishta; one, true eye of the heart (Sioux)
dagulku; goose
dayi; beaver
digalungunyi; where it comes up, common

word for the east
dilstayati; scissors - name for water spider
galagina; buck deer, turkey gobbler
galeshka; spotted (Sioux)
galunky'ti'yu; sacred
galunlati; Sky Father
geyaguga; moon
gili; dog
gule; acorn
gulegi; climber, blacksnake
hetchetu, welu; "it is done" (Sioux)
heyoka; One who is chosen by thunder. Backwards one
hokshichankiya; spiritual seed
igaehinvdo; sun
igaguti; the great magickal crystal, daylight, cl
inali; black fox
kagu; crow
kananeski; spider, watch or clock
kanasdatsi; Water monster
kanunnawu; pipe
kanunsita; dogwood, also spelled kanvsita
kinnikinnik; aromatic herb
kiyaga; ground squirrel, also spelled kiyuga
kunstutsi; sassafrass
kyaiyo; grizzly bear (Blackfoot)
maka ina; Grandmother Earth (Sioux)
manatu; Great Spirit (poss. Shawnee)

ma'hpi'ya; sky
miaheyyun; total universe
mitakuye oyasin; "all are relatives" (Sioux)
momoy; Jimson weed
mudjekeewis; bear (Chippewa?)
natsi; pine tree
nihoestsan; Earth Mother (Navajo)
nunahe; spirits of all
nundagunyi; the sunland, the east
onikari; sweatlodge
ozisigobimic; willow (Chippewa)
paksikwoyi; "sticky-mouth" Honey Bear
peta owihankeshni; The Eternal Fire (Sioux)
quanah; eagle (Comanche)
sagwali; horse, literally burden bearer, soquili
salali; squirrel, also spelled saloli, salili
saligugi; turtle, water
sasa; goose
saynday; Coyote (Kiowa)
selu; corn
shawnodese; coyote (Chippewa)
siyu; "good"
tatanka; Buffalo (Sioux)
tatsuhwa; redbird
tewa; flying squirrel
tlanuwa; hawk
tlayku; blue jay, also spelled tsayoga
tluntutsi; panther, also spelled tlvdatsi
tsalagayunli; old tobacco, Tabacum rustica
tsaliyusti; mullein, literally " like tobacco"
tsalu; tobacco
tsisdetsi; rat
tsiskwaya; sparrow, literally " the real bird"
tsistu; rabbit
tsitsi; mouse
tsiyu; "good"
tskiki; katydid
tsula; fox
tuksi; box turtle

tulanawa; the legendary great hawk
tunkayatakapakah; "Ancient Stones" (Sioux)
Ubaba ungulu; Grandfather/Great Spirit (Zulu)
uguku; hoot owl
uktena; mythical snake; dragon
uk'denok; Thunderers
ulanawa; soft-shelled turtle
ulunsu; crystal
ulunsuti; the great magic crystal
unchi; Grandmother
unega; strangers, Europeans
usdi; small, little
usdiga; another grammatical form of small
usunhiy; darkening land, the west commonly
utsanati; rattlesnake, literally he has a bell
wabeno wusk; yarrow (Chippewa)
waboose; Buffalo (Chippewa)
wabun; eagle (Chippewa)
wahunu; screech owl
wakan; sacred, as to perform in a wakan
wakan tanka; Great Spirit
walasi; frog, also spelled walosi
wanbli; Eagle (Sioux)
wapani; give-away (Sioux)
waya; wolf
welo (see hetchetu welo)
wesa; cat
wudeligunyi; west, where it dies
wusuhihunyi; darkening place, west
yanash; Buffalo (Choctaw)
yanasi; Buffalo (Hitchitee)
yanu; bear
yenasa; Buffalo (Creek)
yunsu; buffalo
yunwi; man
yunwi usdi; little man, genseng
yunwi usdiga adawehi; most powerful
 magician, ceremonial name for genseng

THE SHADOWLIGHT MEDICINE CLAN

In the intent for mutual support, optimum growth and ultimate personal balance, the Brotherhood of Staffs and the Sisterhood of Shields have been formed - not as separate organizations within the Clan, but very much as the two halves of one common heart — each distinct in purpose but existing, bonded together, as the beating, vital life-force of the Shadowlight nation. Listed below are the common goals of these groups - delineated by gender for clarification only and not for segregation or the promotion of gender separation within the Clan, it's teachings and/or ceremonies. There are many roads on the Path - ultimately leading for all to the center of the Sacred Wheel - that place of total growth, love, harmony and balance within Self.

1.To uphold, practice and promote all stated purposes of the Shadowlight Clan.

2.To encourage and assist all women/men in a spirit of Sisterhood/Brotherhood to actively step into each one's individual medicine, balance and path of personal power.

3.To band together in mutual caring, healing, teaching and support.

4.A) To encourage and practice women's Sacred ceremonies, i.e. Moon Lodge.
  B) To encourage and practice men's Sacred cereemonies, i.e. Men's Lodge and Talking Stick.

5.To step into personal male/female balance with the purpose of self-healing, growth, knowing, wholeness: knowing ultimately that as we heal and balance ourselves, we heal and balance the Mother for we are flesh of Her flesh and blood of Her blood.

6.To become fully aware of and actively practicing the Medicine-Wisdom Women/Men that we already are.

7. To honor all of our ancestors who have walked this Path before us, who stand with us at all times, and every second counsel us and continue to show us the Way.

8.To actively honor, nurture, heal and support the Sacred Child within Self and within all of creation

9.A) For all women to actively step into the Sacred Male Shield to manifest all creative energies.
  B) For all men to actively step into the Sacred Female Shield to reach that point of ultimate creativity.

10. For all to actively free self, all and all energies from all forms of enslavement (psychic, emotional, etc.) that cause and promote personal and universal bondage in any form.

MEDICINE HAWK
Chief
Shadowlight Clan